Learning and Governance in the EU Policy Making Process

This book takes stock of learning theories in the European Union (EU) integration literature and assesses what insights the concept of 'learning' has added to our understanding of the European integration processes. Given the European integration dynamics since 2000 (including enlargement and new governance approaches and instruments), learning and learning-related theories have gained major EU significance. The book addresses the less noticed micro level patterns of behavioural change that deserve more visibility in the EU's theoretical toolbox. It focuses on the conditions under which EU actors in various decision-making processes learn or do not learn.

In asking this question it raises issues about the EU's nature. Do the EU conditions that favour learning outweigh the EU conditions that inhibit learning? Is the EU system too complex for learning processes to have a discernible, concrete impact? To assess the degree that the EU system and its member states learn, the authors selected for this volume are all explicitly comparative in their approach, and have been encouraged to look at differences across political systems. In doing so, the authors study how EU member states, EU institutions, and other groups and organisations pursue learning across the multi-level EU policy process.

This book was previously published as a special issue of the *Journal of European Public Policy*.

Anthony R. Zito is Reader in Politics at Newcastle University and is currently Politics Research Director and Co-Director of the Jean Monnet Centre at Newcastle University. His broad research interests focus on the European Union decision-making process, policy-making processes and expert networks. Dr. Zito was a 2007 Leverhulme Fellow, conducting a comparative analysis of EU and United States environmental agencies. He has authored *Creating Environmental Policy in the European Union* (Palgrave 2000) and articles in *Political Studies, Public Administration, Governance, Journal of European Public Policy* and other journals, focusing on the EU policy process and environmental actors and policy-making.

Journal of European Public Policy Series

Series Editor: Jeremy Richardson is a Professor at Nuffield College, Oxford University

This series seeks to bring together some of the finest edited works on European Public Policy. Reprinting from Special Issues of the 'Journal of European Public Policy,' the focus is on using a wide range of social sciences approaches, both qualitative and quantitative, to gain a comprehensive and definitive understanding of Public Policy in Europe.

Towards a Federal Europe
Edited by Alexander H. Trechsel

The Disparity of European Integration
Edited by Tanja A. Börzel

Cross-National Policy Convergence: Causes Concepts and Empirical Findings
Edited by Christoph Knill

Civilian or Military Power?
European Foreign Policy in Perspective
Edited by Helene Sjursen

The European Union and New Trade Politics
Edited by John Peterson and Alasdair R. Young

Comparative Studies of Policy Agendas
Edited by Frank R. Baumgartner, Christoffer Green-Pedersen and Bryan D. Jones

The Constitutionalization of the European Union
Edited by Berthold Rittberger and Frank Schimmelfenig

Empirical and Theoretical Studies in EU Lobbying
Edited by David Coen

Mutual Recognition as a New Mode of Governance
Edited by Susanne K. Schmidt

France and the European Union
Edited by Emiliano Grossman

Immigration and Integration Policy in Europe
Edited by Tim Bale

Reforming the European Commission
Edited by Michael W. Bauer

International Influence Beyond Conditionality
Postcommunist Europe after EU enlargement
Edited by Rachel A. Epstein and Ulrich Sedelmeier

The Role of Political Parties in the European Union
Edited by Björn Lindberg, Anne Rasmussen and Andreas Warntjen

EU External Governance
Projecting EU Rules beyond Membership
Edited by Sandra Lavenex and Frank Schimmelfennig

EMU and Political Science
What Have We Learned?
Edited by Henrik Enderlein and Amy Verdun

Learning and Governance in the EU Policy Making Process
Edited by Anthony R. Zito

Learning and Governance in the EU Policy Making Process

Edited by Anthony R. Zito

LONDON AND NEW YORK

First published 2010 by Routledge

2 Park Square, Milton Park, Abingdon, Oxon OX14 4RN
711 Third Avenue, New York, NY 10017, USA

Routledge is an imprint of the Taylor & Francis Group, an informa business

First issued in paperback 2016

Copyright © 2010 Taylor & Francis

Typeset in Minion by Value Chain, India

All rights reserved. No part of this book may be reprinted or reproduced or utilised in any form or by any electronic, mechanical, or other means, now known or hereafter invented, including photocopying and recording, or in any information storage or retrieval system, without permission in writing from the publishers.

Notice:
Product or corporate names may be trademarks or registered trademarks, and are used only for identification and explanation without intent to infringe.

British Library Cataloguing in Publication Data
A catalogue record for this book is available from the British Library

ISBN13: 978-0-415-57180-7 (hbk)
ISBN13: 978-1-138-97958-1 (pbk)

Contents

	Abstracts	vii
	Notes on contributors	x
1	Learning theory reconsidered: EU integration theories and learning *Anthony R. Zito and Adriaan Schout*	1
2	Organizational learning in the EU's multi-level governance system *Adriaan Schout*	22
3	Measuring policy learning: regulatory impact assessment in Europe *Claudio M. Radaelli*	43
4	EU policy towards other regions: policy learning in the external promotion of regional integration *Mary Farrell*	63
5	Governance and policy learning in the European Union: a comparison with North America *Éric Montpetit*	83
6	The power of institutionalized learning: the uses and practices of commissions to generate policy change *Patrik Marier*	102
7	European agencies as agents of governance and EU learning *Anthony R. Zito*	122
8	Governance and learning in the post-Maastricht era? *Michelle Egan*	142
	Index	152

Abstracts

Learning theory reconsidered: EU integration theories and learning

Anthony R. Zito and Adriaan Schout

This article introduces this special issue by contextualizing learning theory within European integration studies. There are important empirical and theoretical gaps in the study of European integration which necessitate a greater attention to learning theory. This article deploys a number of conceptual distinctions about learning and non-learning processes, drawing from political science, international relations, public administration and sociological/organizational studies. It traces 'learning' in its political science context and how learning has been inserted into EU integration studies. In relating this evolution, the article examines the conditions that define the type and likelihood of learning and surveys the special issue. The article argues that studying learning in the EU is difficult, but integration requires an understanding of the micro policy processes that learning seeks to address.

Organizational learning in the EU's multi-level governance system

Adriaan Schout

The European Union's (EU's) governance reform does not match the expectations of its promoters; the 'new' instruments seem to under-perform. One explanation, explored here, is that governance has been discussed without much attention to capacities at operating levels. Analyses are needed of how instruments are used and designed within the EU's multi-level administrative system. To move from governance to capacities, three interrelated levels of learning are distinguished to examine whether changes in governance are supported by developments in organizational capacities: 'governance learning', 'instrument learning' and 'organizational learning'. One hypothesis is that these need to develop simultaneously. The second hypothesis is that, in the EU's multi-level administration, learning along these dimensions has to take place in parallel at EU and national levels. This article analyses the capacities which the Commission and the Netherlands have created to support the better regulation agenda. It concludes that there is a match between the three levels of learning in the Commission but a mismatch between learning in the Commission and the Netherlands.

Measuring policy learning: regulatory impact assessment in Europe

Claudio M. Radaelli

Do analytic approaches to policy appraisal, specifically regulatory impact assessment (RIA), enable complex organizations to learn? To answer this question, this article distinguishes between types of learning (instrumental, legitimacy-seeking emulation, and political), spells out their micro-foundations, and formulates expectations about evidence drawing on the literature on knowledge utilization. Findings from Denmark, the Netherlands, Sweden, the UK and the EU corroborate emulation and to some extent political learning rather than instrumental learning. The conclusions explain why some types of learning prevail over others.

EU policy towards other regions: policy learning in the external promotion of regional integration

Mary Farrell

Since the 1990s, the European Union (EU) has renewed its support for regional integration in other parts of the world, and incorporated this objective as a part of European external policy. Compared to the embryonic Common Foreign and Security Policy (CFSP), the support for regional integration and co-operation has been much less controversial, having been publicly endorsed by European Commission officials, and identified in the policy publications emanating from the various Directorate Generals (DGs). This article adopts a policy learning perspective to investigate this departure in external policy by the EU, and to identify the explanatory capacity of collective learning for the core beliefs, preferences, and policy instruments eventually adopted by European policy-makers. The article identifies what types of learning have taken place, and assesses the impact of learning on the policy outputs and outcomes.

Governance and policy learning in the European Union: a comparison with North America

Éric Montpetit

Several scholars argue that policy-making in the EU occurs in horizontal networks more frequently than in nation states. They add that EU networks, unlike networks in nation states, are not subordinated to any formal structure of authority. Moreover, EU networks seek consensus as their actors are concerned about the EU's democratic deficit. Consequently, learning features prominently as a method to make policy decisions in EU governance. This article tests this proposal. The test rests on a comparative survey yielding 666 completed questionnaires from actors involved in biotechnology policy development in Europe and North America. The survey was conducted twice, once in 2006 and once in 2008, and provides information on policy learning intensity, on consensus formation and on policy transfers. The survey fails to provide evidence that policy actors involved in EU governance learn more than those involved exclusively in European and North American nation states.

The power of institutionalized learning: the uses and practices of commissions to generate policy change

Patrik Marier

This article analyses the conditions under which commissions succeed in influencing policy change. The paper tackles three questions: What do governments gain by establishing a commission? What are the tools employed by commissions in order to make their recommendations and ensure that their output will have political significance? And how do commissions influence policy outcomes? Five different types of influence are introduced and tested by focusing on the role of pension commissions in France, Sweden, and the UK.

European agencies as agents of governance and EU learning

Anthony R. Zito

This article asks how the EU as a regional organization manages to learn and adapt to policy challenges. It investigates the evolution of one regional level and one national environmental agency (the European Environment Agency and the Environment Agency of England and Wales) which have distinct roles in influencing EU environmental policy performance. The article examines the role of agencies and bureaucracies more generally, investigating some of the assumptions made in the bureaucracy literature, particularly concerning principal–agent models. The focus on agencies helps to illuminate two potential dimensions of the EU process: overcoming the original institutional design and the role of organizational and policy learning.

Governance and learning in the post-Maastricht era?

Michelle Egan

There has been an expansion of research on policy learning in different subfields. The methodological and empirical work continues to face challenges in determining the constitutive elements that foster such transformations in governance through learning. Careful attention needs to be paid to the regularities and patterns, as well as the limits, contingencies and incongruities that shape or hinder the diffusion of cross-national and cross-temporal rules, norms and institutions. In looking at the policy cycle, the process of policy learning focuses predominantly on the organizational environment, the modes of learning, and the implementation effects, without acknowledging the normative implications in terms of accountability and legitimacy.

Notes on Contributors

Anthony R. Zito is Reader in Politics at Newcastle University, UK.

Adriaan Schout is Director of the European Studies Programme at the Netherlands Institute of International Relations ('Clingendael'), the Hague, and Research Professor at the Institut Universitari d'Estudis Europeus (IUEE), Universitat Auto'noma de Barcelona, Spain.

Claudio M. Radaelli is Professor of Political Science (Anniversary Chair in Politics), Jean Monnet Chair in EU Policy Analysis, and Director of the Centre for European Governance, University of Exeter, UK.

Mary Farrell is Reader in European and International Politics at the University of Greenwich, UK.

Éric Montpetit is Associate Professor of Political Science at the Université de Montréal, Canada.

Patrik Marier is Canada Research Chair in Comparative Public Policy at Concordia University, Canada.

Michelle Egan is Associate Professor, Director of Comparative and Regional Studies, and Jean Monnet Chair of European Integration, School of International Service, American University, Washington, DC, USA.

Learning theory reconsidered: EU integration theories and learning

Anthony R. Zito and Adriaan Schout

INTRODUCTION

There are numerous macro approaches within European integration studies, including some based on intergovernmental negotiations and power relations (Moravcsik 1993) or convergence in policies (Knill and Lenschow 2005). We assert that such undoubtedly important 'macro' integration approaches will miss the ubiquitous, important European Union (EU) micro changes. Although the highest political level will address, for instance, carbon dioxide reduction, behind this policy-making are a myriad of 'micro' processes of civil servants and politicians interacting concerning problems, hopes, norms, symbols, instruments, etc. Understanding European integration requires focusing at the micro level of the individuals and their social interactions. Over time, these exchanges generate changes in information, goals, values, behaviours, structures, policies and outcomes.

These micro processes are the realm of learning theory. Learning in policy analysis can be defined as a process of exercising a judgement based on an experience or some other kind of input that leads actors to select a different view of how things happen ('learning that') and what courses of action should be taken ('learning how' – see May 1992; Breslauer and Tetlock 1991). Learning theories vary on what exactly is being learnt: some focus on complex belief change while others focus on more simple instrumental changes. Learning emphasizes change at the level of individuals, but also within the intersubjective process whereby human interaction leads to group/organization understanding.

This special issue takes stock of learning theories in the EU integration literature and assesses what insights 'learning' has added to our understanding of the integration processes. Political science learning approaches originated from the United States, but seem to have largely halted conceptual development before 1995. Some of these concepts have entered the EU academic discussion, but not in a sustained or systematic manner. Nevertheless, given the European integration dynamics around 2000 (including enlargement and the governance 'turn' of exploring new instruments), learning and learning-related theories have gained major EU significance. But now, a decade later, have learning approaches resulted in anything more than confusion over terminology?

Addressing learning is not easy because of the widely varying approaches in which it features. Concepts of learning overlap, and there are difficulties in specifying whether or not learning has occurred given the many possible intervening variables and alternative explanations (James and Lodge 2003; Bomberg 2007). But there are further difficulties with learning, particularly relating to its foundations: why do actors learn and what conditions prevent or facilitate learning? If crisis and dissatisfaction mostly drive learning, should one expect learning to exist in the many EU policy preparations and decisions occurring away from the public eye (Rose 1991)?

Although doubts surround 'learning', the main conceptual advantage of learning is its explicit emphasis on change. It underlines that negotiations between states are not merely about redistributing power (zero sum games) but potentially also positive sum games by changing the context and perceptions (Bennett and Howlett 1992; Schout 2009). With this interest in evolutionary processes, learning contrasts with rational policy theories in which optimal policy conclusions are derived from static analysis.

The special issue assumes that there are core dynamics that integration studies must examine. This is more important now than ever before. The EU has invested heavily in 'learning' both internally (within the EU) and externally (in relations between the EU and other regional blocs). In 2000, the EU faced several difficulties. The fall of the Santer Commission marked a Commission organizational crisis, a wider EU legitimacy crisis regarding policies and instruments, and a communication crisis in terms of public involvement. New structures, instruments and organizations – including a reformed Commission, agencies and networks – were needed. The 2004/07 accession's near doubling of EU membership demanded a shift from the traditional – legal – instrument of integration towards learning-oriented instruments such as the open method of co-ordination (OMC). The turn towards network-based governance marks a paradigm shift in thinking from networks as second-best options in policy areas where EU competencies failed (Hancher 1996) towards becoming first-order instruments.

Reviewing the past ten years, the EU has been surprisingly resilient (Schout and Van den Berge 2009). Although 'macro' reforms faltered or failed with the Lisbon Treaty placed on hold (depriving the EU of institutional innovations) and the referenda failures, new instruments (particularly the OMC) have been used en masse (Zito *et al.* 2003), and the Commission has been reformed (Kassim 2008). Whilst the debates about the endurance and precise effects of the reforms continue, there is sufficient evidence to conclude that the EU, its organization and its instruments, have not halted (Heidenreich and Zeitlin 2009; Peterson 2008; Schout and Van Den Berge 2009). Different forms of learning have occurred, although academia finds it hard to recognize and conceptualize these developments (particularly the OMC; see Scharpf 2001; Lodge 2007; Citi and Rhodes 2007). Exploring the relevance of learning concepts may illuminate the integration process and offer insights into learning in the (EU's) multi-level context. Without this concept, there remains an unsatisfying puzzle about how the EU process has rebounded from its many challenges.

This resilience reflects a number of factors, including leadership, institutional path dependency and protracted global problems, that make integration a more attractive alternative. This issue addresses the less noticed micro level patterns of behavioural change that deserve more visibility in the EU's theoretical toolbox. This issue focuses on the conditions under which EU actors in various decision-making processes learn or do not learn. In asking this question, questions are raised about the EU's nature. Most importantly, how well do the EU's positive conditions nurture learning as opposed to the hindrances of the negative conditions? Is the EU system too complex for learning processes to have some tangible, isolatable impact? Moreover, what do the findings say about learning theories more generally – whether, for example, learning in the EU differs from learning in the USA? To assess the degree to which the EU system and its member states learn, the authors selected for this issue are all explicitly comparative in their approach, and have been encouraged to look at differences across political systems.

The following section traces the evolution of the political science approaches. The third section examines how learning has been incorporated into European integration theory. The fourth section systematizes the questions and the propositions about learning that have been developed in the previous section. Finally, the section draws conclusions on the current state of learning literature and gives the issue overview.

LEARNING THEORY STRANDS

A great variety of learning theories have enriched the study of politics. This article focuses on four core threads that are a product of a post-1945 interdisciplinary development, centred heavily but not exclusively in the United States. The first prominent notion of 'learning' came arguably from Deutsch (1963), who incorporated it in his relatively rationalist decision-making theory.

Learning theories moved into psychological and sociological processes and motivations largely grounded in the 'behaviouralist turn', which this issue largely follows. This section traces through the threads from the founding US theories to define the basic concepts.

This special issue does acknowledge the growing importance of constructivist approaches in the last decade. They emphasize the change in language and intersubjective communication rather than changes in cognition and accumulation of facts. Thus learning occurs when words are situated in a new and different relationship to one another, giving rise to a new context for understanding (Nedergaard 2006: 314).

Organizational learning

Scholars working at the intersection of organization studies, psychology, political science and public administration and sociology initiated the pioneering work in political studies' learning theory. Most notably, Herbert Simon harnessed his psychology background to investigate the behavioural patterns of organizations. Emphasizing the limits of rationality, the incompleteness of knowledge and the organization practices imposed on individuals, Simon explored how organizations move beyond individuals' limitations by building structures that guide behaviour. This learning dynamic harnessed knowledge of organizational technology and a greater understanding of the social sciences (Simon 1961: 246).

Building on Simon's work, various scholars elaborated notions of organizational learning. Cyert and March, together and separately, tackled how organizations learn. Their notable book on firms emphasizes short-term adaptation by organizations, the parameters that organizations set to assess their environment, and changes in the rules governing how they search for information (Cyert and March 1992). Argyris and Schön (1996) discuss in more detail the learning process where organizations seek to improve their learning capability. Borrowing from Ross Ashby's theories for designing a brain, they break organizational learning into three types: (1) 'organizational inquiry', an instrumental learning that leads to improved task performance; (2) organizational exploration to redefine performance standards; and (3) an organization's ability to enhance its capability for 'single-loop' and 'double-loop' learning (Argyris and Schön 1996: 20–1). Single-loop learning stresses learning that is instrumental without changing the fundamental organizational values whilst double-loop learning conceptualizes that feedback triggers a value change transforming organizational behaviour.

The interaction between the individual and the organization has remained a critical strand in organizational learning theories. Crossan *et al.* (1999) detail how the transmission process moves from the individual to groups and organizations. While individuals (as opposed to organizations) shape insight and innovative ideas, ideas have to be shared, given intersubjective meaning and then adopted for action, with the ultimate aim of being embedded in the organization and made routine. Learning involves multi-level interaction between individuals, groups and organizations, but it is important to accept the wider innovation process that occurs for networks beyond one individual organization. Accordingly, individuals intuit patterns based on their personal experience but then must interpret and explain them to others in a way that triggers integrated thinking (i.e. a shared understanding within the group). This learning is then institutionalized within the organization (Crossan et al. 1999: 524–30).

This communication, integration and routinization must then happen at the level of the wider network (Knight 2002: 446–7). This is not a unidirectional, bottom-up process: organizations do not passively accept learning – they influence the learning of their members and retain layers of past learning (Hedberg 1981: 6). These insights into organizational learning and network learning are closely linked to EU research on the OMC and uploading (Padgett 2003), but this line of inquiry has not yet been fully developed in terms of organizational learning.

Policy learning

Building on Deutsch's work, Heclo (1974: 307) raised the concept of 'political learning' in relation to policy changes. In this concept he differentiated between group learning, where organizations internally learn from their experiences, and social learning (encompassing the transformation of ideas). Rather than assuming self-organization in learning, Heclo emphasizes that the injecting of these ideas into a society and its policy-making process requires a 'network of policy middlemen' (1974: 311). Heclo also raised the importance of 'non-learning' by acknowledging that policy-makers and institutions may be unwilling or unable to adapt to new information (1974: 312). The idea of networks – which appears in most theories either in a more or less explicit fashion – carrying and inserting ideas is an extremely critical dimension to the learning process.

Sabatier's advocacy coalition framework (ACF) takes Heclo as its starting point, elaborating on the ideational dimension and the policy community dimension (Sabatier 1988: 130). Sabatier's ACF refashions the notion of policy community to argue that, within any given policy subsystem, there are advocacy coalitions, comprising actors with similar core beliefs or values. The ACF separates beliefs according to how fundamental they are to an individual's basic philosophy (Sabatier 1988: 148–9). The more core the beliefs are to the individual, the more they are resistant to change. Hall (1993) constructs a similar differentiation of core ideas and instruments.

Diffusion

Moving deeper into the processes of change across space and time, comparative studies have emerged on how ideas and knowledge have diffused across organizations and political systems. Diffusion studies portray the agents of transfer within broader political structures while the knowledge transferred may relate more to social learning (e.g. paradigms) or lesson drawing (e.g. instruments). The actual process may be rational and voluntary or more coercive (Dolowitz and Marsh 1996). Diffusion studies have, however, mainly treated change as a rational process and have been concerned with the objects of change (whether – not how – objectives, instruments or values change) rather than the process (Bomberg 2007).

Rural sociologist Everett Rogers' 1962 book *Diffusion of Innovations* gave a huge impetus to this study. Rogers defined this diffusion process as one by 'which (1) an innovation (2) is communicated through certain channels (3) over time (4) among the members of a social system' (Rogers 1983: 10). Most significant for this special issue has been the American scholarship on how individual states have acted as policy innovation laboratories (Walker 1969; Volden 2006). Diffusion studies have a long, fruitful history in explaining variation in policy innovation adoption across political systems through examination of the political systems' characteristics and the different diffusion processes (Berry and Berry 1999; Volden 2006: 310).

One of the main issues for diffusion theory was specifying the causal forces that led to convergence around particular innovations. Bennett (1991: 220–9) suggested several different explanations for convergence. These processes include convergence through voluntary emulation or borrowing from other political systems, through interaction, through external actors imposing innovation, and through the entrepreneurship of expert networks (see also Busch and Jörgens 2005). Dolowitz and Marsh (1996) and others have elaborated this stream of work, emphasizing policy transfer and lesson drawing.

International relations networks

Cybernetics and cognitive psychology has informed international relations approaches to decision-making for decades, including Steinbrunner's 1974 examination of the decision-making process and Jervis's 1976 study of how perception and misperception influence actors. Ernst Haas' original, path-breaking formulation of neofunctionalism builds on a social learning argument in international relations (E. Haas 1968: 13). Over time, the focus of the population's loyalty shifts towards the supranational level. The political élite (particularly those in supranational institutions) and transnational interest groups (an implicit network) instigate this shift. Haas' second major statement explores a learning process through which power-oriented states reorientate their values towards policies that benefit the welfare of groups within and across states (E. Haas 1964: 47–8); this would now be labelled 'political learning'. The learning and shifts in loyalty originate from changes in ideas about what issues are possible and beneficial, about international co-operation. It involves changes in 'consensual knowledge' in addition to perceptions of self-interest (Cornett and Caporaso 1992: 238–40). That recognition leads to the scope of integration to expand from one policy area to other related issue areas that could benefit from integration, a process called 'spillover'.

When Haas abandoned neofunctionalism, he focused more on explaining how learning shapes politics and how problems are 'nested' – interconnected with institutions, processes, value systems and other policies (E. Haas 1991: 84). Central to this argument was the generation of 'consensual knowledge' through communities. This argument takes heavily from the organizational approach of Simon, March and others (E. Haas 1990). Haas' most definitive statement on collective learning differentiates adaptation from learning (E. Haas 1991: 72–4). Adaptation reflects how organizations change behaviour and adopt new purposes without changing their underlying theories, values and belief systems; learning involves organizations having to make behavioural changes that reflect a question of the core theories and values.

Peter Haas (1990) elaborated the epistemic community concept, defining it as a network of professionals/experts that participate in a common set of beliefs about how causal relationships work in any given political area. The later work of Haas and Haas (1995) more explicitly embraces a more constructivist view of how learning and communication works.

Tying the threads

Learning theory seemed to have reached a plateau before 1995. Several eminent overviews, drawing together the threads in the learning literature, acknowledged both the strengths and the limitations of learning (particularly Bennett and Howlett 1992: 278–88; see also Argyris and Schön 1996). Frustrated by the wealth of concepts, they synthesized the learning literature by asking: what is learned, by whom and to what effect? Who learns and who promotes learning is discussed in the next section which outlines conditions for learning.

Table 1 reflects a number of learning overviews circa the early 1990s; it underlines that learning can be double as well as single loop, but also political (leading to maximization of support), or even non-existent or merely symbolic (mainly related to the 'spinning' of the argument). With this, one can explain the behaviour of decision-takers as a combination of social conflict, rational analysis, institutional incentives and symbols (Levitt and March 1981). This interplay of dimensions makes learning both powerful in producing change and hard to decompose (Bennett and Howlett 1992; James and Lodge 2003).

Table 1 differentiates organizational, political and instrumental learning, all of which Ernst Haas would label 'adaptation'. Organizational learning focuses on changes in understanding of the administrative process with resulting organizational change. Lesson drawing encapsulates instrumental/adaptational learning. A different form of single loop learning may involve political actions (trying to please specific audiences with changes in political strategy in order to advance a political idea (Heclo 1974; May 1992: 336) and highly symbolic efforts to legitimize actions (DiMaggio and Powell 1983). The special issue articles are

Table 1 Learning modes (partly adapted from Bennett and Howlett 1992)

Learning types		Literature thread/authors	Learns what	To what effect
'Learning'	Organizational Learning	Organizational learning: Simon, Cyert, March	Process-related behaviour and strategy	Organizational change and political positioning
	Lesson drawing (instrumental learning)	Policy learning and diffusion: Rose, Bennett, Rogers	Instruments	Programme change
	Social learning	Policy learning and international networks: Heclo, Sabatier, Haas, Hall	Ideas, worldviews	Core paradigm, value shift
	Political learning; also symbolic learning	May, Heclo, DiMaggio and Powell	Understand preferences of others; sell the argument	Win elections (politicians) or maximize budgets (bureaucrats) to gain legitimacy
	Unlearning	Implicit in most threads but especially organizational learning: Argyris and Schön	Abandonment of particular ideas	Actors seek to substitute with new ideas perceived to be better
'Non-learning'	'No' learning	Organizational and policy learning: Simon, Rose	No change in cognition and behaviour	Actors in process are satisfied with status quo
	Blocked learning	Organizational learning: Crossan, Hedberg	Cognitive change occurs but structures, interests and current worldviews block behavioural change	Learning remains at individual or group level, and is not embedded into organization and network routines

influenced by many of the theoretical threads described above. In order to give the authors some frame of reference, Table 1 is offered as a starting point.

The review should not stop at the discussion of learning. A key element of all learning is 'unlearning', where actors subtract particular knowledge which they deem false and/or obsolescent (Argyris and Schön 1996: 3). 'Unlearning' old lessons and moving away from past successes requires time and effort (Hedberg 1981: 9). Similarly, all Table 1 categories may reflect flawed/bad learning (e.g. 'competency traps' – see Levitt and March 1988: 322–3). Learning can enslave and harm (Hedberg 1981: 4). Hence, learning does not necessarily involve an improved understanding of knowledge and a commensurate improvement in policy.

'Blocked learning' acknowledges that individual learning is not enough. It must permeate the thinking of key decision-makers of the group or organization to reflect on the group; busy policy-makers tend to stick to routine (Rose 1991: 11–12). Hence, as some of the articles show, there is a time dimension in learning. Learning may also taper off, but equally learning may take time to build. Judgements about blocked learning therefore need careful consideration.

The reviews also underline that learning is contingent on the conditions so that policy processes reveal different forms of learning and non-learning (see Table 1). There must be both a cognitive change of actor understanding, as well as a behavioural adaptation to this new knowledge. Hedberg (1981: 12–13) notes how both relatively unchanged environments and rapidly changing environments with information overload create poor conditions for learning. Where cognitive and behavioural processes fail due to misperception or too comfortable (or too hostile) conditions, no learning is transmitted (Jervis 1976: 117–216). Rose (1991: 10–13) has stated elegantly that people do not want to learn when they are satisfied. Actors are expected to have limited time, information and other resources; there is no expectation of systematic preference formation and evaluation. Hence, Table 1 summarizes types of learning as well as the outcomes.

EUROPEAN INTEGRATION THEORIES AND LEARNING

'Learning' has been a much less specific research topic in EU integration theory. Notable exceptions include Eising (2002), Padgett (2003), Bomberg (2007), Kerber and Eckardt (2007) and Bulmer *et al.* (2007). This list shows that the explicit attention for learning is fairly new and seems to be increasing (Egan 2009). Owing to developments such as enlargement and the search for new instruments, scholarly attention has been shifting from interest in the EU institutions towards the impact on the member states (Bauer *et al.* 2007). This, however, does not mean that earlier EU studies have been unrelated to 'learning'. Without striving for completeness, some of the connections between integration theories and learning are explored below.

Neofunctionalism and learning

Ernst Haas' work, discussed above, is relevant to international organizations generally but the importance of nested issues has particular relevance to the EU and requires management of spillover effects. The lessons learnt from the financial crisis have led to reinvigorated discussions over the need to interconnect integration in the financial market and the internal market (Larosière Report 2009). Nested issues create incentives for transnational actors seeking solutions for cross-border problems. Haas' work points to the EU's institutionalized actors who drive change processes forward. He highlights integration networks of élites, drawing crucially from supranational institutions that garner support and credibility from managing spillover processes. Bomberg (2007) similarly views the Commission as being highly skilled 'teachers'.

Elaborating on this idea of institutionalized actors, there are more drivers for change, particularly the rotating presidency that has been a source of 'semi-supranational' leadership alongside the Commission (Schout 2008), as well as the interconnected non-governmental organizational (NGO) networks (see governance discussion below). The EU's leadership is open and shared across the Commission, Council and European Parliament which implies not only an open system with many points of access but also a great leadership capacity at multiple levels (Haywood 2008).

Some EU scholars have explicitly adopted the epistemic community explanations whilst others have adopted the parallel ACF framework. Verdun (1999: 320–2) emphasizes the importance of divergent national interests driving the Delors Committee, and leading to a blueprint for European monetary union (EMU). Zito (2001) studied the behaviour of epistemic communities in changing EU acid rain policy. Such examples support the argument that epistemic communities shape the EU discourse and form consensual ideas when conditions for a particular issue are complex and full of ambiguous choices. The openness of the EU arena with its multiple member states and institutions does present strong advantages for the agenda-setting to reflect learning.

Dudley and Richardson (1999) find that the combination of repeated interaction within advocacy coalitions has driven change (see also Parrish 2003). Particularly important in their study of EU steel policy was the presence of policy problems, the ideas that could be potential solutions, and the presence of multiple leadership roles which introduced and brokered these ideas. Moving beyond these EU characteristics, a discussion emerged as to whether the EU as a 'laboratory' with its continued and increasing effort to develop co-ordination processes provides an environment to induce adaptive behaviour among administrations based on imported information and insights (Radaelli 2000).

Diffusion studies

Neofunctionalism highlights the role of EU actors involved in learning either as learners or teachers. 'Diffusion' has centred around a discussion on whether its specific conditions make the EU particularly suitable to policy transfer and diffusion. Arguably the EU, like other complex federal systems, is relatively well suited to the development of new learning ideas (Kerber and Eckardt 2007). Nevertheless, the EU's conditions also create layers of veto points of which oppositional groups can take advantage. Morgan (1997), for example, suggests that member state central governments can act as significant constraints to such learning processes. Also, Marier (2009) underlines that lessons learned from other countries have proved hard to implement when major national interests are at stake, as seen in pension reform. It is one thing to set the agenda in one stage of the EU decision-making chain, but how one sustains learning and change across a number of levels is a fundamental EU challenge owing to interdependencies between policy reforms and administrative reform, and between EU and national reforms (Schout 2009).

More subtle are Kerber and Eckardt's (2007) qualifications of the EU's learning capacities. They compare 'laboratory federalism' and the EU's OMC instrument. Laboratory federalism based on competition seemingly has substantial advantages over the EU's OMC centralized system of providing best practice. 'Benchmarks' are a type of optimal policy displaying an implicit preference for convergence while limiting the incentives for states to experiment and compete.

Moving on from the broad discussion on the EU's learning conditions, enlargement and the increasing use of OMCs have more or less forced detailed attention to conditions for diffusion. The new member states having to adapt to the EU's *acquis* and related institutions and the investments in OMC processes have delivered a stream of insights into the favourable conditions for diffusion. First, these studies are focusing more or less explicitly on whether convergence takes place – rather than on learning which is more mutually adaptive (Bomberg 2007). The causalities stimulating diffusion include whether financial support is given in relation to adaptation, the EU's capacities to monitor actual implementation, political sensitivities concerning integration, whether pre-existing systems exist (if not, then adaptation is easier) and the type of governance mode (compliance, competition or communication) (Bauer *et al.* 2007).

In terms of isolating conditions, Radaelli (2000) finds evidence for national convergence and policy transfer under conditions where national models provide a source for transfer but also where EU institutions, particularly the Commission, can manufacture solutions and exercise entrepreneurship. Bulmer *et al.* (2007) studied three EU regulatory regimes in the utilities sector and conclude that policy transfer has been pivotal in the evolution of Europe's utilities in these sectors. Institutional dynamics are particularly significant, with the most hierarchical and institutionalized regime (air transport) providing the most evidence for emulation.

Moreover, the EU diffusion-related theories have generated considerable attention to the importance of the 'shadow of the hierarchy'. The extent to which new member states incorporate the *acquis* depends partly on the EU capacities to enforce legislation (Bauer *et al.* 2007). Moreover, OMC processes and voluntary co-operation tend to misfire if they are not strongly guided either by Commission leadership (Schout and Jordan 2005) or the threat of imposing legislation if soft co-ordination fails (Héritier and Lehmkuhl 2008). This raises the question centring on the extent to which diffusion theories are about learning or squarely about coercion (Radaelli 2009).

To understand the true extent of EU policy transfer, Padgett (2003: 228–9) argues that it is insufficient to study how policies are transferred from the member states to the EU ('uploading' of a policy). One must analyse the 'downloading', which is dependent on how well the policy idea fits with domestic institutions and interests and the configuration of the national institutions. Padgett's (2003: 242–3) empirical findings suggest that the EU leads to weaker forms of hybrid transfer. Uploaded policies must first survive the bargaining process and then subsequently be downloaded and adapted to the national level.

This underlines the strengths and the weaknesses of the EU's capacity to diffuse. Policy transfer is more likely to involve labels rather than beliefs. This is in addition to the difficulty of getting policy ideas through the complex 'veto' points of the EU multi-institutional system. In this process, the adaptation pressures triggered by the European-level policy ideas may redistribute resources and affect the political balance within the domestic constituency; furthermore, the interaction of the national representatives with the EU process may cause the national actors to redefine how they view a problem (Padgett 2003). This underlines conditions where strong domestic coalitions perceive gains from a policy shift and where the national representatives have more continuous interaction. The EU's system of continuous interaction where the same actors often meet in multiple arenas indicates that the system may be geared towards uploading but face inherent difficulties with downloading.

If one extends the policy transfer analysis to EU influence on other regions, this dynamic may be even more limited. Grugel (2007) studied the impact of EU efforts to export notions of social citizenship to the Mercosur region. The actual learning was extremely limited as the South American élites shared very little in the way of social norms (Grugel 2007: 56–61). Farrell's arguments suggest similar limits in extending diffusion processes to Africa (Farrell 2009). This confronts the EU with some difficulties as the international UN-based regulatory fora (e.g. for aviation safety) are country-based whereas the EU prefers promoting 'regional blocs', but this will only succeed if more blocs such as the EU appear (Schout 2008). The EU's place at international negotiating tables is therefore conditional on the prior diffusion of integration experience with its inherent difficulties.

Current EU literature is highly critical of concepts of policy transfer and convergence (e.g. Citi and Rhodes 2007; Lodge 2007; Scharpf, 2001 have labelled the learning-based OMC turn in the EU as 'mere talk'). Others see more significant dynamics, as the above examples have shown. Yet, if one brings in the time dimension, one can see major mutual adaptation processes in areas such as consumer policy or competition policy (e.g. Kassim and Wright 2009). Eising (2002) pointed out that consensus-building norms and consensual knowledge lead to policy learning, and change may be possible in the latter stages of the EU policy process. In the highly sensitive area of energy liberalization, routine interaction in the EU's multi-level system has triggered policy learning. The incremental nature of Council proceedings forced member states to aggregate their preferences and build solutions in a sequential manner, while increasing the knowledge of member state representatives about the questions at hand and the consequences of policy change (Eising 2002: 109–13). Nevertheless, the ambitious Lisbon process seems to have been a failure for a decade, and the 'Cardiff' learning process has simply conflated (Jordan and Schout 2006). In other words, there are successes and failures to report, suggesting that scholars should avoid jumping to conclusions.

Governance and learning

Although originating from a different thread, 'EU governance' is closely related to the notion of epistemic communities. The success of the internal market programme and the enlargement from 15 to 27 member states triggered a profound examination of EU governance. Much of the 'governance turn' from hierarchical steering (legislation) towards particular networks (or communication-based instruments more generally) centres on networks such as the OMC and agencies (or 'networked governance'; see Kohler-Koch 2002; Jordan and Schout 2006). Moving beyond legislation, network-based instruments depict problem recognition and problem-solving as core elements of policy-making. Networked governance crosses subnational, national, European and international levels and involves a multitude of stakeholders across these levels (Eising and Kohler-Koch 1999: 5–6).

The EU, with its diffused structure and party structures, is geared to consensus-building governed by persuasion (Kohler-Koch 2002: 88–9) with the hope that, through knowledge transfer, convergence with the benchmark emerges (Bomberg 2007). However, others are much less concerned with a static form of convergence but see the EU institutions and other actors cooperating and competing in a process of collective learning as they seek support from society. Eberlein and Kerwer (2004) posit that governance, framed in terms of 'democratic experimentalism', can address policy stalemates as actors become exposed to ideas from outside and transform their understanding of their own interests.

Essentially, governance is about *process* – bringing actors together assuming this leads to action – but the drivers and conditions for success have garnered little attention. Schout and Jordan (2005) discuss the implicit assumption in governance that networks are self-organizing on the basis that actors learn almost automatically because they recognize their interdependence and the value added of mutual adaptation. Ostrom (1986) deducts a list of preconditions for successful self-organization including small size, a tradition of cooperation and a common culture. This would emphasize the limits of network learning in an increasingly differentiated EU and help to explain why OMC-type learning has mixed results. It also emphasizes the need to start taking the management of networked governance seriously.

CONCLUSIONS AND SPECIAL ISSUE OVERVIEW

The first conclusion of this review is that the extension of policy analysis into learning theories started in the US and seemed to have reached a plateau in the early 1990s: major reviews of learning theories emerged, concluding that learning has to be decomposed in questions around who learns, what is learnt and under what conditions. As such, learning theories had not become a serious component in European integration studies. However, with the initiation of the governance 'turn' around 2000, integration theories shifted from macro theories towards analysing the micro processes in EU decision-making. Pragmatic considerations following enlargement and a change in preferences ('a paradigm shift'; see Schout 2009) in favour of networks and related learning-driven instruments – mainly the OMC – have made learning a major theme on the EU academic and political agendas. The increased differentiation in the EU and swing towards 'new' governance made it even more important to understand whether and how member states learn to operate in the more competitive internal market, and whether and how they adapt to policies elsewhere in the EU. With this renewed interest in learning theories, the attention increased for conditions for learning and diffusion.

Second, there seems to be a mismatch between the extent to which learning instruments are now applied in the EU and our understanding of learning in complex multi-level systems. At the political level, networked governance banks strongly on the capacities of member states to learn rapidly whilst academic literature is strongly divided over the extent to which member states learn. The OMC has been warmly perceived by those claiming that its communication-based instruments are the new preferred instruments. Others suggest that these institutions amount to little more than just talk. This special issue, however, has shown that scholarly literature is trying hard to become more precise regarding conditions for learning and questions about whether the time dimension of learning has been underestimated – allowing for more time, the EU's abilities to learn may be a source of its resilience.

Third, networks have always played a major role in learning theories. In the EU, however, networks were first less the focus of attention and even seen as a second best option compared to more community approaches to integration in the pre-subsidiarity days. But, with the governance 'turn', networks developed into the top league. With this, learning-related governance theory was equated with self-organization. Hence, the EU literature had a different emphasis compared to the earlier learning theories that were more concerned with organizational learning and leadership.

Fourth, although still in an early phase, conditions that influence learning in the EU are becoming clearer. Characteristics of the EU that foster learning include its diversity of member states locked in repeated interactions and its multiple and multi-level leadership which makes the EU open to new ideas. The EU's operational basis organized in networks (including advocacy coalitions or epistemic communities) offers multiple possibilities to exchange ideas and knowledge. Yet, with its diversity of actors, layers and phases (including uploading, downloading and implementation) the EU also offers multiple obstacles to learning and implementation. This implies an inherent tension between institutional innovation and path dependence.

In sum, there are those who are equivocal about whether learning is a relevant subject or whether the EU system has substantial advantages for learning over individual states and subnational regions. Some scholars view diffusion of power across EU institutions and levels as enhancing the possibility for learning as states are forced to consensus, whilst other scholars see this diversity as multiplying veto points that block learning and the implementation of lessons learned. Yet, rather than having left it as a debate between the EU as facilitating or frustrating learning, the literature has been identifying the contingencies involved in learning and singling out the leadership provided by the (formal and informal) EU institutions including the 'shadow of the hierarchy'.

Reconsidering learning and taking stock of the current trends, learning now combines longer-term perspectives for understanding changes and specification of learning contingencies with clearer distinctions between types of learning. With the differences in nuances between learning, diffusion, governance and lesson drawing, and with the multitude of intervening variables, learning is not developing into an elegant, parsimonious theory. Fortunately, elegance is not a requirement for relevant theories. Understanding European integration beyond crude institutional theories requires working with more differentiated concepts such as 'learning'. What the discussions above and in this special issue show, however, is that the body of EU learning literature is growing and opening up the change patterns.

Issue overview

To highlight the insights in learning conditions and the specificities of learning in the EU, the editor explicitly selected authors working with inter- and intra-EU comparisons. The special issue starts with two empirical papers examining the consequences of the EU's key administrative feature, i.e. its multi-level nature, and emphasizing the difficulty of instrumental learning. *Schout's* article isolates two sets of interdependencies. First, learning at the EU and national levels are interdependent. In the EU's multi-layered administration, administrative changes at the international level are dependent on the match between learning at EU and at national levels. Second, the EU's 'governance learning' is interdependent on its 'instrument learning' and 'organizational learning'. These conceptual and administrative interdependencies underline that in a multi-level system learning needs to develop in parallel at the EU and national administrative levels, as seen in the implementation failure at the EU level.

Radaelli (2009) examines the nature of learning itself by asking whether analytic approaches to policy formulation, specifically regulatory impact assessment (RIA), enable complex organizations to learn. He distinguishes between types of learning, their micro foundations, and the implications for knowledge utilization. The article assesses four countries (Denmark, the Netherlands, Sweden, and the UK), controlling for both domestic and multi-level effects. Radaelli concludes that, in the case of RIA systems, mutual learning has a high level of symbolic learning due to emulation (to gain legitimacy by trying to appear more like the benchmark countries) and political learning (improved policy salesmanship rather than substantially learning about policies through RIA).

The next two papers gauge how the EU system compares with external systems. *Farrell* (2009) examines the extent to which the European model has been exported to other regional integration projects. The article incorporates a historical institutionalist approach with the policy learning framework. Like Schout and Radaelli, Farrell points to limitations in relation to instrumental learning. Farrell's explanation is largely based on internal and external stabilizing power conditions. However, she also points to changes emerging over time as new actors, particularly NGOs, appear on the scene.

Montpetit (2009) questions whether EU policy processes are particularly conducive to policy learning. His statistical analysis rests on a survey of actors in Europe and North America. Despite claims that the EU involves more learning than the US and that the EU has specific policy styles, Montpetit does not find such differences. Differences in learning seem to be between policy fields, not between geographical areas. This also speaks to those who are concerned with a legitimacy gap particularly in the EU due to learning-based instruments.

Demonstrating that key learning processes may happen within the EU but without large EU input, *Marier's* (2009) article reveals that, in the area of pension reforms, where the EU member states have retained control, instrumental learning has been highly path dependent. Although European governments have created special public inquiries (such as commissions) to provide an in-depth analysis of pensions policy problems and learning from abroad, substantive learning from abroad has remained very limited.

Picking up the theme of the EU's learning abilities, *Zito's* (2009) article investigates the evolution of two environmental agencies (the European Environment Agency and the England and Wales Environment Agency) which have distinct roles in improving EU environmental performance. Traditional agency theories are based on principal–agent models and examine the ability of agencies to shirk. Zito, however, looks more at micro level changes by examining two dimensions of the EU learning process: organizational learning and policy learning. The article provides insights into the subtleties of how both agencies have been able to reformulate their roles by using among others, budget reforms and outcomes of evaluations. In line with Montpetit's findings, the EU level does not seemingly offer more learning abilities than the national level.

Egan (2009) discusses the special issue papers by asking under what conditions the need for solutions to political and societal problems leads to the transferral of a policy designed for another political system and/or ideas taken from other contexts. She interrogates the use of terminology in the special issue and compares the value added of the learning approach to other plausible mechanisms for policy diffusion. This discussion paper assesses the extent to which this issue can provide analytic leverage and historical narratives about policy change given the several complementary, yet distinct, notions of policy learning found in this emerging area.

The authors all point to the enormous ambition of even contemplating the possibility of cross-border learning and to the major difficulties and interdependencies involved. Yet they also show that time is an underestimated factor in learning studies which should warn scholars about jumping to conclusions about refuting or embracing learning theories. Moreover, they underline that, depending on the areas, changes *are* taking place influenced by shifts in perceptions of problems and solutions. By decomposing the many forces at work, slowly but surely our insights into what drives change in the complex EU integration process increases. Finally, and counter to intuitive and counterclaims elsewhere, the EU does not seem particularly better at learning than other administrative systems – although it seems to be relying on such expectations more.

ACKNOWLEDGEMENTS

The authors thank Michelle Egan, the other special issue authors and the two anonymous referees for their invaluable suggestions. Anthony Zito also thanks the Leverhulme Trust and the British Academy for their support.

REFERENCES

Argyris, C. and Schön, D. (1996) *Organizational Learning II*, Reading, MA: Addison-Wesley Publishing.
Bauer, M., Knill, C. and Pitschel, D. (2007) 'Differential Europeanization in Eastern Europe: the impact of diverse EU regulatory governance patterns', *Journal of European Integration* 29(4): 405–23.
Bennett, C. (1991) 'What is policy convergence and what causes it?', *British Journal of Political Science* 21(2): 215–33.
Bennett, C. and Howlett, M. (1992) 'The lessons of learning: reconciling theories of policy learning and policy change', *Policy Sciences* 25(3): 275–94.

Berry, F. and Berry, W. (1999) 'Innovation and diffusion models in policy research', in P. Sabatier (ed.), *Theories of the Policy Process*, Boulder, CO: Westview Press, pp. 169–200.

Bomberg, E. (2007) 'Policy learning in an enlarged European Union: environmental NGOs and new policy instruments', *Journal of European Public Policy* 14(2): 248–68.

Breslauer, G. and Tetlock, P. (1991) 'Introduction', in G. Breslauer and P. Tetlock (eds), *Learning in US and Soviet Foreign Policy*, Boulder, CO: Westview Press, pp. 3–19.

Bulmer, S., Dolowitz, D., Humphreys, P. and Padgett, S. (2007) *Policy Transfer in the European Union Governance*, London: Routledge.

Busch, P.-O. and Jörgens, H. (2005) 'The international sources of policy convergence: explaining the spread of environmental policy innovations', *Journal of European Public Policy* 12(5): 860–84.

Citi, M. and Rhodes, M. (2007) 'New modes of governance in the EU: a critical survey and analysis', in K.E. Jørgensen, M. Pollack and B. Rosamund (eds), *Handbook of European Union Politics*, London: Sage, pp. 463–82.

Cornett, L. and Caporaso, J. (1992) '"And still it moves!" State interests and social forces in the European Community', in J. Rosenau and E. Czempiel (eds), *Governance without Government: Order and Change in World Politics*, Cambridge: Cambridge University Press, pp. 219–49.

Crossan, M., Lane, H. and White, R. (1999) 'An organizational learning framework: from intuition to institution', *Academy of Management Review* 24(3): 522–37.

Cyert, R. and March, J. (1992) *A Behavioural Theory of the Firm*, 2nd edn, Oxford: Blackwell.

Deutsch, K. (1963) *The Nerves of Government*, New York: Free Press.

DiMaggio, P.J. and Powell, W.W. (1983) 'The iron cage revisited: institutional isomorphism and collective rationality in organizational fields', *American Sociological Review* 48(2): 147–60.

Dolowitz, D. and Marsh, D. (1996) 'Who learns from whom?', *Political Studies* 44(2): 343–57.

Dudley, G. and Richardson, J. (1999) 'Competing advocacy coalitions and the process of "frame reflection": a longitudinal analysis of EU steel policy', *Journal of European Public Policy* 6(2): 225–48.

Eberlein, B. and Kerwer, D. (2004) 'New governance in the EU', *Journal of Common Market Studies* 42(1): 121–41.

Egan, M. (2009) 'Governance and learning in the post-Maastricht era?', *Journal of European Public Policy* 16(8): 1244–53.

Eising, R. (2002) 'Policy learning in embedded negotiation: explaining EU electricity liberalization', *International Organization* 56(1): 47–84.

Eising, R. and Kohler-Koch, B. (1999) 'Introduction: Network governance in the European Union', in B. Kohler-Koch and R. Eising (eds), *The Transformation of Governance in the European Union*, London: Routledge, pp. 3–13.

Farrell, M. (2009) 'EU policy towards other regions: policy learning in the external promotion of regional integration', *Journal of European Public Policy* 16(8): 1165–84.

Grugel, J. (2007) 'Democratization and ideational diffusion: Europe, Mercosur and social citizenship', *Journal of Common Market Studies* 45(1): 43–68.

Haas, E. (1964) *Beyond the Nation-State: Functionalism and International Organization*, Stanford, CA: Stanford University Press.

Haas, E. (1968) *The Uniting of Europe: Beyond the Nation State*, Stanford, CA: Stanford University Press.

Haas, E. (1990) *When Knowledge is Power: Three Models of Change in International Organizations*, Berkeley, CA: University of California Press.

Haas, E. (1991) 'Collective learning: some theoretical speculations', in G. Breslauer and P. Tetlock (eds), *Learning in US and Soviet Foreign Policy*, Boulder, CO: Westview Press, pp. 62–99.

Haas, E. and Haas, P. (1995) 'Learning to learn: improving international governance', *Global Governance* 1(3): 255–85.

Haas, P. (1990) *Saving the Mediterranean: The Politics of International Environmental Cooperation*, New York: Columbia University Press.

Hall, P. (1993) 'Policy paradigms, social learning and the state', *Comparative Politics* 25(3): 275–96.

Hancher, L. (1996) 'The regulatory role of the European Union', in H. Kassim and A. Menon (eds), *The European Union and National Industrial Policy*, London: Routledge, pp. 52–69.

Hayward, J. (ed.) (2008) *Leaderless Europe*, Oxford: Oxford University Press.

Heclo, H. (1974) *Modern Social Politics in Britain and Sweden*, New Haven, CT: Yale University Press.

Hedberg, B. (1981) 'How organizations learn and unlearn', in P. Nystrom and W. Starbuck (eds), *Handbook of Organizational Design*, Oxford: Oxford University Press, pp. 3–27.

Heidenreich, M. and Zeitlin, J. (2009) 'Introduction', in M. Heidenreich and J. Zeitlin (eds), *Changing European Employment and Welfare Regimes – The Influence of the Open Method of Coordination on National Reforms*, New York: Routledge, pp. 1–9.

Héritier, A. and Lehmkuhl, D. (2008) 'Introduction: the shadow of hierarchy and new modes of governance', *Journal of Public Policy* 28(1): 1–17.

James, O. and Lodge, M. (2003) 'The limitations of "policy transfer" and "lesson-drawing" for public policy research', *Political Studies Review* 1(2): 179–93.

Jervis, R. (1976) *Perception and Misperception in International Politics*, Princeton, NJ: Princeton University Press.

Jordan, A. and Schout, A. (2006) *The Coordination of the European Union: Exploring the Capacities of Networked Governance*, Oxford: Oxford University Press.

Kassim, H. (2008) '"Mission impossible", but mission accomplished: the Kinnock reforms and the European Commission', *Journal of European Public Policy* 15(5): 648–68.

Kassim, H. and Wright, K. (2009) 'Network governance and the European Union: the case of the European competition network'. Paper for 'The Transformation of the Executive Branch of Government in Europe', ARENA, University of Oslo, 4–6 June.

Kerber, W. and Eckardt, M. (2007) 'Policy learning in Europe: the open method of co-ordination and laboratory federalism', *Journal of European Public Policy* 14(2): 227–47.

Knight, L. (2002) 'Network learning: exploring learning by interorganizational networks', *Human Relations* 55(4): 427–54.

Knill, C. and Lenschow, A. (2005) 'Compliance, competition and communication: different approaches of European governance and their impact on national institutions', *Journal of Common Market Studies* 43(3): 583–606.

Kohler-Koch, B. (2002) 'On networks, travelling ideas, and behavioural inertia', in T. Conzelmann and M. Knodt (eds), *Regionales Europa – Europäisierte Regionen*, Frankfurt: Campus Verlag, pp. 87–103.

Larosière Report (2009) *The High-level Group on Financial Supervision in the EU: Report*, Brussels: Commission of the European Communities, 25 February.

Levitt, B. and March, J. (1988) 'Organizational learning', *Annual Review of Sociology* 14: 319–40.

Lodge, M. (2007) 'Comparing non-hierarchical governance in action: the open method of co-ordination in pensions and information society', *Journal of Common Market Studies* 45(2): 343–65.
Marier, P. (2009) 'The power of institutionalized learning: the uses and practices of commissions to generate policy change', *Journal of European Public Policy* 16(8): 1204–23.
May, P. (1992) 'Policy learning and failure', *Journal of Public Policy* 12(4): 331–54.
Montpetit, E. (2009) 'Governance and policy learning in the European Union: a comparison with North America', *Journal of European Public Policy* 16(8): 1185–1203.
Moravcsik, A. (1993) 'Preference and power in the European Community: a liberal intergovernmentalist approach', *Journal of Common Market Studies* 31(4): 473–522.
Morgan, K. (1997) 'The learning region: institutions, innovation and regional renewal', *Regional Studies* 31(5): 491–503.
Nedergaard, P. (2006) 'Policy learning in the European Union', *Policy Studies* 27(4): 311–23.
Ostrom, E. (1986) 'An agenda for the study of institutions', *Public Choice* 48(1): 3–25.
Padgett, S. (2003) 'Between synthesis and emulation: EU policy transfer in the power sector', *Journal of European Public Policy* 10(2): 227–45.
Parrish, R. (2003) 'The politics of sports regulation in the European Union', *Journal of European Public Policy* 10(2): 246–62.
Peterson, J. (2008) 'Enlargement, reform and the European Commission. Weathering a perfect storm?', *Journal of European Public Policy* 15(5): 761–80.
Radaelli, C. (2000) 'Policy transfer in the European Union: institutional isomorphism as a source of legitimacy', *Governance* 13(1): 25–43.
Radaelli, C.M. (2009) 'Measuring policy learning: regulatory impact assessment in europe', *Journal of European Public Policy* 16(8): 1145–64.
Rogers, E. (1983) *Diffusion of Innovations*, 3rd edn, New York and London: The Free Press.
Rose, R. (1991) 'What is lesson-drawing?', *Journal of Public Policy* 11(1): 3–30.
Sabatier, P. (1988) 'An advocacy coalition framework of policy change and the role of policy-oriented learning therein', *Policy Sciences* 21(2–3): 129–68.
Scharpf, F. (2001) 'Notes toward a theory of multilevel governing in Europe', *Scandinavian Political Studies* 24(1): 1–26.
Schout, A. (2008) 'Beyond the rotating presidency', in J. Hayward (ed.), *Leaderless Europe*, Oxford: Oxford University Press, pp. 269–88.
Schout, A. (2009) 'Organizational learning in the EU's multi-level governance system', *Journal of European Public Policy* 16(8): 1124–44.
Schout, A. and Jordan, A. (2005) 'Coordinated European governance: self organising or centrally steered?', *Public Administration* 83(1): 201–20.
Schout, A. and Van den Berge, M. (2009) 'The resilience of the Union: European integration 1999-2009'. Paper presented at 'Enlargement – Five Years After: The State of European Integration and New Challenges for the Discipline', Central European University, Budapest, 8–9 May.
Simon, H. (1961) *Administrative Behavior*, 2nd edn, New York: Macmillan.
Steinbrunner, J. (1974) *The Cybernetic Theory of Decision*, Princeton, NJ: Princeton University Press.
Verdun, A. (1999) 'The role of the Delors Committee in creating EMU: an epistemic community?', *Journal of European Public Policy* 6(2): 308–28.
Volden, C. (2006) 'States as policy laboratories: emulating success in the children's health insurance program', *American Journal of Political Science* 50(2): 294–312.
Walker, J. (1969) 'The diffusion of innovations among the American states', *American Political Science Review* 63(3): 880–99.

Zito, A.R. (2001) 'Epistemic communities, collective entrepreneurship and European integration', *Journal of European Public Policy* 8(4): 585–603.
Zito, A.R. (2009) 'European agencies as agents of governance and EU learning', *Journal of European Public Policy* 16(8): 1224–43.
Zito, A., Radaelli, C. and Jordan, A. (2003) 'New policy instruments in the European Union: better governance or rhetorical smoke', *Public Administration* 81(3): 509–606.

Organizational learning in the EU's multi-level governance system

Adriaan Schout

1. INTRODUCTION

The learning literature underlines that politics is more than a conflict and a struggle for power. Politics also involves dealing with uncertainty, gathering and processing information, and building new structures (Bennett and Howlett 1992). The learning perspectives point towards these dynamic changes in the contexts in which power struggles take place.

The European Union (EU) governance literature more or less assumes a 'governance turn' (Kohler-Koch and Rittberger 2006) and hence presumes that policy-making in the EU has been raised to a higher level by moving away from ('hierarchical') legislation towards networked governance. In the governance literature, hierarchical norm-setting, which has been the EU's preferred mode of governance, is regarded as a zero-sum game in which sectors and member states fight over static obligations (e.g. over the percentage of waste recycling). Instead, it is hoped that 'new' modes of governance based on communication and networks will offer win–win situations through interactive processes in which objectives are identified and problems solved (Kooiman

2003). But is this what has happened? Moreover, has the 'governance turn' delivered on its promises and if not, why not?

Reviews of EU governance show, first, that there has not been so much of a shift from legislation to new instruments and, second, that the results of new instruments fall behind expectations (Citi and Rhodes 2007; Schout and Jordan 2008). However, equating the governance debate with a shift to 'new' instruments does not do justice to the governance reforms and the attempts to upgrade quality of legislation. This article argues that to understand the state of play in the governance reforms, we have to take a much closer look at what has happened in terms of instruments and examine the changes on the 'shop floor' of the administrative systems (Hanf 1994).

To see how governance has changed and where things may have become stuck, we distinguish three levels in the governance debate: governance learning, instrument learning and organizational learning. In learning terms, the governance 'turn' suggests nothing less than a shift in paradigm in the EU's preferred steering modes, i.e. in preferences for broad categories of governance instruments (Lascoumes and Le Galès 2007). This paradigm shift is referred to here in the context of the EU's governance debate as 'governance learning' and is defined as learning about the major governance modes and how they can be employed effectively. It involves 'instrument learning', defined as the development in instruments and entailing lessons about the viability of the individual policy instruments (May 1992: 332). Accounting for the performance of particular instruments requires access to the operational details. It is at this level of 'organizational learning' that we can see whether governance has changed and where we can find explanations for performance.

The organizational learning literature is rich, examining sociological aspects, information technology, leadership and processes. The definition of organizational learning used here follows Common's (2004: 36): 'making practical use of ... knowledge to achieve particular government objectives, usually accompanied by organizational change'. This definition relates to the organizational science literature studying capacities for information gathering, lowering co-ordination costs, and steering the behaviour of individuals and groups (Cyert and March 1963). Organizational learning takes place when organizations develop structures and procedures ('capacities' as elaborated below) to upgrade information processing and improve problem-solving (Olsen and Peters 1996).

Of the different learning approaches, organizational learning is probably the least developed. The different views on the usefulness of the 'hard' organizational aspects in relation to more political views on organizations partly explain this lacuna (Dawson 1992; Rhodes 1997). Typically, Easterby-Smith and Lyles (2003), who utilize organizational learning, emphasise 'process' and 'power'. Important as these perspectives are, they need not deny the relevance of studying organizational structures.

By distinguishing three layers of learning, this paper analyses the match between changes in governance and the redesign of administrations. For reasons discussed below, in the context of the EU's multi-level administration this match has to be analysed in at least two ways. The innovations in the use of instruments at EU level have to be matched by developments in administrative capacities in the EU institutions. Second, the capacities that are being built at the EU level require parallel adaptations in national administrations. Organizational learning offers an approach to studying the development of organizational capacities and to comparing these between levels of administration.

As a case study, we take impact assessments (IAs). Being the key component in the EU's better regulation (BR) policy, the IA should lead to better argued policies in terms of objectives such as consequences for the environment and for administrative costs, and to a careful selection of instruments (see Radaelli 2009). Yet, after 15 years of experimenting with different types of assessments, the evaluations of the results achieved are still lukewarm (EVIA 2008). There are several explanations for this and the paper argues that multi-level organizational design issues are part of them. This case study is part of a wider research studying the administrative challenges of the governance debate (Monda et al., forthcoming).

Section 2 defines organizational learning and discusses the links between learning at governance, instrument and organizational levels. This leads to a model to operationalize and assess organizational learning. Placing this study in the context of EU governance as a multi-layered learning challenge, section 3 moves from the higher level of abstraction (the EU's governance debate) to a specific, relatively new instrument in the EU (IAs). The subsequent sections explore the development of organizational capacities in the Commission (4) and the Netherlands (5). Given obvious difficulties of multi-level organizational studies, this article only discusses the Commission (the EU level) and the Netherlands (as a sample of the Council). This offers a reasonable flavour of EU organizational learning dilemmas. The Dutch government is an obvious candidate as it has invested heavily in BR and has been presented as a world leader (World Bank 2007). Moreover, the Dutch are acutely aware of the need for further EU steps to ensure better policies nationally. The Netherlands is a critical case and raises the question, if they have difficulty in matching capacities to policy innovations, whether IAs are feasible in the EU. The conclusions follow in section 6.

For information on how the IA system is structured and used, this article draws on reports and on interviews with officials at the Commission (Directorate-Generals (DGs) and the Secretariat General (SG)), the European Parliament (administrators and Members of the European Parliament (MEPs)) and the General Secretariat of the Council, as well as with officials at various Dutch ministries and at the independent watchdog for administrative burden (ACTAL). Two senior officials from the Dutch administration and the Commission have read earlier drafts and have confirmed the findings.

2. LEVELS OF LEARNING IN THE EU GOVERNANCE DEBATE

Differentiating three levels of learning helps to position organizational learning in the EU governance debate (see Table 1). The first level is governance learning.

Table 1 Organizational learning in the context of governance learning

Governance learning	Instrument learning (without being exhaustive)	organizational learning
A switch between governance modes or an upgrade of these modes individually: • Markets (competition) • Networked governance (communication) • Hierarchies (coercion or legislation)	Law • Regulation as hierarchical steering • Law as stick to support soft co-ordination • Development of horizontal requirements for EU law as specified by the BR agenda (proofing, subsidiarity, 25 per cent reduction of administrative costs, IAs, etc.) • Planning, priority-setting and budgeting Soft co-ordination • OMC • Steering through information Tax incentives, fiscal policy and budgets Agencies • As independent regulatory authorities (e.g. the trade mark agency) • As network organizations (e.g. the European Environment Agency)	Hierarchy Bureaucratic capacities Standardization of objectives Training Horizontal co-ordination mechanisms (informal relations, task forces, teams, integrating managers (with limited arbitration powers or with strong decision-taking powers))

At the highest level of abstraction, governance is about broad steering modes originally summarized in the literature as 'markets and hierarchies' but developed into 'markets, networks and hierarchies' when networks became fashionable (Powell 1990). The governance debate marks a shift from government ('hierarchy' or legislation as understood in the EU governance debate; Héritier and Lehmkuhl 2008) to governance through interactions within networks ('processes'; Kooiman 2003) and economic incentives ('markets'). Governance learning may involve improvements in the existing mode or a 'turn' towards another mode. To be complete, governance learning includes increasing insights into instruments and their designs but the levels are treated separately for heuristic reasons.

The second level relates to the instruments associated with the governance modes. Moving from governance to instruments immediately points to some confusion as 'markets', 'networks' and 'hierarchies' are not categories but instruments. Knill and Lenschow (2005) therefore use the broader labels of competition, communication and coercion (see Table 1).

Although the EU governance debate focuses on the broadening out of instruments from legislation towards network-based modes and incentive-based mechanisms such as tax measures (Jordan *et al.* 2003), governance is mainly discussed in relation to network-based instruments such as the open method of co-ordination (OMC), IAs (EVIA 2008), and agencies and their networks (Majone 1996; Monda *et al.*, forthcoming). The EU has seized on networks to circumvent or complement legislation. 'Networked governance' is a system where governments are 'dependent upon the cooperation and joint resource mobilization of policy actors outside their hierarchical control' (Börzel 1998: 260). Networks may nurture a greater sense of ownership for horizontal objectives such as subsidiarity, competitiveness, regulatory quality and sustainability and allow flexibility in the post-enlargement era (Schout and Jordan 2005).

Linking governance to instruments is, however, not straightforward. In reality, the modes are interconnected. The OMC may not mean less legislation and legislation may be part of the move towards networked governance (Héritier and Lehmkuhl 2008). Moreover, markets are complex systems which cannot be seen independently from hierarchical regulation or networks (Powell 1990). The modes need several or even all of the instruments but in different formats. Markets as well as soft co-ordination need laws but in specific forms and with different functions (laws as rules guiding market interactions or as sticks behind OMC processes). IAs can be seen as ways to improve hierarchical governance but can also be employed as a network type of steering. Similarly, agencies can support hierarchical legislation by providing better information but agencies can also be part of networked governance. EU agencies are organized differently when supporting the Commission in law-making, compared to EU agencies facilitating interactions between social partners (Monda *et al.*, forthcoming). Confusion arises when agencies are presented as governance innovation in the form of independent authorities whereas their design offers the Commission tight controls on agencies with a view to supporting the traditional Community method (Schout and Pereyra, forthcoming). Hence, to understand shifts in governance it is essential to see how instruments are designed.

By the same token, the design has to be in accordance with governance objectives. For example, if a network has to foster co-operation between energy regulators, we need to see whether it is granted sufficient powers and resources to do so (Coen and Thatcher 2008). Reviews of the new instruments show mixed results. While there are successes to report (e.g. Knill and Lenschow 2005; Gornitzka 2006), many studies have drawn critical conclusions. New governance instruments do not seem to work as hoped as underlined by the critical assessments of IAs (TEP 2007; EVIA 2008), networks (Eberlein and Newman 2008; Coen and Thatcher 2008) and agencies (CEC 2008). Several explanations have been explored for the levelling off of performance including unrealistic expectations, the lack of leadership, the suitability of administrative cultures, the differentiation between the administrations and functional difficulties (the OMC threatens harmonization, Holzinger *et al.* 2006). However, organizational learning has received hardly any attention.

Unpacking organizational learning

Lascoumes and Le Galès (2007: 2) conclude that instruments are generally seen in a functionalist way and treated as 'natural' and as being 'at our disposal' – suggesting that all that needs to be considered is what the best instruments are to meet objectives. These authors note that policy-makers think that by changing the instruments they change the world but the results generated by the EU's new instruments show that this has not been the case. Hence, broadening the governance tools neither implies automatic changes in governance nor success. The details of how instruments are shaped and used in the EU are now beginning to be explored (Kassim and Le Galès 2008).

Studying organizational learning requires a model to operationalize administrative capacities. The basis of any organization is the definition of the unit structure and of the co-ordination mechanisms that glue it together ('differentiation and integration'; Lawrence and Lorsch 1967). The workload involved in designing and using EU instruments imposes a need for the co-ordination capacities in the Commission and national administrations to be efficient (for details, see Schout and Jordan 2005).

The organizational literature discusses mechanisms through which information is gathered and shared, and problems are solved. Borrowing from Mintzberg's synthesis (1979), different types of co-ordination mechanisms can be distinguished. These capacities influence the co-ordination costs and co-operation in the organization. As with all governance mechanisms, these are mutually reinforcing (Rhodes 1997):

- *Hierarchical co-ordination* is defined here as supervision by the political apex. In practice, there is only so much the hierarchy can supervise so that contributions from the hierarchy often take the form of mission statements (e.g. 'ensure early co-ordination' of IAs, CEC 2009). The starting point of any administrative study is the political commitment but amidst other objectives and dynamics this can, in practice, be more symbolic than real (DiMaggio and Powell 1983).
- *Bureaucratic capacities* (roles, rules, procedures, guidelines and resources) reduce transaction costs by making information exchanges cheap and reliable and by defining the margins of manoeuvre. They help to define who has the right to information and take decisions.
- *Standardization of objectives* involves setting clear and measurable objectives to allow decentralization. Management by objectives is an essential new public management technique but has proved to be hard to apply in the public sector (Bouckaert and Pollitt 2004). This form of standardization

is closely linked to divisionalization as it makes divisions ('DGs' in public sector terminology) responsible for reaching targets. In terms of organizational capacities it implies that DGs have their own units not just for implementing policies but also for monitoring achievements. In terms of the BR discussion below, if DGs are made responsible for IAs they would need to set up units in which IA expertise is combined and where assessments are monitored. In addition, the apex has to have a unit to monitor whether targets are being met with a view to creating commitment to these targets.

- *Training (professionalization)* influences working methods, culture or objectives. Training – for example, on how to use IAs – is probably most used in reform programmes as it is fairly straightforward to apply.
- *Horizontal co-ordination mechanisms* unload hierarchies in decision-making and allow richer and more flexible communications. They include informal contacts, task forces at the operating core, teams and integrating managers. Teams are committees at a higher level with a broad overview and are able to resolve conflicts. Integrators are the chairs of the teams and have potentially weaker (mediating) or stronger (decision-taking) powers. Using the IA example, assessments will require task forces combining information from different fields as well as teams to solve problems and take decisions.

This model makes it possible to assess and compare organizational learning in the EU's multi-level administrative system (Table 1, third column). As a hypothesis, the introduction of new policy instruments requires careful attention to each of these organizational capacities. Moreover, if we know how instruments are designed and whether there is a match between instrumental learning and organizational learning, we know whether governance learning has taken place and in which direction (reinforcement of existing governance mechanisms or a shift in mode of governance).

Evidently, there is no automatic link between changes in the use of instruments and organizational redesign. Explanations for discongruencies are many (Zito and Schout 2009). Moreover, not all reforms in relation to new instruments will be an improvement. The Commission interviews show that officials are not necessarily experienced in thinking through how changes in instruments should be complemented with organizational changes, and they may fear design questions particularly when obligations on other DGs are involved. Hence, organizational learning should not simply be assumed. With this model we can at least analyse change in capacities and discuss its effects.

3. BETTER REGULATION AS GOVERNANCE LEARNING AND INSTRUMENT LEARNING

Has there been a governance turn? Apparently, the direction of governance learning was undecided for some time. While academic literature focused on open co-ordination, the Commission's official line favoured clearer legislation

(CEC 2001). Although the EU has become increasingly active in OMC projects such as 'Lisbon', the EU's output has not drastically changed. Legislative output hardly diminished and soft instruments have not really increased (Kurpas *et al.* 2008). Nevertheless, a more complementary use of instruments can be deduced as a result of a broadened instrumental toolkit with agencies, networks and OMCs (Treib *et al.* 2007).

Although no paradigm shift can be discerned, there has been governance learning, especially as a result of the BR agenda (Radaelli 2009). BR, particularly because of the IA system, has resulted in better argued Commission proposals and a 'change in culture' (according to several interviews) from DGs working independently towards co-operation. What started out as a variety of objectives cherished by different DGs (sustainable development, reduction of administrative costs, gender equality), a series of unrelated IA systems developed by different DGs and a search for 'good governance' by the SG (related to, among others, exploring new instruments) has resulted in an IA system in which these objectives are integrated.

Radaelli (2007: 191) defines better regulation as 'a type of meta-regulation because of its emphasis on standards and rules which, instead of governing specific sectors or economic actors, steer the process of rule formulation, adoption, enforcement, and evaluation'. An interviewee defined it simply as a 'policy policy'. With the integrated IA as a core instrument, the lines between governance and BR faded. The BR agenda now comprises a range of objectives including subsidiarity, proportionality, providing empirical proof for policies, sustainability, reducing administrative burdens by 25 per cent, priority-setting and using the least disruptive instruments (such as OMCs and voluntary agreements). These are now well founded in the Commission's IA system (2009) and have resulted in a common approach with the European Parliament and the Council on better law-making (CEC 2006) by which the EU institutions committed 'themselves to take the IAs of the Commission into full account' and to carry out assessments of substantial amendments.

BR is a political spearhead on the EU agenda equal to the '1992' programme or the Lisbon processes. With the 'completion' of the internal market, BR has emerged as the priority in the post-Delors era of 'less but better' (Peterson 2008). Having figured at the top of the Commission and Council agendas for some time (Radaelli and De Francesco 2007), the hierarchical commitment is beyond doubt. Underscoring the political commitment, assessment systems are now increasingly organized in units closely connected to the political apex of the Commission and national administrations (EVIA 2008).

Superficially, one can see the IA as a tool to arrive at better legislation but, more fundamentally, BR can be seen as part of a process of depoliticization or scientification of politics. The elaboration of instruments such as agencies, consultation of independent experts and IAs, increasingly binds the hands of politicians. The use of regular independent evaluations of policies and sunset clauses also underlines this trend. BR alters the nature of EU governance more fundamentally than stability in the use of instruments suggests. Hence, some form of paradigmatic shift has taken place in the sense of better argumentation of policies and instruments.

Nevertheless, the assessment system has remained problematic. The Commission's efforts now cover more than 15 years of trial and error, evaluation and reformulation. The latest 'integrated impact assessment' system has already gone through several reviews and modifications (TEP 2007; CEC 2009). Comparisons to earlier evaluations of European IA systems reveal persistent problems (Wilkinson 1995; Kraemer *et al.* 2002) such as:

- Postponement of assessments until proposals are nearly finalized.
- Lack of assessments of alternatives.
- Difficulty in gathering data.
- Lack of political commitment (from MEPs and ministers in the Council) to actually pursue the assessment methodology throughout the negotiations.

Yet, Commission officials were positive about the influence of the assessments on policy-making because there is now more internal co-operation. MEPs also underlined in interviews that they consider Commission proposals as being better argued and offering better information as to why one alternative was chosen compared to others. On the whole, the interviews underlined changes in the Commission proposals but also expressed doubts as to whether the assessments make a difference in the final outcomes. To Summarize, there are major instrumental developments but their performance has continued to be mediocre (EVIA 2008).

4. ORGANIZATIONAL LEARNING IN THE COMMISSION

Integrated BR ambitions assume that the Commission is able to co-ordinate matters in order to deliver proposals that are sustainable, respect the ambitions of minimum administrative burdens, etc. This contrasts sharply with the Commission's reputation for being internally fragmented (Mandelkern Group 2001: 64). Policy making was an informal process where officials – often in co-operation with the cabinets – worked in relative isolation from other Commission units. The Commission work programme as such was long and rather non-committal. Programme items could easily be ignored while proposals not in the programme were pursued. One interviewee suggested that sometimes items were left outside the programme to shield them from colleagues. Acknowledging that large organizations will be hard to reform, BR may not have been much more than symbolic politics.

However, the BR agenda coincided almost by accident with the Kinnock reforms which resulted in a successful reform of the Commission (Peterson 2008). The Commission introduced a system of activity-based management together with the strategic planning and programming (SPP) cycle to focus activities and resources (see Table 2). With a view to reinforcing the BR agenda in its work planning, the Legal Service was involved at an earlier stage. Moreover, IAs became an obligatory step in the legislative process

Table 2 The Commission's BR-related organizational learning

Hierarchy	Bureaucracy	Management by objectives (divisionalization)	Professional organization	Horizontal co-ordination
Strong commitment and leadership from Barroso, the SG and from sector DGs	SPP cycle	Obligation of DGs to carry out IAs and to create in-house expertise	Major training programmes	Participation of the SG and Legal Service in inter-service consultations ('task forces')
	Guidelines on IAs and how they are connected to the policy process ('roadmaps', etc.)			Impact Assessment Board (a team chaired by the deputy SG as powerful integrating manager)
	Regular evaluations SG: Elaboration of staff and powers			IA working group Stoiber Group
	Budgets for IAs Internet portal			

(CEC 2006). To include a legislative proposal in the work programme, it had to be complemented by at least an initial assessment ('roadmap'), and all legislation going to the College for a decision had to include a full IA. Hence, the reforms resulted in an overhaul of policy planning in which the IA – and the objectives it embodies on BR – was incorporated. In addition, DGs have reserved budgets in their work plans for the use of consultants to carry out IAs and the use of consultants is regulated by guidelines incorporated in the IA system. Consultants can gather information but should not write the proposal and DGs must give them clear questions. These measures have resulted in new rules and organizational roles and therefore implied a much needed bureaucratization of the Commission (see Table 2).

This – positive – bureaucratization of planning has been reinforced by the elaboration of the position of the SG. Originally, the SG was never as powerful as the nationally appointed Commissioners who exercised strong control over 'their' DGs. It operated more as a post box for the College. The SG's horizontal authority has been greatly upgraded with Barroso's more presidential style (Peterson 2008), the formalization of the SG role in work planning and IAs, and its staff expansion.

The Commission also established an Impact Assessment Board (IAB) in 2006. The IAB is a high-level team to cement horizontal co-ordination. It monitors the development of the IAs of the DGs and checks the assessments when proposals are sent to the College. The IAB's comments are presented on the Commission website – a remarkably high level of transparency as this means that the Commission has opened up its internal deliberations. The Deputy SG chairs the IAB, which consists of directors from: DG Employment, Social Affairs and Equal Opportunities; DG Economic and Financial Affairs; DG Enterprise and Industry; DG Environment. The chair sees that the directors participate themselves to ensure the necessary strategic level and commitment.

The IAB scrutinized about 180 proposals in 2008. The interviews indicate that the Deputy SG spends up to 40 hours per month on IAs (reading the IAs and notes from his staff, participating in IAB meetings and, when necessary, meeting with the lead DGs to follow up the IAB report). The interviews show him as a driving force behind the IAB and its 'critical' and 'rigorous' reviews. This suggests that he is not just a mere committee chair but more of a forceful integrating manager. The way this position is designed, close to the apex of the Commission and well resourced, contributes to the success of the IAB. The IAB's verdict can take the form of approval, conditional approval, no agreement or a suspended agreement. In the latter case the proposal will not go to the College (unless Barroso decides otherwise). This, together with the openness of its comments, underlines the IAB's procedural power (Peterson 2008).

The SG has committed approximately eight officials for the IA-related tasks: to write the guidelines, and be involved in the work planning and reviewing of the IAs before IAB examination. In addition, other officials from the SG who are involved in internal policy co-ordination – approximately 40 officials – also work on assessments in one way or another. They participate in the early inter-service consultations where they support the use of the IA guidelines and monitor the search for alternative options and instruments. Moreover, they ensure that the consultants are used in appropriate ways and that the final IAs adhere to the guidelines.

The BR agenda has also resulted in an external monitoring body (the Stoiber Group), created in September 2007. Its objective is to add external political pressure and to help set priorities for cost reduction. This group of experts from business, environmental and social organizations scrutinizes EU policies from an integrated perspective. It is too early to establish this group's influence. Other support facilities include an internal Impact Assessment Working Group and an intra-Commission Internet portal with practical information on conducting an IA (TEP 2007).

The support mechanisms for the IA system include, first, the guidelines (a bureaucratic rule system) which specify standards and operational procedures. Second, the Commission organizes internal and external training seminars to broaden and professionalize the use of the IA system. Third, the DGs are expected to provide support functions for the IAs (divisionalization). Each DG has a unit or one or two experts for support and to ensure the first line of quality control on IAs. The TEP (2007) evaluation found that only three out of the 21 DGs were able to conduct or follow the relevant IAs in sufficient detail. However, this evaluation was done early in the establishment of the IA system. More recent interviews show that the DGs have continued to invest in the necessary IA structures and training.

In terms of organizational capacities, these measures amount to fundamental changes from fragmentation towards a mature bureaucracy, a reinforcement of the Commission's divisionalized form and stronger horizontal co-ordination. Compared to the fragmentation before the Kinnock reforms, the work of the Commission is now structured by work planning and control mechanisms, and internal networks are being set up to ensure integrated perspectives on policies. These are not mere quantitative ('more of the same') but real qualitative organizational changes.

To summarize, the results of the developments of the Commission's IA system have been mixed. On the one hand, there has been considerable instrument and organizational learning to report and MEPs have indicated that they think that the quality of Commission proposals has improved as a result. On the other hand, there is still considerable reservation in the DGs to really apply the logic of the IAs. As the evaluations and interviews indicate, IAs have an element of window dressing by reserving them for the final stages, and using them for clarification rather then as a tool to 'think outside the box'. Part of the explanation can be found in the functioning of the Council.

5. BETTER REGULATION IN THE NETHERLANDS – INSTRUMENT AND ORGANIZATIONAL LEARNING

In a multi-level system, success also depends on the capacities of the Council. Even if the Commission offers an integrated proposal, the inherently fragmented Council – and the EP – can still focus on sectoral interests without giving consideration to, for example, administrative costs, sustainability or proportionality. Moreover, if the Council does not signal to the Commission a desire for integrated proposals, the Commission has fewer incentives to invest in horizontal BR objectives. This may offer an important explanation for the limited actual significance of IAs. Hence, the EU's multi-level context requires examination of instrument and organizational learning in both the Commission and Council as well as of the design of the interplay between the levels.

The Netherlands has been one of the frontrunners in the EU's BR debate, together with the UK and other member states (Radaelli and De Francesco 2007). It has uploaded its national objectives, but has it also aligned its policy and structures to those of the Commission? Has it considered the implications of the EU's IA system for its own policy and EU policy co-ordination?

In terms of governance learning, the Dutch BR agenda has not developed in parallel with the EU's integrated agenda and has focused heavily on deregulation. Against the background of the Dutch consocational welfare state, the reform processes have concentrated from the early 1980s onwards on reducing the size of government and liberalizing the market. Although concerns were expressed at regular intervals about not ignoring quality, BR has been mainly concerned with quantity (i.e. deregulation and assessing costs of legislation). The first cabinet of Wim Kok in 1994 formulated the 10 per cent cost reduction ambition. This ambition was raised to 25 per cent (1998) and has been continued by successive Balkenende cabinets from 2002 onwards.

The government created a structure based on a number of organizational features to support the 25 per cent reduction, acclaimed by the World Bank (2007) as being a 'world leader' because of its clear and simple structure. Dutch success stems from the following:

- Political commitment and leadership of the Ministry of Finance ensured by connecting the 25 per cent objective to the budget cycle.
- Bureaucratic rules in the form of a simple quantitative tool – the standard cost method – to measure the administrative burden of new proposals and independent procedural control by a supervisory body (ACTAL), which reviews all legislation before it goes to cabinet and parliament. Its comments are published.
- Standardization of objectives through the objective of 25 per cent net reduction. This objective is distributed over the ministries so that each has a specific reduction target. Each ministry has set up internal contact points for burden reduction, monitoring progress and support.
- As regards capacities related to the professional organization, ACTAL organizes training sessions and workshops for the ministries on the application of the standard cost model.

These features imply strong hierarchical steering within cabinet, a strong bureaucratic procedural framework, an independent agency controlling performance, and a reinforcement of the divisional structure by giving ministries individual objectives (see Table 3).

Table 3 The Netherlands BR-related organizational learning (weakening of system in italics)

Hierarchy	Bureaucracy	Divisionalized organization	Professional organization	Horizontal co-ordination
Strong political commitment for cost reduction (cabinet level)	ACTAL monitors administrative costs before legislation goes to parliament. *The position of ACTAL is unclear in relation to integrated assessments*	25 per cent reduction target with specification of targets per ministry. *With the move towards integrated assessments, targets diversify and become more qualitative*	Training sessions on cost reduction	Inter-ministerial meeting of co-ordinators for cost reduction (now also discussing developments towards IAs)
Strong political leadership (Ministry of Finance). *After 2008 leadership seems to become more diffuse and co-operation to become voluntary*	Zero-base measurement as basis for the overall evaluation of achievements			
	Elaboration of rules for integrated assessments			

Despite discussions on whether business actually notices any reductions and on the dangers of ignoring the benefits of regulation, the assessment of costs in 2002 (16.4 billion euro) compared to the administrative costs in 2007 (approximately 13 billion euro) shows that the 25 per cent target was almost reached. This amounts to a benefit of 3.6 per cent of gross domestic product (GDP) (Ministerie van Financiën (2006)). Moreover, the BR policy has contributed to a culture that is more conscious of the costs policies imposed on business (Ministerie van Financiën (2007); Linschoten *et al.* 2008).

The focus on the reduction of administrative costs and deregulation should not suggest that there have been no policies related to administrative quality. The administrative burden programme has, however, been the only one with a real impact. The traditionally highly fragmented Dutch administration (Andeweg 1988) has seen many different kinds of BR-type policies. The Department for Home Affairs has a programme concerning the administrative burden on citizens. The Economic Affairs Ministry has been responsible for projects dealing with contradictory regulations, simplification of permits and 'gold plating' (adding requirements when implementing EU policy). The Ministry of Justice launched a framework project with various goals, including stimulating the use of alternative instruments. The Environment Ministry has been active in promoting sustainable development tests. These programmes have been (much) less visible for different reasons – including lack of political backing.

This system is currently being changed to an integrated system. The progress with the 25 per cent programme implied that, with cost reduction on its way, new targets had to be found to keep the BR agenda alive. This resulted in an assessment of approaches in the various departments and a debate on moving towards integrated assessments. An overview of departmental efforts uncovered 110 tests that the departments had created. Many are unknown or of little consequence. This figure underlines the high level of administrative fragmentation of the Dutch BR agenda.

Developments towards an integrated assessment have not been promising. An inter-ministerial meeting, originally set up to discuss cost reductions, is trying to broaden the assessment system but the ministries have difficulty in agreeing on an integrated system. Typically, the IA model now on the table assumes that departments adhere to it on a voluntary basis, and therefore seems to erode hierarchical co-ordination (see Table 3). In addition, it will be more qualitative (eroding the management by objectives). Furthermore, it is unclear how the external watchdog – ACTAL – can be remodelled into an integrated set of objectives (eroding the bureaucratic capacities of the previous system). Hence, the design features that made the 25 per cent programme successful will probably cease to exist. It is too early to evaluate the newly emerging system, but this seems to be, so far, an example of learning leading to the breakdown of a rather successful, although one-dimensional, system.

With the move towards integrated assessments, the Dutch and the EU's BR agendas become more alike. However, instrument learning in the Netherlands has been not matched by organizational learning. Capacities for burden reduction were successful but a system for integrated assessments has not been created (so far).

The Dutch BR agenda and EU policy-making

Moving beyond the EU and Dutch BR agendas individually, we need to address whether Dutch BR ambitions have also altered Dutch EU policy co-ordination. What organizational learning has taken place in this interface between EU policies and the definition of the national position at the various phases of EU policy-making? Building on Jordan and Schout (2006), the administrative demands of a multi-level IA system require that the member states incorporate the IA logic in the negotiations in the Council. Otherwise, the Commission will have few incentives from the Council to perform assessments or to guard a variety of objectives requiring (occasionally painful) co-ordination between DGs. Moreover, it would be a waste of time and resources for the Commission if their carefully assessed proposals, in which sustainability, administrative costs, etc., are incorporated, were watered down by the rather fragmented sectoral Councils. These Councils sometimes tend to focus on traditional sectoral interests without much interest in the broader BR agenda. Therefore, whether the BR succeeds depends also on whether the Councils incorporate the IA logic. This, in turn, will depend on whether the member states have incorporated this logic in the preparation of their negotiation positions.

Moreover, the Commission will need information from the member states to produce IAs. In an ideal situation, national officials follow the Commission agenda, early drafting of proposals and IAs so that they can have an impression of how policies will affect the national situation in terms of subsidiarity, environment conditions, administrative costs, etc. This will also help the Commission in determining how proposals affect the member states. Moreover, they should consider the consequences of national negotiating positions in relation to integrated objectives, and they should ensure with their colleagues in the Council that major changes proposed by the Council are assessed. In other words, the logic of the IAs should be part of the formulation of the national position and of input in the Council.

Dutch EU policy co-ordination has been structured on the basis of three interdepartmental co-ordination committees: the BNC (committee to assess new Commission proposals), the Committee of Permanent Representatives (COREPER) instruction meeting, and the CoCo (senior co-ordinating committee for EU and international affairs more generally). The Ministry of Foreign Affairs chairs these committees but can only assume a weak co-ordination and arbitration role. Apart from these committees, departments co-operate informally or operate independently. The latter two committees finalize the formal Dutch instructions and solve problems. The BNC sets out the major lines by defining who is involved in the co-ordination and the initial perspective on a proposal (politically, financially and legally). It is a junior committee and located early on in the Council process (when the Commission sends the proposal to the Council). This committee has to present a *fiche* within six weeks to the government summarizing the proposal and the initial perspective. It has been a long-held objective that this committee would make Dutch EU policy co-ordination less reactive but, given its junior nature, it has remained mainly an information exchanging body and, as such, hardly threatens the independence of departments (ROB 2004).

Responding to the increasing importance of BR, the *fiche* has been revised after long drawn-out discussions (2007). This debate was difficult as it concerns the question of which tests merit the attention of the inter-ministerial meeting and relates to a recurring discussion on questions in the *fiche* on gender equality, impact on development co-operation, sustainable development, etc. Ministries have developed a reflex response to preventing additional questions. Nevertheless, discussions on the Commission's assessment regarding information obligations and consequences for subsidiarity and proportionality are now incorporated in the *fiche*. What is subsequently done with the information in the *fiches* is difficult to determine as it only aims at information exchange. The interviews indicate that the discussion on assessments can sometimes be serious but more often remains a box-ticking exercise (compare also EVIA 2008).

This does not mean that the Commission's IAs are totally unco-ordinated. Some ministries, such as Environment and Transport, have started to take an interest in the Commission work programme and to create task forces (sometimes interdepartmental and with representatives from regional governments and non-governmental organizations) to see whether and how Commission IAs need to be anticipated and influenced. These developments are, however, still rare and very new. As far as our limited analysis can show, only Environment has arranged for a proactive assessment on a Commission proposal, and is now regularly in discussion with stakeholders as to which issues on the Commission agenda may need particular attention.

The Ministry of Finance monitors the attention to burden reduction in the preparations of the Dutch EU positions and can involve ACTAL to assess the costs of Commission proposals. Finance officials also try to monitor subsequent developments on the dossiers, but the interviews show that this ministry operates at a junior level when monitoring EU dossiers and influence is otherwise limited owing to the workload involved and the knowledge required.

This shows that the Commission's IAs may be taken more seriously in the future, and may lead to more and earlier interdepartmental teams to assess forthcoming Commission proposals. But, for the time being, the actions of the Netherlands to steer the EU's administrative burden policy are not matched with a strategy to incorporate this more fully in the day-to-day preparations of negotiating positions. Nor does the value system (brain frame) seem to have changed. Whereas the Commission is now concerned with proof and evaluations up to the point where there are too many and too early evaluations (interviews), this quality control or search for proof is much less developed in the Netherlands where it concerns EU policies. The preparation of the Dutch position is still oriented towards finding interdepartmental consensus.

Confronted with the challenge of how to reinforce the agreed BR objectives in Dutch EU policy co-ordination, one interviewee simply commented along the lines of 'we are optimistic that some pragmatic solutions will emerge'. This underlines the difference between formulating integrated objectives politically and understanding the multi-level organizational learning this requires.

6. CONCLUSIONS

The EU has made great strides in governance learning but has there been a governance turn, and has this turn been successful? At a superficial level, the EU has witnessed a governance turn but this requires two qualifications. There has been considerable stability in the use of instruments and the results of the governance experiments have not been successful across the board. To place organizational learning in the context of governance learning, this article distinguished governance learning, instrument learning and organizational learning, and assumed that these types of learning have to develop in parallel. Moreover, in the EU's multi-level context and depending on the instrument, organizational learning at the national level has to match the EU's capacity-building.

The first conclusion is that the Commission has shown considerable governance learning not so much in terms of a paradigm shift towards new instruments but by making progress particularly with improving legislation. Second, in terms of instrument learning, the shares of networked governance and legislation have remained stable. However, remarkable instrument learning has taken place through better planning and arguing new proposals. Third, the case of BR, and focusing particularly on IAs, shows that instrument learning at the EU level has been matched by considerable organizational learning in the form of additional bureaucratic, divisionalized, professional and horizontal co-ordination capacities. Fourth, despite the country being a great supporter of BR, the Netherlands case reveals that similar organizational learning may not have taken place in the Council. Organizational learning tends towards a breakdown of the existing system.

Finally, the Dutch BR agenda and related organizational learning have concentrated on Dutch policy-making. The BR principles are not structurally incorporated into the Dutch positions defended in the Council. Hence, there are two incongruities: a mismatch between instrument learning and organizational learning, and a separation between national BR policy and national EU policy co-ordination. If this can be generalized to the Council, this would explain the lack of political attention for BR and the lack of national input into Commission IAs. Therefore, the Commission has a dilemma. It has made the necessary organizational adaptations, but may now have to put on the agenda the – sensitive – question of how member states prepare their negotiating positions. Insufficient connection between EU and national IA systems may explain the limited progress with EU IA systems. With these findings, the organizational model presented above proves to be useful in assessing and comparing organizational learning in the EU's multi-level administrative system.

ACKNOWLEDGEMENTS

I would like to thank Andrea Lenschow, Duncan Liefferink, Tony Zito and the anonymous referees for their comments on earlier versions.

REFERENCES

Andeweg, R.B. (1988) 'Centrifugal forces and collective decision-making; the case of the Dutch cabinet', *European Journal of Political Research* 16: 125–51.
Bennett, C. and Howlett, M. (1992) 'The lessons of learning: reconciling theories of policy learning and policy change', *Policy Sciences* 25: 275–94.
Börzel, T. (1998) 'Organizing Babylon: on different conceptions of policy networks', *Public Administration* 76(2): 253–73.
Bouckaert, G. and Pollitt, C. (2004) *Public Management Reform*, Oxford: Oxford University Press.
CEC (Commission of the European Communities) (2001) *European Governance: A White Paper*, COM(2001)428, Brussels.
CEC (Commission of the European Communities) (2006) *Better Lawmaking 2005*, COM(2006)289, Brussels.
CEC (Commission of the European Communities) (2008) *European Agencies – The Way Forward*, COM(2008)135, Brussels, 11 March.
CEC (Commission of the European Communities) (2009) *Impact Assessment Guidelines*, SEC(2009)92, Brussels.
Citi, M. and Rhodes, M. (2007) 'New modes of governance in the EU: a critical survey and analysis', in K.E. Jørgensen, M. Pollack and B. Rosamund (eds), *Handbook of European Union Politics*, London: Sage, pp. 463–82.
Coen, D. and Thatcher, M. (2008) 'Network governance and multi-level delegation: European networks of regulatory agencies', *Journal of Public Policy* 28: 49–71.
Common, R. (2004) 'Organisational learning in a political environment: improving policy-making in UK government', *Policy Studies* 25(1): 35–49.
Cyert, R. and March, J.G. (1963) *A Behavioral Theory of the Firm*, Englewood Cliffs, NJ: Prentice Hall.
Dawson, S. (1992) *Analysing Organizations*, London: University of London.

DiMaggio, P.J. and Powell, W.W. (1983) 'The iron cage revisited: institutional isomorphism and collective rationality organizational fields', *American Sociological Review* 48(2): 147–60.
Easterby-Smith, M. and Lyles, M. (2003) 'Organizational learning and knowledge management: agendas for future research', in M. Easterby-Smith and M. Lyles (eds), *The Blackwell Handbook of Organizational Learning and Knowledge Management*, Oxford: Blackwell, pp. 639–53.
Eberlein, B. and Newman, A. (2008) 'Escaping the international governance dilemma? Incorporated transgovernmental networks in the European Union', *Governance* 21(1): 25–52.
EVIA (Evaluating Integrated Impact Assessments) (2008) *Improving the Practice of Impact Assessment;* http://web.fu-berlin.de/ffu/evia/EVIA_Policy_Paper.pdf
Gornitzka, A. (2006) *The OMC as Practice: A Watershed in European Education Policy?* Oslo: Arena, Working Paper 16.
Hanf, K. (1994) *The International Context of Environmental Management from the Negotiating Table to the Shop Floor*, Den Haag: Cip-Data.
Héritier, A. and Lehmkuhl, D. (2008) 'The shadow of hierarchy and new modes of governance', *Journal of Public Policy* 8(1): 1–17.
Holzinger, K., Knill, C. and Schafer, A. (2006) 'Rhetoric or reality? "New Governance" in EU environmental policy', *European Law Journal* 12(3): 403–20.
Jordan, A. and Schout, A. (2006) *The Coordination of European Governance*, Oxford: Oxford University Press.
Jordan, A., Wurzel, R. and Zito, A. (eds) (2003) *New Instruments of Environmental Governance? National Experiences and Prospects*, London: Frank Cass.
Kassim, H. and Le Galès, P. (2008). 'Introduction – Governing the EU: policy instruments in a multi-level polity'. Paper presented at the CONNEX workshop, 'Governing the EU: Policy Instruments in a Multi-Level Polity', University of East Anglia, 28–29 May.
Knill, C. and Lenschow, A. (2005) 'Compliance, competition and communication: different approaches of European governance and their impact on national institutions', *Journal of Common Market Studies* 43(3): 583–606.
Kohler-Koch, B. and Rittberger, B. (2006) 'Review article: the "governance turn" in EU studies', *Journal of Common Market Studies* 44: 27–49.
Kooiman, J. (2003) *Governing as Governance*, London: Sage.
Kraemer, R., Klassing, A., Wilkinson, D. and von Homeyer, I. (2002) *EU Environmental Governance: A Benchmark of Policy Instruments, Final Report*, Berlin: Ecologic.
Kurpas, S., Grøn, C. and Kaczyński, P. (2008) *The European Commission after Enlargement: Does More Add Up to Less?*, Brussels: CEPS Special Report.
Lascoumes, P. and Le Galès, P. (2007) 'Introduction: understanding public Policy through its instruments', *Governance* 20(1): 1–21.
Lawrence, P.R. and Lorsch, J.W. (1967) *Organization and Environment; Managing Differentiation and Integration*, Boston: Harvard Business School Press.
Linschoten, R., Nijland, J. and Sleifer, J. (2008) 'Institutions for better regulation: the example of the Netherlands 2002–2007', in A. Nijsen, J. Hudson, C. Muller, K. van Paridon and R. Thurik (eds), *Business Regulation and Public Policy*, New York: Springer.
Majone, G. (1996) *Regulating Europe*, London: Routledge.
Mandelkern Group on Better Regulation (2001) *Final Report;* http://ec.europa.eu/governance/better_regulation/documents/mandelkern_report.pdf
May, P. (1992) 'Policy learning and failure', *Journal of Public Policy* 12(4): 331–54.
Ministerie van Financiën (2006) Vaststelling van de begrotingsstaten van het Ministerie van Financiën (IXB) voor het jaar 2007, Tweede Kamer, vergaderjaar 2006–2007, 30 800 hoofdstuk IXB, nr. 2.

Ministerie van Financiën (2007) *Merkbaar minder regeldruk!*, Kabinetsplan aanpak administratieve lasten, Tweede Kamer, vergaderjaar 2006–2007, 29 515, nr.202, Den Haag, 19 juli.

Mintzberg, H. (1979) *The Structuring of Organizations: A Synthesis of the Research*, Englewood Cliffs, NJ: Prentice Hall.

Monda, C., Schout, A. and Vos, E. (eds) (forthcoming) *EU Agencies in Between the EU Institutions and Member States*, Dordrecht: Kluwer Law International.

Olsen, J. and Peters, G. (1996) 'Learning from experience', in J. Olsen and G. Peters (eds), *Lessons from Experience*, Oslo: Scandinavian University Press, pp. 1–35.

Peterson, J. (2008) 'Enlargement, reform and the European Commission. Weathering a perfect storm?', *Journal of European Public Policy* 15(5): 761–80.

Powell, W. (1990) 'Neither market nor hierarchy: network forms of organization', *Research in Organizational Behaviour* 12: 295–336.

Radaelli, C. (2007) 'Whither better regulation for the Lisbon agenda?', *Journal of European Public Policy* 14(2): 190–207.

Radaelli, C. (2009) 'Measuring policy learning: regulatory impact assessment in Europe', *Journal of European Public Policy* 16(8): 1145–64.

Radaelli, C. and De Francesco, F. (2007) *Regulatory Quality in Europe*, Manchester: Manchester University Press.

Rhodes, R. (1997) *Understanding Governance*, Buckingham: Open University Press.

ROB (Raad voor het Openbaar Bestuur) (2004) *Nationale Coördinatie van EU-beleid: een Politiek en Proactief Proces*, Den Haag: Raad voor het Openbaar Bestuur.

Schout, J.A. and Jordan, A.J. (2005) 'Coordinated European governance: self organising or centrally steered?', *Public Administration* 83(1): 201–20.

Schout, A. and Jordan, A. (2008) 'The European Union's governance ambitions and its administrative capacities', *Journal of European Public Policy* 15(7): 957–74.

Schout, A. and Pereyra, F. (forthcoming) 'The institutionalization of EU agencies – agencies as "mini Commissions"', *Public Administration*.

TEP (The Evaluation Partnership) (2007) *Evaluation of the Commission's Impact Assessment System*, Brussels: Commission of the European Communities, April.

Treib, O., Bähr, H. and Falkner, G. (2007) 'Modes of governance: towards a conceptual clarification', *Journal of European Public Policy* 14(1): 1–20.

Wilkinson, D. (1995) *Approaches to Integrating the Environment into Other Sectoral Policies: An Interim Evaluation of Experience in the European Commission and Parliament*, London: Institute for European Environmental Policy.

World Bank (2007) *Review of the Dutch Administrative Burden Reduction Programme*, Washington: World Bank.

Zito, A. and Schout, A. (2009) 'Learning theory reconsidered: EU integration theories and learning', *Journal of European Public Policy* 16(8): 1103–23.

Measuring policy learning: regulatory impact assessment in Europe

Claudio M. Radaelli

INTRODUCTION

Several years ago, Carol Weiss showed that very rarely does an individual policy appraisal shape a public decision. However, she carried on, problem definitions, instruments, and paradigms that constantly feature in policy appraisals carried out over time do 'percolate' into public policy-making processes, and gradually foster learning by changing the way policy-makers and institutions think (Weiss 1979). More recently, Susan Owens and her collaborators reminded us of the importance of taking a longitudinal approach to find out how appraisal tools change those who use them. There is knowledge utilization, they argue, when those involved in policy appraisal learn (Owens *et al.* 2004). A recent lead article in this journal has qualified knowledge utilization, distinguishing among instrumental, legitimacy-seeking, and substantiating usages (Boswell 2008). In the meantime, the debate on policy instruments has been rekindled, drawing attention to the 'theorizations' about the political world implicit in analytic approaches to policy formulation. When instruments are institutionalized, their implicit theorizations affect the way policy-makers think about policy (Hood 2007; Lascoumes and Le Galès 2004: 27).

Regulatory impact assessment (RIA, or simply impact assessment, IA) provides an appropriate empirical reference for the analysis of learning over a long period of time. This instrument consists of a systematic and mandatory appraisal of how proposed primary and/or secondary legislation will affect certain categories of stakeholders, economic sectors, and the environment. Essentially, RIA is a type of administrative procedure, often used in Europe for pre-legislative scrutiny of legislation and in delegated rulemaking. The impacts analysed may cover administrative burdens or compliance costs, or more complex types of costs and benefits, including environmental benefits, distributional effects, and the trade effects. RIA can also be used to appraise the effects of proposed regulations on public administration (e.g. government departments, schools, hospitals, prisons, universities) and local government.

Once adopted, RIA is used by governments and regulators to scrutinize proposed regulation no matter what the substance of the policy problem may be. Thus, over the years the regulators experiment with the same set of procedures and economic techniques – an ideal experimental condition to test the arguments put forward by Carol Weiss and Susan Owens. Some European countries have experimented with RIA for at least ten years, a fairly long period of time to observe some of the 'knowledge utilization' effects related to learning. Further, RIA draws significantly on economics and the socio-environmental sciences – yet its utilization takes place in a very political context, that is, policy formulation within key agencies and government departments. The whole question of informing the decision-maker by dint of economic analysis raises constitutional issues of power in law-making (Meuwese 2007; Nilsson *et al.* 2008).

In terms of case selection, these considerations suggest the inclusion of the European countries that have a long experience of RIA (at least ten years). These countries are Denmark, the Netherlands, Sweden, and the UK. Given the scope of this special issue and the multi-level nature of the European Union (EU), and the fact that the European Commission has used different types of RIA since the mid-1990s, from the early *fiche d'impact* to the current impact assessment procedure, it is useful to add the EU. The methodology includes desk research on academic and primary documents (including translation of written governmental guidance documents, and administrative law), systematic process-tracing since the early 1990s, examination of individual RIAs, cross-country regulatory indicators and 52 semi-structured interviews (October 2006–March 2008). On average, each interview lasted 75 minutes. All interviews were face to face and taped, with the exception of three questionnaires (two in the UK and one in Sweden) that were answered in writing because this was the choice of the interviewee.

The organization of the paper is as follows. After a short overview of the main difficulties encountered in the measurement of learning, I discuss different learning types, their micro-foundations, and how they can be measured. Next I present the empirical analysis. The conclusions summarize the findings and make suggestions for future research.

WHAT HAVE WE (NOT) LEARNED ABOUT LEARNING?

In public policy analysis, learning is a process of updating beliefs about key components of policy (such as problem definition, results achieved at home or abroad, goals, but also actors' strategies and paradigms). Updating, in turn, is the result of analysis and/or social interaction. Professional knowledge and lay knowledge are often combined in learning processes.

The state of the academic debate on policy learning is somewhat disappointing (James and Lodge 2003). True, several projects have documented policy learning (for two excellent reviews, see Biegelbauer 2007; Grin and Loeber 2007). This literature has also crossed roads with policy diffusion (Weyland 2005; Zito and Schout 2009), knowledge utilization (Boswell 2008) and the role of information as symbol, signal, and cognitive device (Levitt and March 1988; March 1981). Other studies have diagnosed the role of specific actors as agents of learning (Calvert 1985; Stone 1996; Dunlop, forthcoming, 2010).

Yet, the frustration with learning studies arises out of *specific* problems of research design. First, the null hypothesis of lack of learning is rarely tested. One consequence is that the measurement of the dependent variable is flawed. Second, there is the problem of the time-dimension. If we examine learning over a fairly narrow time-frame, we may not see the learning buds that are about to blossom. Yet, if we consider a long time-frame, it is almost impossible *not* to find instances of learning. Organizations, political systems, actors must learn, at least if they are to survive in a dynamic environment.

Third, when measurement is carried out via qualitative interviewing, policy-makers overestimate the role of learning as opposed to coercion and classic notions of power politics. Sometimes interviewees make references to learning to protect their organization from critiques ('we have learned – hence the case is closed'; see Alam 2007). This benevolent, non-political view of learning is a source of bias.

Fourth, learning is a compound concept (Bennett and Howlett 1992; Hall 1993; May 1992), underlying different mechanisms and micro-foundations that have to be made explicit before measurement takes place. May (1992) and more recently Gilardi have stressed the importance of distinguishing between learning about policy improvement and learning what is useful for political purposes like winning elections, expanding the bureau, or shifting the blame (Gilardi 2008). Turning to micro-foundations, why on earth would an actor (be it an individual or a complex organization) want to learn? This invites a specification of the payoffs of learning and a consideration of the environment external to the organization. An environment that puts pressure on delivery, results, performance would lead an organization to pursue instrumental uses of knowledge (Boswell 2008). The organization will therefore try to learn from the empirical analysis of policy proposals. Other hypotheses about the environment lead to different types of learning.

GETTING TO GRIPS WITH THE EMPIRICAL ANALYSIS OF LEARNING

In short, there is plenty of room for improving on measurement. To begin with, it is advisable to consider the full range of the dependent variable, including zero learning. As for the bias generated by the time-dimension, it is useful to follow Sabatier's heuristic to consider a decade or so (Sabatier 1993) – in our case from the mid-1990s to 2007. In relation to the issue of 'where' to look for learning (actors, instruments, institutions, and so on; see Zito and Schout 2009), instruments like RIA are different from the broader setting of policy. In fact, RIA is an instrument of a type of regulatory reform known as 'better regulation' (Wiener 2006).

A fundamental step is to distinguish between policy learning, social learning, political learning (Hall 1993; May 1992), and perhaps reflexive learning (Grin and Loeber 2007; Sanderson 2002). 'Social learning' refers to large society-wide paradigmatic changes of policy that cannot possibly be induced by RIA. Reflexive learning about governance cannot be expected since this would require advanced, sophisticated, participatory usages of RIA that previous studies have not found in Europe (Hertin *et al.* 2007; Nilsson *et al.* 2008; Hertin *et al.* 2009 found a few cases that occurred, however, despite rather than because of RIA). We end up with instrumental learning versus political learning (Gilardi 2008), and, drawing from organizational theories and the diffusion studies previously mentioned, emulation or symbolic learning (Boswell 2008; Weyland 2005) – see Table 1.

Instrumental learning, based on rational policy-making, is triggered by analysis of what seems to work. This is different from emulation, where the aim is to seek legitimacy, not to improve policy (DiMaggio and Powell 1991). Banerjee (1992) has demonstrated that this type of symbolic learning does not make efficient use of information – yet another reason to distinguish it from instrumental learning.

Qualifying Peter May's original insights, political learning can lead to three different usages of knowledge: 'strategic' (i.e. to increase control on the regulators), 'substantiating' (i.e. to support a prefabricated position pro or against regulation; we borrow this term from Boswell 2008), and 'symbolic' (i.e. using RIA to send signals or for blame-shifting purposes).

Turning to micro-foundations, an organization under pressure to deliver will care about instrumental uses of knowledge and learn instrumentally. If there is pressure to become or remain a respectable member of international environments, we will expect symbolic learning as described by emulation models. Politically competitive environments will bring organizations to learn how to use RIA to exercise control, implement broad political trajectories such as deregulation, increase popularity in the polls, and alter power relations (Table 1, third column).

In Table 2, we clarify how evidence corroborates one type of learning or another – drawing on Peter May (1992: 344) – looking at the macro-level of better regulation (the policy dimension) and RIA (the instrument-setting dimension).

Looking at Table 2 by row, we start with two manifestations of the null hypothesis, that is coercion (e.g. RIA is introduced in a country because of pressure from external organizations) and partisan effects (e.g. new elections

Table 1 Types of learning, mechanisms, micro-foundations, and usages of knowledge

Type of learning	Mechanism: up-dating beliefs on the basis of ...	Micro-foundations	Use of knowledge	Role of regulatory impact assessment
Instrumental	Evidence about policy. This mechanism works via updating subjective probability assessments when the information set available to actors changes	Organization under pressure to deliver	Instrumental	With RIA, policy-makers seek to improve on the efficiency and effectiveness of regulation
Cross-national emulation	What seems to provide legitimacy. The mechanism works via fora for facilitated co-ordination (OECD, EU) and/or bilateral exchange and/or informal networking (e.g. standard cost model network)	Dense, institutional international environment (e.g. EU) → the organization seeks legitimacy	Symbolic	RIA used to increase legitimacy, not to improve policy
Political	Evidence and conjectures about the strategies pursued by other actors. This mechanism works via interaction in political environments	Politically competitive environment → three possible micro-foundations: (a) to increase the core executive control on the regulators (b) to support a specific regulatory policy paradigm (c) to increase popularity of the incumbent	(a) Strategic (b) Substantiating (c) Symbolic = sending signals to the business community	(a) RIA used to stack the deck (b) RIA tweaked to support broad policy trajectories (c) Stripped-down RIA used as signal

Table 2 Types of learning and expectations about evidence

	Policy-setting level (better regulation policy)	Instrument-setting (RIA)
Null hypothesis (no learning)	• Coercion, donor requirements • Partisan effects	• OECD regulatory reviews accelerate the introduction or redefinition of RIA • International consultants paid by donors design RIA guidance • New incumbents change the nature of RIA to pursue their party-political goals
Instrumental learning	• Cost–benefit analysis, welfare economics • Focus on success of policy when introducing changes in better regulation • Systematic evaluation • Watchdogs care about the quality of analysis • Presence of epistemic communities • Common set of regulatory quality indicators	• Single template for RIA • Benefits justify costs rules • RIA Guidance is reformulated on the basis of empirical evidence • Regulatory decisions informed by economic analysis
Emulation	• Diffusion of better regulation triggered by the explicit intention to emulate what has been done by the 'leaders' • EU-level networks • Co-ordination across EU Presidencies	• EU-level targets for RIA matched by national targets • Rapid convergence across the EU on specific tools for impact assessment, such as the standard cost model • RIA stripped down to basic types of assessment that can be easily diffused across the EU • RIA guidance is reformulated on the basis of foreign models
Political learning	• Focus on electoral feasibility of reform • Innovations are pushed down • Watchdogs care about the policy paradigm of the incumbent	• RIA as information obligation monitored by core executive structures • RIA as fire alarm for constituencies of support • Resistance to RIA from some departments

(*Continued*)

Table 2 Continued

	Policy-setting level (better regulation policy)	Instrument-setting (RIA)
	• Link between better regulation targets and economic resources	• RIAs used to systematically favour the policy paradigm of the incumbent
	• Better regulation as signal that 'we care about business'	• The implementation of highly publicized campaigns against administrative burdens does not go beyond low-hanging fruits

bring in a new administration which resets better regulation in order to implement the manifesto). Some qualifications are in order. Coercion is not entirely absent from the European scene. Downstream, some EU governments, especially in new member states, have adopted RIA systems under pressure from the Organization for Economic Co-operation and Development (OECD) and the European Commission. Upstream, the EU offers an opportunity structure to the most active finance ministers and the EU Presidency to put pressure on the European Commission to adopt smart regulation tools.

The second row shows that there is instrumental learning when cost–benefit analysis plays a large role in the design of regulation, the focus is on policy success (i.e. what works and what doesn't), and regulatory quality bodies perform systematic evaluations. We also expect to find epistemic communities that have developed around common beliefs concerning the economic analysis of regulation. We would also expect the adoption of a common set of regulatory quality indicators across the EU to stimulate learning from the others and convergence of outcomes.

At the micro-level, evidence should point to the presence of a single coherent template for RIA, the preference for benefit–cost principles (i.e. rules are introduced or revised on the basis of whether they deliver benefits that justify or, in a stronger formulation, outweigh the costs), and the role of evaluation in the revision of RIA guidelines (as opposed to, say, the partisan effect of a new administration). Another important way to learn instrumentally is to use RIA to inform policy decisions.

With the third row we move to emulation – in a cross-national and often transnational dimension. Diffusion processes are channelled by social networks across countries and international organizations. The main trigger is the search for legitimacy, rather than the rational evaluation of success. In the EU, this type of learning may be produced by co-ordination activities across EU Presidencies and the creation of ad-hoc networks to support diffusion of best practice and tools. At the micro-level, we should find evidence that RIA templates are copied, translated, and imitated widely. Over time, we expect rapid adoption of those tools that are easier or simply more politically amenable to diffusion – arguably, not the complicated cost–benefit analytic RIAs, but some stripped down versions, such as the appraisal of administrative burdens. EU targets should be set and matched by domestic targets – so that the whole train of diffusion is not slowed down by slow coaches.

On political-strategic use of learning, we expect better regulation policy goals to be set in accordance with their electoral feasibility, with policy performance as secondary goal. Innovations in better regulation are used to increase the political control of the core executive over the regulating departments. Thus, innovations are pushed down rather than pulled up. Further, quality assurance is about limiting agency drift. Turning to expectations about the micro-level, evidence should show that RIA is essentially an information obligation monitored by core executive structures – and a fire-alarm for constituencies (McCubbins *et al.* 1987). Pressure groups use RIA to gather information, and alert the principal that regulators are drifting away. Departments with constituencies for support different from the ones of the core executive will probably resist RIAs. Finally, guidance should be strict on oversight requirements.

On political-symbolic use of learning, we should see campaigns for better regulation that are highly publicized but not implemented beyond the collection of low-hanging fruits. When political learning goes in the direction of substantiating knowledge, RIAs will be an instrument to create support for the ideology of the incumbent – such as risk-tolerant deregulation in the UK (Dodds 2006).

To sum up then, the concept of policy learning can be broken down into different types, categorized, and measured. Since we are working with ideal-types, a single country may well display evidence of more than one type of learning. It is to this kind of empirical question that we now turn.

INSTRUMENTAL LEARNING

In this section we appraise instrumental learning. One thing we can immediately rule out is the presence of epistemic communities. Although there are RIA experts in all the countries we have examined, especially in the UK and the Netherlands, there is no professional community (compared to the one active in the US) with shared beliefs about the nature, content, and purposes of the economic analysis of regulation.

Similarly scarce is evidence matching the ideal-type of instrumental learning, although the UK has evolved from an early emphasis on the assessment of compliance costs faced by business to a template informed by the systematic analysis of how benefits and costs affect different stakeholders. Since the mid-1990s, the UK has looked at cost–benefit criteria for inspiration on how to set better regulation policy, although it has not gone as far as the US in the implementation of cost–benefit techniques. Departments such as Defra, Transport, and to some extent the DTI (then BERR – Department of Business Enterprise and Regulatory Reform; since June 2009 Department of Business, Innovation and Skills) have invested resources in the analysis and in some cases monetization of benefits. BERR has taken a sophisticated approach to the cost-side of the equation, looking into the option of introducing regulatory budgets for departments, but Peter Mandelson abandoned the project in 2009.

Further, most of the initiatives launched on RIA and better regulation have not been formally and independently evaluated, with the exception of the National Audit Office annual reports on RIA. Up until recently, the Better Regulation Executive (BRE) has been somewhat reluctant to publish annual reports on RIA and there have been few BRE indicators in the public domain. In 2008, the House of Commons recommended 'regular parliamentary scrutiny of the BRE through annual reporting to parliament' (Regulatory Reform Committee, HC 474-I, 2007–2008: 3). The government agreed (November 2008), asking BRE to publish an annual overview of the whole regulatory reform agenda.

New initiatives on reducing administrative burdens and simplification plans were introduced by the cabinet office in 2005–2007 without an ex-ante evaluation of their costs and benefits, and whether resources invested in these new exercises could crowd out other desirable initiatives – indeed some departments had problems in carrying out their RIAs because their resources were being absorbed by the measurement of administrative burdens (NAO 2006).

Turning to the micro-level, there is a single template for RIA in the UK. In the period we are examining, the UK has been the only country in Europe to insist that benefits of regulatory proposals justify the costs. However, the National Audit Office has revealed that the quality of economics in English RIAs (Scotland performs its RIAs independently) is well below the standards set in the guidelines. Studies for business organizations have also been critical (Ambler *et al.* 2007). We scored 131 RIAs carried out in 2005 and found that quantification of benefits and the application of cost–benefit criteria are poor. Systematic analysis of alternative options is often lacking giving the impression that most RIAs started at a late stage, with one option already chosen outside the RIA. Even transparency on data sources is on average low or absent. One cannot conclude that sound economics informs regulatory decisions systematically (Bartle 2008; section 4; NAO 2006; Russel and Turnpenny 2009 find that 98 per cent of RIAs in their sample do not appear to drive policy). Indeed, one of the arguments put forward by the BRE to change guidance and format for RIA in 2007 was that the role of economics in regulatory decisions was well below expectations.

Turning to Denmark, this country has set better regulation policy with the aim of improving the business environment for firms. In some areas Denmark is a leader in Europe – panels of firms to test the costs of proposed regulation were first introduced in this country. But the idea of scrutinizing regulatory proposals on the basis of rigorous cost–benefit principles is not embedded in policy formulation. The interviewees involved in the preparation of legislation do not feel constrained by benefit–cost principles and techniques. Informal, pragmatic co-operation among departments is decoupled from the detailed provisions of the official RIA guidelines. Calculations on costs (other than administrative burdens) and benefits, when they both exist, do not end up in a final public document summarizing the net impact of proposals. Instead, they inform a discussion that hinges on informal co-operation. External accountability is therefore low. When asked about how the Danish system would cope with an Anglo-Saxon RIA template, an interviewee answered: 'the system would come to a grinding halt in two weeks' (interview in Copenhagen, November 2006).

There are, however, written RIAs available for public discussion and analysis – but they cover only one aspect of proposed regulation, that is, the administrative costs for firms. The Danish Commerce and Companies Agency contributes directly to the analyses of burdens in proposed regulations, by performing some calculations of the burdens for the department in charge of developing the rule. Other calculations and analyses are contracted out to consulting firms. Interestingly, although Denmark has a pretty good record in terms of ex-post evaluation of policies, better regulation was evaluated only in 2009 by Fias-World Bank and a team of peer reviewers organized by the OECD with financial backing from the European Commission. Independent watchdogs and single strong co-ordinating units with the size and functions of BRE do not exist.

Overall, Danish policy-makers do not see a separation between an analytic phase (supported by RIA) and informal co-operation of a more political-administrative nature. RIA is not the mainstream vehicle for the analysis of proposals, since it has the same status as other evidence-based forms of appraisal, such as background studies, hearings (consultation has a long tradition that predates the advent of better regulation), discussions of scenarios with experts, and so on. To identify the impact of an individual RIA on a given decision is impossible. In most cases, it would also be impossible to find the RIA as a written document with a narrative explaining how initial options were identified, how the costs and benefits were calculated, and how the analysis supports the choice of a given option (with the exception of the administrative burdens analyses and the assessment of large infrastructural projects).

We found the same problem of distinguishing between technical-economic and political appraisal in Sweden. Here, although the situation is changing towards a single RIA template, for many years there have been different systems of appraisal (Nilsson *et al.* 2008). When legislation is being developed by one or more departments, the lead Ministry organizes a committee to appraise the impact of proposals. For major proposals, the committee will include representatives from different parties represented in Parliament, as well as civil servants. The choice of the committee chair is obviously very political, and so is the drafting of the mandate given to the committee. The committee then produces a report that blends both empirical evidence and political deliberation. For major proposals, the reports are quite lengthy. For minor proposals, the lead department may well decide (with the consensus of the ministers involved) to have a small committee of civil servants, even only one civil servant. In this case, the 'committee' will perform its inquiry with a less political-deliberative orientation. However, there is no expectation that this type of committee will confine the inquiry to the economic analysis of costs and benefits. The recommendations of the committee are expected to be directly useful to the government, by showing which option will be most likely backed by a parliamentary majority. 'The key function of the committee is not learning but building political consensus' (Hertin *et al.* 2009, forthcoming). As several interviewees remarked, the entire work of the committees could be called 'appraisal' or 'impact assessment' but this is broad in scope and political in orientation.

There is another type of Swedish RIA, this time carried out by some 550 agencies. Agencies are quite independent, arguably the most independent in the four countries. In some cases it is the government that asks agencies to look into the impact of proposed regulation, in others it is the agency itself that performs an analysis of consequences within the scope of their regulatory power. The regulations issued by agencies are supported by an 'analysis of consequences' that in some cases follows the template of an Anglo-Saxon RIA, in others is more similar to large background studies. Finally, every year there are some 200 assessments of the effects of regulation on small business. They are mandatory, but the format varies. They can be as short as one page, or even less – a simple box on 'no major administrative burden' ticked.

The guidance produced by the Swedish government used to be quite general and dispersed, being contained in three different ordinances. The government introduced a single template in 2007 – perhaps a signal of the intention to move closer to the Anglo-Saxon approach. On 15 May 2008 the Swedish government set up an advisory Regulatory Board, with the instruction to assist the government as well as the agencies in simplifications aiming at cutting the administrative burdens of enterprises. The Regulatory Board will also examine the quality of RIAs with possible effects on enterprises. It is too early to say whether this board will produce effective quality assurance or not. In the interviews, the officers remarked that quality assurance needs improvement (see also OECD 2007).

Overall, evidence pointing towards instrumental learning is scarce. Recent institutional changes may well go in this direction. But up until now RIA has not been the vehicle of standardized economic analysis of regulation. Economics plays a role, of course, but largely outside RIA; for example, in classic economic reports and sustainability reports. Basic economic analysis also plays a role in the initiatives on administrative burdens. Both in Sweden and Denmark the measurement of burdens is carried out following the template of the Dutch standard cost model.

The Netherlands is yet another case in which we find different RIA formats – although this is yet another case moving towards a single template for appraisal. Up until recently, there was a checklist-based analysis of regulatory-legislative proposals monitored by the Department of Economic Affairs, an ex-ante analysis of regulatory burdens monitored by an independent body called Actal, and an ex-post plan to reduce administrative burdens via simplification of legislation monitored by Ipal within the Department of Finance. The first segment was weak. It was impossible to track down and score individual RIAs arising out of the checklist analysis – the only written trace of the exercise is the explanatory memorandum. By contrast, Actal's examinations are entirely public, including the reports on the quality of analysis. In late 2007, the first segment was moved to a new unit, the Regulatory Reform Group, which effectively combines the first and the third segment under the leadership of the Ministry of Finance. The director of the Regulatory Reform Group, Jeroen Nijland, is also the main source of inspiration behind the cross-national standard cost model network (http://www.administrative-burdens.com/). Nijland's team is supported by the Minister of Finance at home and within the Economic and Financial Affairs Council (ECOFIN). The standard cost model is a basic technique that provides information on how administrative obligations impact on business costs. It is not based on comprehensive rationalities of the benefit–cost types, indeed its strength is all about being practical and limited to one category of costs.

EMULATION

Diffusion triggered by emulation is supported by networks (Evans and Davies 1999), especially in a multi-level system like the EU. Since the late 1990s, intense networking activity to promote adoption and implementation of better regulation tools has taken place through bilateral exchange between governments, informal bodies such as the Directors of Better Regulation of the EU, the co-ordination of EU Presidencies, and peer review/benchmarking exercises. Implementation levels vary markedly. Governments have implemented different types of RIA. Some have only launched pilot projects and do not use it systematically (Jacob *et al.* 2008).

However, the stripped-down version of impact assessment based on the measurement of administrative burdens has become popular (Wegrich 2009). All the countries examined here (and the European Commission) have invested significant resources in this area. In the first stage, diffusion has focused on the tool used by the Dutch, that is, the standard cost model. But over the last four years or so other components of the Dutch approach have been discussed with a view to emulating them, specifically independent bodies like Actal. Thus, we have a clear leader, the Netherlands, a process of emulation, and a specific network of developers and implementers of the standard cost model, with its own website, bilateral visits, and co-ordinated campaigns.

At the EU level, co-ordination has stepped up a gear. By using the opportunity structure of the EU Presidency, the UK and the Netherlands set the agenda in terms of targets for the reduction of administrative burdens at the EU level as well as in the member states. Vice-President Verheugen worked in tandem with the German Presidency of 2007 to secure at the March 2007 European Council a commitment to the reduction of burdens arising out of EU legislation.

Initially, the campaign to focus on red tape was not well received by the European Commission. The Commission, in fact, established in 2002 a template for RIA based on three pillars (economic, social, and environmental) and on the consideration of a large set of benefits and costs. This agenda did not contemplate major efforts on administrative burdens, in contrast with the expectations of the Dutch and British finance ministers of the time (Zalm and Brown). Gradually, the Commission started to reason that the war on red tape was the only practical way to make progress. Decisive was the attitude of the other member states, certainly they were more prepared to wage war on red tape than to carry out complex RIA initiatives.

In the meantime, the UK had deliberately imported the standard cost model in an attempt to demonstrate 'what seems to work elsewhere' (BRTF 2005). Denmark was already developing initiatives on measuring regulatory costs that were then channelled into the burdens-reduction national plans. Sweden adopted its own administrative burden programme as a result of emulation.

In addition to intense bilateral and multilateral exchanges, sections and handbooks regarding RIA guidance have been reformulated in Sweden, Denmark and the UK to take the standard cost model into consideration. The Commission's guidelines were changed specifically to include a section on administrative burdens. In the January 2009 guidelines, the Commission inserted an Annexe (no. 10) on how to assess administrative costs arising out of EU rules. Overall, these features of emulation support Wiener's argument that better regulation in Europe has been an exercise in legal borrowing, both horizontal and vertical (Wiener 2006).

POLITICAL LEARNING

Political learning covers (a) *strategic* usage of knowledge to improve political control over the regulators, (b) *symbolic* use of better regulation and RIA to increase popularity, and (c) *substantiating* knowledge. There is systematic evidence of political learning only in the Netherlands and the UK.

Let us start with the link between policy-setting and electoral feasibility. As mentioned, the war on administrative burdens and the Dutch standard cost model have achieved momentum in Europe. The question is why? It would be simplistic to argue that the main reason is the scientific robustness of the instruments or the obvious gains in terms of policy performance. There are serious and valid concerns about the conceptual validity of the exercise (Helm 2006). Yet, politically it is attractive to target burdens, less attractive to invest in complex RIA systems (Wegrich 2009). The war on burdens captures the political imagination. It delivers over a single electoral cycle – the programmes for the reduction of burdens are timed to provide results in three to four years, whilst full RIA programmes produce effects over a decade or so. Finally, at the level of public discourse at least, the campaigns on administrative burdens have anchored the better regulation agenda to the redefined Lisbon agenda for growth and jobs (Radaelli 2007).

Another manifestation of the political aspects of learning is how innovations have been 'pushed down' by the core executive. Both the Netherlands and the UK present plenty of evidence of changes that, as one interviewee put it, 'are foisted on us' (interview in London, October 2006). Actal, the Regulatory

Reform Group and the BRE are there to assist the core executive in the implementation of this control agenda. As Dr Duncan Russel said to the Environmental Audit Committee, the BRE officers do not exactly design guidance on appraisal by 'sit[ting] down with the people who have to write the RIAs and say "What do you need?"'(EAC, HC 740, 2006–2007, Ev 11).

Three more aspects complete the picture of policy-setting in terms of 'controlling the regulators' – to use a term originally applied to compliance cost assessment techniques in the UK (Froud *et al.* 1998) and oversight via administrative procedure. First, in the UK a panel for regulatory accountability was created, originally with the idea of looking at the regulatory agenda across departments, but then refocused on RIA. The panel then became a formal cabinet committee, chaired by the Prime Minister and with a fairly high-level representation from the Treasury. It is essentially a mechanism of oversight based on anticipated reactions – knowing that scrutiny takes place at a high level, proposals are not sent to the panel unless there is confidence in the quality of RIA.

Second, Actal and the Regulatory Reform Group use sanctions against recalcitrant departments. Actal's officers examine the quality of proposed regulation. If they find that the analysis of administrative burdens is poor, they issue a negative opinion. Anticipated reactions work well in this case too, as no one wants to be named and shamed by a (public) negative opinion issued by Actal. The Regulatory Reform Group (and previously Ipal) de facto operates from within the powerful Ministry of Finance. This enables the Dutch Minister of Finance to remunerate a department that is delivering on the reduction of burdens by giving this department additional economic resources during the preparation of the finance bill. The link is not automatic – it is not based on a formula connecting departmental burdens and financial budget. Yet it has established a mechanism of sticks and carrots (Jansen and Voermans 2006).

Third, in an attempt to secure consistency for the burdens reduction programmes beyond the electoral cycle, in 2006 the Dutch Ministry of Finance asked the World Bank and the OECD to evaluate its initiatives and make recommendations. The OECD and the World Bank praised the work done by oversight bodies. They suggested that the next government set the same target (an additional 25 per cent reduction of burdens), and confirm (indeed possibly upgrade) the oversight bodies. Unsurprisingly, then, although Zalm is no longer Finance Minister, the coalition pact signed by the parties in government on 7 February 2007 includes a commitment to an additional 25 per cent reduction.

Turning to the instrument-setting level, the evidence on how policy-makers have learned to use RIA politically is less convincing. True, there has been resistance to RIA from some departments, but there is no hard evidence that the central units have been willing (and have managed) to use impact assessment to steer the regulatory agenda of the departments to support a specific policy paradigm. The UK is the case where policy paradigms seem to matter most, with RIA originally set in the context of a deregulation exercise, then reformulated to advance an inclusive governance agenda pointing to wide social legitimacy, and recently, perhaps, redirected towards risk-tolerant deregulation (Dodds 2006).

Overall, we found no evidence that the constituencies supporting the core executive use RIA as information/alert on whether the regulators are going too far. European courts have not developed jurisprudence on how RIA should be used. Although the argument on this possible use of RIA has been made at the theoretical level in the literature on the political economy of administrative law, and may have empirical leverage in the US, there is no evidence in our cases.

If this is the broad RIA picture, there is no doubt that for certain departments the current enthusiasm of the core executive for the reduction of burdens has been a less than welcome redirection of the political agenda. Simplification plans and targets for the reduction of burdens have been seen as manifestations of political steering from the centre. An interviewee from a department said, 'Probably my comment, though, is that the pressure [on us] has been applied very crudely through the standard cost model.' Interestingly, the interviewee carried on observing that 'we have responded to that, we've been working very hard to broaden the agenda so that we get the right outcomes' (interview in London, October 2006).

To conclude, there is strategic use of RIA but limited evidence of substantiating knowledge in the sense of Boswell (2008). The question is whether the burdens reduction campaigns are yet another symbolic turn of the better regulation movement or not. At the moment, surveys suggest that the business community is not latching on (NAO 2007) – thus supporting the symbolic interpretation.

THE NULL HYPOTHESIS

To control for the null hypothesis, we have to look at coercion and partisan effects. At the policy-setting level, partisan effects should be pronounced, with right-of-centre governments linking better regulation to neo-liberal economic policies. Although there are instances in which this has happened (the Swedish government elected in 2006 was somewhat challenging the social-democratic orthodoxy on regulatory priorities), there has been a pretty even diffusion of better regulation principles across Europe. The Dutch Balkenende 4 government has not changed the trajectory of the previous, more neo-liberal, administration. Nor has the UK changed the party in government in the period examined here, yet better regulation has been redefined more than once.

In a sense, there is a partisan effect at the level of the Commission. The Barroso Commission (November 2004–October 2009) was closer to business regulatory priorities than the previous Prodi Commission, arguably more interested in open governance and a balanced approach to sustainable development, social cohesion and growth. This is consistent with the political affiliation of Barroso's Commissioners (Hix 2007).

At the instrument-setting level, there has been more than one episode in which the most active Finance Ministers, such as Gordon Brown and Gerrit Zalm, have put pressure on the Commission to move forward with better regulation innovations consistent with the goals pursued by the ministers at home. This is partly in connection with the mobilization of better regulation networks at the EU level (and therefore falls in the category of diffusion and emulation), but it has also partly taken the shape of explicit political pressure on Brussels.

CONCLUDING REMARKS

This article has contributed to the literature on policy learning by improving on conceptual analysis, micro-foundations, and the specification of the null hypothesis. Empirically, the strongest learning effects are in the category of emulation (the Netherlands as leader in the diffusion process, the UK, Denmark, Sweden and the Commission as importers), followed by political learning, especially in the Netherlands and the UK. There is limited evidence pointing towards instrumental learning (most of the evidence is from the UK) and the null hypothesis. Indeed, the findings for partisan effects are limited. In Sweden, the centre-right administration elected in 2006 was somewhat inclined to break with some social-democratic regulatory taboos and has given a more distinct pro-business colour to simplification and regulatory oversight. The European Commission provides evidence of pressure from governments to redefine the priorities of better regulation in the direction of business and administrative burdens – thus falling at least in part within the null hypothesis.

These results stimulate some concluding remarks. At the macro-level, to produce instrumental learning is a very difficult, and rare, event in politics (Olsen and Peters 1996). It requires a 'learning group' of politicians and experts at the top of the executive, with the right mix of motivation and opportunity to learn from experience (Olsen and Peters 1996). At the micro-level, individual RIAs cannot possibly produce instrumental or reflexive learning if they are carried out at the late stages of policy formulation (Russel and Turnpenny 2009), are focused on a narrow range of regulatory costs (Hertin *et al.* 2009), and there are no political-administrative incentives to think creatively about problem definition, causality, risk and uncertainty (Baldwin 2005; Black 2005).

Second, the presence of symbolic and some forms of political learning is consistent with basic tenets of rational policy analysis (although in the literature symbolic behaviour is often contrasted with rational choice). For top bureaucrats and politicians, it makes sense to adopt those innovations, like the standard cost model and the burdens reduction targets, that seem less complicated, less context-sensitive, and easier to transfer. If these innovations then seem to provide legitimacy gains and popularity-boosting signalling devices, a rational actor should adopt them. Burdens reduction plans provide concentrated benefits to the business community and diffuse their high costs. A full RIA system provides diffuse benefits (its main regulatory quality principle is to introduce only regulations that improve the welfare of the community) and diffuse costs. With a full RIA system it is impossible to predict ex-ante whether a social group will be adversely affected by proposed regulation or not. Hence its political attractiveness is low. Classic regulation theory (Wilson 1980) will therefore predict that burdens reduction plans are preferred to complex RIA systems.

Third, instrumental learning is particularly difficult if the theories of the policy process embedded in policy instruments are wrong. Most European RIA guidelines draw on a rationally synoptic theory of the policy process – implying a separation between means and ends, root-and-branch analysis of options, trivial information costs. They also assume separation between the technical and the political aspects of choice. Wrong theoretical assumptions about policy-making hinder instrumental learning – rather than facilitating it (Hertin *et al.* 2009).

Finally, learning should not be correlated with policy improvement. It is obvious that policy-makers have learned symbolically and politically. But this does not necessarily mean that the quality of rules has increased. The latter is a proposition that requires its own research design to be tested. Future research could usefully look into the relationship between better regulation, learning, and the implications for the quality of the regulatory systems in Europe, as well as contrasting the European cases with the North American experience.

ACKNOWLEDGEMENTS

The theoretical underpinnings of this article are shaped by my European Research Council advanced grant on Analysis of Learning in Regulatory Governance. Empirical research was funded by the project on Regulatory Impact Assessment in Comparative Perspective funded by the Economic and Social Research Council, grant RES-000-23-1284. I am grateful to Fabrizio De Francesco for research assistance and to the participants in seminars at UCL London, the University of Edinburgh and the European Research Institute (Birmingham University) where earlier drafts were presented. I am particularly grateful to Christina Boswell, Peter Biegelbauer, Fabrizio De Francesco, Michelle Egan, Anne Meuwese, Colin Provost, Tony Zito and two anonymous referees for their comments. The usual disclaimer applies.

REFERENCES

Alam, T. (2007) *Quand la vache folle retrouve son champ. Une comparaison transnationale de la remise en ordre d'un secteur d'action publique*, Lille: CERAPS.

Ambler, T., Chittenden, F. and Xiao, D. (2007) *The Burden of Regulation: Who is Watching Out for Us?*, Report for the British Chambers of Commerce, London.

Baldwin, R. (2005) 'Is better regulation smarter regulation?', *Public Law* (Autumn): 485–511.

Banerjee, A.V. (1992) 'A simple model of herd behavior', *Quarterly Journal of Economics* 107: 797–817.

Bartle, I. (2008). 'Risk based regulation and better regulation in the UK: towards what model of risk regulation?', ECPR Standing Group on Regulatory Governance, Biennial Conference, 5–7 June, Utrecht.

Bennett, C.J. and Howlett, M. (1992) 'The lessons of learning: reconciling theories of policy learning and policy change', *Policy Science* 25: 275–94.

Better Regulation Task Force (2005) *Regulation – Less is More*, Report to the Prime Minister, March, London: BRTF.

Biegelbauer, P. (2007) 'Ein neuer Blick auf politisches Handeln: Politik-Lernansätze im Vergleich', *Österreichische Zeitschrift für Politikwissenschaft* 3: 231–47.

Black, J. (2005) 'The emergence of risk-based regulation and the new public risk management in the United Kingdom', *Public Law* (Autumn): 512–48.

Boswell, C. (2008) 'The political functions of expert knowledge: knowledge and legitimation in European Union immigration policy', *Journal of European Public Policy* 15(4): 471–88.

Calvert, R.L. (1985) 'The value of biased information: a rational choice model of political advice', *Journal of Politics* 47(2): 530–55.

DiMaggio, P.J. and Powell, W.W. (1991) 'The iron cage revisited: institutional isomorphism and collective rationality in organizational fields', in W.W. Powell and P.J. DiMaggio (eds), *The New Institutionalism in Organizational Analysis*, Chicago and London: University of Chicago Press, pp. 63–82.

Dodds, A. (2006) 'The core executive's approach to regulation: from "better regulation" to "risk-tolerant deregulation"', *Social Policy and Administration* 40(5): 526–42.

Dunlop, C.A. (forthcoming, 2010) 'The temporal dimension of knowledge and the limits of policy appraisal: biofuels policy in the UK', *Policy Sciences*, forthcoming.

Evans, M. and Davies, J. (1999) 'Understanding policy transfer: a multi-level, multi-disciplinary perspective', *Public Administration* 77(2): 361–85.

Froud, J., Boden, R., Ogus, A. and Stubbs, P. (1998) *Controlling the Regulators*, Basingstoke: Macmillan.

Gilardi, F. (2008). 'Who learns from what in policy diffusion processes? Evidence from unemployment benefits retrenchment in OECD countries', paper presented at the American Political Science Association Annual Meeting, Boston, MA, 28–31 August.

Grin, J. and Loeber, A. (2007) 'Theories of policy learning: agency, structure, and change', in F. Fischer, G.J. Miller and M.S. Sidney (eds), *Handbook of Public Policy Analysis: Theory, Politics, and Methods*, Boca Raton, FL: CRC Press, pp. 201–19.

Hall, P. (1993) 'Policy paradigms, social learning and the state. The case of economic policy-making in Britain', *Comparative Politics* 25(3): 275–96.

Helm, D. (2006) 'Regulatory reform, capture, and the regulatory burden', *Oxford Review of Economic Policy* 22(2): 169–85.

Hertin, J., Pesch, U. and Jacob, K. (2007). 'The production and use of knowledge in regulatory impact assessment – an empirical analysis', ECPR General Conference Pisa, 6–8 September.

Hertin, J., Turnpenny, J., Jordan, A., Nilsson, M., Russel, D. and Nykvist, B. (2009) 'Rationalising the policy mess? Ex-ante policy assessment and the utilization of knowledge in the policy process', *Environment and Planning A*, forthcoming.

Hix, S. (2007) *What's Wrong with the European Union and How to Fix It*, London: Polity.

Hood, C. (2007) 'Intellectual obsolescence and intellectual makeovers: reflections on the tools of government after two decades', *Governance* 20(1): 127–44.

Jacob, K. *et al.* (2008) *Improving the Practice of Impact Assessment*, Berlin: EVIA Consortium.

James, O. and Lodge, M. (2003) 'The limitations of "policy transfer" and "lesson-drawing" for public policy research', *Political Studies Review* 1: 179–93.

Jansen, W. and Voermans, W. (2006) 'Procura e destruição nos Países Baixos: políticas legislativas no combate à burocracia', *Legislação*, 44(October–December): 63–79.

Lascoumes, P. and Le Galès, P. (2004) 'L'action publique saisie par ses instruments', in P. Lascoumes and P. Le Galès (eds), *Gouverner par les instruments*, Paris: Sciences-Po Presses, pp. 11–44.

Levitt, B. and March, J.G. (1988) 'Organizational learning', *Annual Review of Sociology* 14: 319–40.

March, J.G. (1981) 'Footnotes to organizational change', *Administrative Science Quarterly* 26: 563–77.

May, P.J. (1992) 'Policy learning and failure', *Journal of Public Policy* 12(4): 331–54.

McCubbins, M.D., Noll, R.G. and Weingast, B.R. (1987) 'Administrative procedures as instruments of political control', *Journal of Law, Economics, and Organization* 3(2): 243–77.

Meuwese, A.C.M. (2007) 'Inter-institutionalizing impact assessment', in S. Weatherill (ed.), *Better Regulation*, London: Hart, pp. 287–309.

NAO (National Audit Office) (2006) *Evaluation of Regulatory Impact Assessment 2005– 2006*, London: National Audit Office.

NAO (National Audit Office) (2007) *Reducing the Cost of Complying with Regulation. The delivery of the Administrative Burdens Reduction Programme, 2007*, London: National Audit Office.

Nilsson, M., Jordan, A., Turnpenny, J., Hertin, J., Nykvist, B. and Russel, D. (2008) 'The use and non-use of policy appraisal in public policy making: an analysis of three European countries and the European Union', *Policy Sciences* 41(4): 335–55.

OECD (2007) *Government Capacity to Assure High Quality Regulation in Sweden*, Paris: Organisation for Economic Co-operation and Development.

Olsen, J. and Peters, G. (eds) (1996) *Lessons from Experience: Experimental Learning in Administrative Reforms in Eight democracies*, Oslo: Scandinavian University Press.

Owens, S., Rayner, T. and Bina, O. (2004) 'New agendas for appraisal: reflections on theory, practice, and research', *Environmental and Planning A* 36: 1943–59.

Radaelli, C.M. (2007) 'Whither better regulation for the Lisbon agenda?', *Journal of European Public Policy* 14(2): 190–207.

Russel, D. and Turnpenny, J. (2009) 'The politics of sustainable development in UK government: what role for integrated policy appraisal?', *Environment and Planning C: Government and Policy*, forthcoming.

Sabatier, P. (1993) 'Policy change over a decade or more', in P.A. Sabatier and H. Jenkins-Smith (eds), *Policy Change and Learning*, Boulder, CO: Westview Press, pp. 13–39.

Sanderson, I. (2002) 'Evaluation, policy learning and evidence-based policy making', *Public Administration* 80(1): 1–22.

Stone, D. (1996) *Capturing the Political Imagination. Think Tanks and the Policy Process*, Ilford: Frank Cass.

Wegrich, K. (2009) 'The administrative burden reduction policy boom in Europe: comparing mechanisms of policy diffusion', CARR, LSE Discussion Paper no. 52, London.
Weiss, C.H. (1979) 'The many meanings of research utilization', *Public Administration Review* 39(5): 426–31.
Weyland, K. (2005) 'Theories of policy diffusion: lessons from Latin American pension reforms', *World Politics* 57(2): 262–95.
Wiener, J.B. (2006) 'Better regulation in Europe', *Current Legal Problems* 59: 447–518.
Wilson, J.Q. (1980) *The Politics of Regulation*, New York: Basic Books.
Zito, A. and Schout, A. (2009) 'Learning theory reconsidered: EU integration theories and learning', *Journal of European Public Policy* 16(8): 1103–23.

EU policy towards other regions: policy learning in the external promotion of regional integration

Mary Farrell

1. INTRODUCTION

Since the 1990s, the European Union (EU) has declared its support for regional integration in other parts of the world, and incorporated this objective as a part of European external policy (European Commission 1995, 2005a, 2008a). In the midst of the more problematical and often contentious areas of the embryonic common foreign and security policy (CFSP), the support for regional integration and co-operation has been much less controversial, having been publicly endorsed by European Commission officials, and identified in the policy publications emanating from the various Directorate Generals (DGs).[1]

The EU now has some 20 inter-regional agreements with the other major regional groupings around the world, including accords with regional groupings in Africa, Asia and the Americas (Alecu de Flers and Regelsberger 2005). While the EU continues to struggle to define its international role, and its identity as an international actor, the bloc-to-bloc diplomacy and inter-regional co-operation does in itself go some way to enhance the actorness of the EU, distinguishing the political processes involved from the more traditional (state-to-state) practices in international relations (Bretherton and Vogler 2005; Hill and Smith 2005; Smith 2008).

The EU has supported regional integration elsewhere in the world since the 1960s. However, this support has become much more explicit since the 1990s, and this article examines the extent to which a qualitative shift in policy can be explained in terms of learning. Policy learning is understood here as a long-lasting change in the perception of policy-related problems, beliefs and attitudes of government (Bandelow 2008). The article identifies what types of learning have taken place with respect to the policy of promoting regional integration, and assesses the impact of learning on the policy outputs and outcomes. The following sections address the conditions that trigger learning in the EU context, and the constraints and limitations that may inhibit learning processes.

Recent research on the EU policy towards the promotion of regional integration elsewhere has tended to contextualize the policy from different standpoints: the export of the EU model of regional integration; the expansion of regional governance; or as the spread of European norms. Moreover, the success of European regionalism has in some cases prompted other countries to imitation, while elsewhere countries have opted for their own form of regionalism firmly rejecting any explicit attempt to replicate the European experience (Fawcett and Hurrell 1995; Hurrell 2007; Gamble and Payne 1996; Telò 2007; Soderbaum and Shaw 2003). Making case study comparisons is often difficult, not least because of the variation in the use of the term 'regionalism' (Hurrell 2007: 130). Among the many regionalism processes that operate, a distinction can be made between formal regional inter-state co-operation for the purposes of creating region-wide regimes and policies in certain issue areas; regional consolidation, where the 'region' takes on 'actorness' to conduct relations between the constituent member states and the rest of the world; and the informal regionalization associated with increased levels of economic and social interaction. Both formal and informal processes may over time lead to the emergence of regional awareness and a sense of regional identity, though such outcomes are never certain in even the most 'regionalized' communities.

Since we are concerned here with an examination of policy learning with respect to regional integration – part of the policy instruments in the EU's external relations policy – the 'narrow' understanding of regional integration as inter-regional/inter-state co-operation will be adopted. However, in practice, it is impossible to conduct this kind of policy without unleashing complex and dynamic processes amidst often competing logics – the logics of economic and societal integration, of power politics, and of security (Hurrell 2007: 130). The European Commission's definition of regional integration would seem to recognize this complexity: 'regional integration is the process of overcoming, by common accord, political, physical, economic and social barriers that divide countries from their neighbours, and of collaborating in the management of shared resources and regional commons' (European Commission 2008a).

The next section establishes the analytical framework based upon a policy learning perspective.

2. POLICY LEARNING – AN ANALYTICAL FRAMEWORK

Learning can be an individual process, and there is an extensive literature dealing with individual learning, largely seen as the product of internal and mental processes and explained by psychological or philosophical approaches or, alternatively, as a product of exogenous processes. Recently, political science and international relations literature has focused on mutual learning, on the collective learning in organizations, recognizing that institutions can, and do, have the potential for learning (Argyris and Schön 1978; Finnemore and Sikkink 1998; Dolowitz and March 2000). Latterly, various areas of EU policy have been subject to analysis under a policy learning framework, including the open method of co-ordination, the European employment strategy, environmental policy, and the policy transfer by national governments as they adapt to European integration (Radaelli 2004; Nedergaard 2006; Bomberg 2007; Bandelow 2008). Greater challenges emanate from the application of a policy learning framework to the analysis of foreign policy, long recognized as an area of conceptual and political complexity (Levy 1994).

Ernst Haas defined learning as 'the process by which consensual knowledge is used to specify causal relationships in new ways so that the result affects the content of public policy (Haas 1990: 23), specifying the conditions for learning in the shared understandings implicit in the notion of consensual knowledge. In essence, for Haas the policy learning depended upon the policy actors sharing a larger and common perspective that allowed them to reach agreement on policy outputs, and even identify radical solutions to existing problems.

Elsewhere in the international relations literature, attention has been given to the role of ideas in shaping and changing public policy (Goldstein and Keohane 1993). Clearly, ideas influence policy by the impact upon political actors, and new ideas can effect policy change where two conditions apply: first, when there are groups and individuals who will promote the new ideas and promulgate them by building coalitions of support; and, second, ideas need to become embedded in institutions by a process of 'social learning' (Hall 1993). According to Hall, social learning occurs as policy-makers seek to find new solutions to policy problems, embarking on a process of changing existing policy instruments to address these policy problems, and experimenting with new policy instruments when existing instruments are considered to be ineffective. In this trial-and-error approach, learning takes place as the policy actors identify what works and respond accordingly. Hall describes the failure to identify appropriate and effective policy instruments as opening up a window of opportunity for new ideas and new instruments, suggesting the appearance of a 'market place for ideas' and the contestation of different ideas and their respective policy solutions/instruments until there is an eventual victory of one idea (and the respective policy instruments). Hence, the new idea becomes institutionalized, and provides the paradigmatic framework for policy-making (Oliver and Pemberton 2001). In his analysis, Hall proposes that the process of social learning will lead to changes at different levels: changes to existing policy instruments (first order change); adoption of new instruments (second order change); paradigm change, with a change of goals (third order change). Third order change is the most radical for it implies a fundamental re-ordering of priorities and goals, as well as policy instruments, and it marks a sea change in the way policy-makers view the problems they seek to address.

Hall's approach to the analysis of policy processes faces a challenge in the rather different and more complex context of European policy-making. A broader range of political actors, including transnational interest groups, supranational institutions, as well as the array of national interest representation, complicates the picture, and requires a more nuanced understanding of the social processes embedded in policy-making and the shared understandings of the common problems facing the European community (Pierson 1998). Jeffrey Checkel adopts a constructivist approach to examine learning in the context of European integration, explaining learning as a process whereby actors, through interaction with broader institutional contexts (norms and discursive structures), acquire new interests and preferences (Checkel 2001). In this approach, what matters to learning is the role of norms and discursive structures, where norms are understood as shared collective understandings that regulate behaviour. Learning comes about when people interact and interpret the world as a socially constructed reality. Language and its meaning matter to the actors, and dominant concepts frame the arguments, even for those actors who may wish to propose counter arguments. This approach to learning recognises the struggle for power that can dominate social relations, and what matters is the capacity to promote a dominant logic of argumentation and to impress it upon the other actors.

Here we can identify certain conditions that are likely to promote learning. First, the actors share a set of normative and causal beliefs; second, the actors engage in an iterative process, a co-ordinated interaction over time. Competition among views and ideas is possible, and a struggle for power and an ensuing dominant idea (or set of ideas) is likely, as we saw above, but there should remain a shared set of fundamental, core beliefs. Third, learning occurs with the changes to actors' preferences, when actors realize that they need to alter strategies in order to achieve certain goals, and ultimately this leads to policy change – acting according to the 'logic of consequentiality'. Fourth, and borrowing from the sociological institutionalist literature, actors learn from on-going cognitive processes, 'taking cues from their institutional environment as they construct their preferences and select the appropriate behaviour for a given institutional environment' (Pollack 2004: 139) – acting according to the 'logic of appropriateness'.

Finally, we can consider the extent of learning and the impact upon the actors' belief systems. Beliefs can be categorized as a hierarchical system based on three levels of beliefs. At the top of the hierarchy are the *fundamental, core beliefs*, normative (and abstract) beliefs that are so fundamental as to be impossible to change. At the second level are the *policy core beliefs* that reflect the cognitive frames of reference shared by policy actors, understandings of the nature and scope of a policy problem and of the priorities across different policy areas. Policy core beliefs are rather difficult to change, and likely only as a result of learning over a long period, or possibly due to pressure from external or unexpected shocks. The third level of the hierarchy contains the *secondary beliefs*, and these relate to narrower policy preferences, where the political actors can make choices between different instruments. Learning is most likely and easier at this level.

The literature on policy learning suggests that political actors (governments, the EU) can react to the success or failure of previous policy instruments; they can also take into account changes to the external (international) environment in which policy operates, and/or take advice from experts (the role of epistemic communities). Adopting the notion of a hierarchical belief system, we can see in the different literature a distinction between levels of learning – first order learning, where there is a change of policy instruments; and second order learning, where there is a change of overall goals (Bandelow 2008: 745). In the case of first order learning, the values, attitudes and perceptions of the problem remain the same, whereas new learning from experience and new knowledge produce a change of goals, thus generating second order learning.

3. PROMOTING REGIONAL INTEGRATION

While other areas of foreign policy have yet to be elaborated coherently, the policy on regional integration attracted little opposition at national or European level, raising no threat to national sovereignty, or to the common interests shared by the community of states. Driven by the European Commission, a number of directorates quickly adopted the regional integration policy and the changing approaches to development policy ('trade not aid') brought the development directorate into closer contact with external relations and trade directorates. Even if this emerging consensus across different areas of the European Commission did not dispel the normal rivalries and competition between them, there was enough common interest among the supranational bureaucracy to drive this policy forward. In practice, the EU policy (implemented largely through the European Commission) has operated not through the kind of common approach to be found in other policy areas (such as trade, competition, agriculture) but instead by a diversified strategy based on a range of policy instruments, a mix of conditionalities and incentives, generally tailored to the economic, security and geopolitical interests of the EU.

Three broad approaches to the promotion of regional integration can be distinguished, exemplified by the differences in instruments and a qualitative distinction in outcomes and strategic intent. First, the promotion of regional integration through enlargement has provided a very direct and comprehensive way of implementing this policy, at the same time spreading the regulatory system and the legal order to new member states. But the use of conditionality in the enlargement process served also to enforce the EU rules and to shape the institutions in the applicant states. Conditionality was coercive, securing compliance to the policy outcome and to the Commission's highly politicized demands that the individual applicant states adopt the full array of rules, regulations, standards and policies in the *acquis communautaire*.

Second, the EU can and has been able to influence regional integration in a broad and general way through normative suasion, where other regional communities adopt certain practices, institutional arrangements, or other forms of governance modelled on the European regional governance system. The role of norms in shaping outcomes has long been recognized in the literature, and even in the absence of a specific policy, agreement, or other form of intervention targeted at a region it can be possible for the EU to exert influence. In practice, the same policy approach is not adopted for all regional groupings and for individual countries, so that the EU's effectiveness as a norm exporter is determined by the nature of each arrangement and how the target region responds to the EU. Agreements that are politically rather than legally binding tend to commit the contracting parties only if there is a strong interest at stake.

Third, the promotion of regional integration has developed through the inter-regional agreements between the EU and other regional groupings, such as the Asia–Europe meeting (ASEM) or the Cotonou Agreement with the African, Caribbean and Pacific group. The inter-regional agreements also take different forms, distinguishing between pure inter-regional co-operation (involving formal regional blocs, such as EU–Mercosur) and hybrid inter-regionalism (co-operation between a formal regional community and a group of countries that do not constitute a formal regional entity). Inter-regional co-operation takes a variety of forms and policy instruments, ranging across aid programmes, regional trade agreements, support for regional integration and more comprehensive regional strategies – sometimes embracing all of these components. Generally, the inter-regional agreements cover a whole range of issues (trade, environment, technical assistance, development, infrastructure, political reform), though the individual agreements tend also to include specified objectives, such as the Cotonou Agreement with its emphasis on the integration of the African countries into the global economy.

Inter-regional co-operation agreements are characterized by complexity and a diversity of content, policy instruments, and outcomes. European Commission official publications do, however, broadly agree on the impetus for this departure in the EU's external relations. The genesis of these agreements is a shift in the EU's strategic priorities, with geographic proximity prioritizing the regions of greatest importance. Newly independent states emerging after the collapse of the Soviet Union generated uncertainty about European security and a threat of instability on the EU's eastern borders, thus posing the question of how to manage relations with these states. Ultimately, the concerns were addressed through the offer of membership. Furthermore, new geo-strategic priorities were emerging, to underline the need for new actions and programmes located in the strategic priorities of the EU rather than those of the individual states. In essence, the policy towards the promotion of regional integration can be seen as part of a dual strategy, the preservation of regional order and the enhancement of the EU's global presence.

In sum, the external promotion of regional integration can be used for various goals: to export the EU model of governance; to exercise international influence through the spread of EU values; and to strengthen the identity of the EU without compromising the national interests of the respective member states. Not all three approaches identified in this section are mutually exclusive: enlargement was about spreading regional integration, and also disseminating European norms to the prospective members; and inter-regional co-operation also facilitates norm transfer, though without the prospect of accession. Conditionality is used pervasively in all the European Commission's negotiations, though its impact is highly variable across countries and regions. Similarly, the link between regional integration and development emerges in both EU–Africa and EU–Asia relations, though clearly there are significant variations not only in the underlying structural conditions but also in the receptivity to European norms and ideas.

For example, the African approach to regional integration reflects much from the European experience, most noticeably in the preference for supranational institution-building, and a proposed new currency in West Africa. Inter-regional co-operation between the EU and Asia is conducted with fewer power asymmetries, and a strong commitment on the part of the Asian states generally to the principle of domestic non-intervention (Forster 2000). Though the EU continues to push the human rights agenda in bilateral and multilateral negotiations with Asian countries, the latter have not been so receptive to the explicitly normative European agenda nor to any extension of policy discussion beyond the trade and economic arena, with the result that the EU has not been able to press conditionality with the same fervour as elsewhere. However, the Association of South-east Asian Nations (ASEAN) grouping has begun in recent years to address regional integration, emphasizing trade, strengthening security and addressing the 'war on terror' in the region, as part of a reappraisal of the regional group's role and relevance in the contemporary Asian and global order (Conde 2007).

In recent years, much inter-regional co-operation involving the EU and other regional groupings has taken the form of trade agreements, a trend to European external policy that contrasts sharply with the failure to secure agreement in the World Trade Organization (WTO) trade liberalization negotiations under the Doha Development Round. Negotiations for a free trade area (FTA) started with the ASEAN group, with the Andean Community, and Central America. These essentially economic inter-regional agreements are supported by a range of bilateral agreements between the EU and individual countries that represent diverse strategic interests – China, India, South Africa, and Brazil rating particularly strong as important partners for the EU. This 'search for partnership' characterizes much of the EU's external relations over the past five years, with the European Commission as principal actor and lead negotiator representing the member states. Mostly, the issues and agenda cover trade and economic matters where the Commission has negotiating authority and a mandate to represent the member states.

Regional integration – the EU representation

In the academic literature, distinctions are made between regional integration and regionalism based on different processes, and different driving forces, though the terms can sometimes be used interchangeably (Sbragia 2008). Both imply some degree of consolidation and pooling of resources, sharing of sovereignty, and a commitment of states to political, economic, and legal objectives. The level of integration can vary, from a loose co-ordination in some area(s), including trade, to deeper integration at the political level, pooling sovereignty, and the creation of supranational institutions. As integration processes continue, a sense of identity emerges from common interests and values, and ultimately a regional (political) community acts as a subject with its own identity, an actor with capability and the structures to facilitate region-wide decision-making.

Despite the many references to regional integration in EU official publications over the past decade, the European Commission was slow to articulate a precise vision of its policy on regional integration. Instead, it appears as part of a range of policy instruments and strategic objectives, from security to trade, to inter-regional co-operation, development policy, EU–Africa relations, and EU–Asia co-operation. In *The EU and Africa: Towards a Strategic Partnership*, adopted by the European Council in December 2005, the primary goals of the EU's Africa strategy are the achievement of the Millennium Development Goals and the promotion of sustainable development, security and good governance in Africa. Regional integration introduced under the heading *Sustainable Economic Growth, Regional Integration and Trade* is linked to the Economic Partnership Agreements, and to a whole array of objectives around the integration of Africa into the global economy, support for improved governance and for compliance with EU rules and standards, aid for trade, and environment and climate policies.

In the case of EU relations with the Middle East, initiatives are very much determined by the former's capacity as an actor reliant upon civilian power, and driven by the two geo-strategic objectives of improved political stability in the region, and the desire to reduce the economic migration from the region into Europe. EU efforts have revolved around the discourse of trade integration among the participating states, fostering intra-regional trade and policy co-ordination between the Middle East states, under the framework of the Barcelona process. In recent years, the promotion of regional trade agreements has been the EU's preferred policy instrument, simultaneously signing bilateral trade agreements with individual countries while pushing for trade liberalization at the intra-regional level. Given the constraints imposed upon the EU as a coherent foreign policy actor, policy towards the Middle East has tended in practice to be ad hoc, with very limited successful outcomes even in the economic arena. Despite the EU's continued support for and encouragement of regional co-operation and integration, the Middle East countries have had little success in intra-regional co-operation and there has been limited economic integration, sometimes characterized by tense political relations between the states.

The security imperative is less influential in shaping the EU's relations with Asia generally. Instead, the economic rationale permeates the programmes and policies that emerged with the European Commission's 1994 publication 'Towards a New Asia Strategy' that marked the European 'rediscovery' of Asia. Trade flows and inter-regional economic co-operation have increased significantly on a regional and bilateral basis, with a few individual countries (China, Singapore, Japan, India) taking the lion's share of economic flows. Market access and strengthening the EU's political and economic presence across the region as a global economic actor are the key objectives in this European strategy. Unlike other regions, the EU has tended to downplay the policy of promoting regional integration in Asia, and mainly confines this discourse on regional integration promotion to the case of south Asia, and the South Asian Association for Regional Co-operation (SAARC) regional grouping. Instead, inter-regional co-operation is conducted in a series of fora and institutional frameworks: the pure inter-regional, or bloc-to-bloc co-operation taking place in EU–ASEAN, EU–SAARC, and the ASEM meetings; and the hybrid inter-regional, bilateral co-operation characterized in EU–China dialogue, EU–India, and EU–Japan. The ASEM (Asia–Europe meeting) continues as a forum for informal dialogue and co-operation between the EU, the European Commission, and the Asian states (Brunei, China, Indonesia, Japan, South Korea, Malaysia, the Philippines, Singapore, Thailand, and Vietnam), and, while the wide-ranging agenda of topics reflects a broad-based set of interests, action is largely confined to economic, technical and trade-related concerns of all actors (Farrell 2009).

In contrast to the case of Africa, discussed in detail in the next section, the mix of bilateral/multilateral co-operative agreements continues to characterize the EU's relations with most other regional communities, and the extent to which emphasis is placed upon the promotion of regional integration per se varies quite considerably from region to region. The next section takes a closer look at the case of EU–Africa relations, where the policy of promoting regional integration has perhaps been pursued most explicitly and where 'the Economic Partnership Agreements remain high on the agenda and, when concluded on a comprehensive regional basis, will be the cornerstone of EU support for regional integration' (European Commission 2008b).

4. EU–AFRICA RELATIONS: POLICY LEARNING OR ADAPTATION?

Inter-regional co-operation between the EU and Africa has a long history, based upon an institutionalized framework that predated any other inter-regional co-operation policies currently implemented by the EU. Stemming largely from colonial ties, the Lomé Agreements provided an institutionalized basis for policy towards the African countries, and a formal framework for the conduct of inter-regional dialogue between what the European side declared as ostensible 'equal partners'. For three decades, the institutionalized framework supported high-level talks between the political representatives of the EU (including member state representatives, and the European Commission) and their counterparts in the countries of the African, Caribbean and Pacific (ACP) region.

The Cotonou Agreement of 2000 marked a departure from its predecessor in several respects.[2] Growing criticism of the Lomé Agreements for the failure to deliver real results (market access for ACP producers, development and modernization of primary production among the countries of the region), combined with a more critical concern within Europe towards the need to secure 'value for money' led to a reappraisal of the agreements. Growing donor fatigue and increased public concern about the effectiveness of European aid expenditure and the appropriate use of public finance in the recipient countries, combined with the shift in EU development policy towards an emphasis on 'trade not aid' as a key route to development, brought European policy into line with the international institutions, notably the World Bank and the International Monetary Fund. By the mid-1990s, there was a strong international consensus favouring a neo-liberal approach to development and the support for market-based activities.

The Cotonou Agreement reflected these various concerns, emphasizing trade liberalization (dropping the non-reciprocity of the predecessor Lomé accords), with the specific proposal for regional economic integration agreements between the EU and groups of countries within the ACP bloc, and in parallel, the establishment of regional integration among the countries of the ACP region. These regional economic integration agreements, now commonly referred to as Economic Partnership Agreements (EPAs), constituted a departure from previous policy in their emphasis on broad-based economic liberalization – across countries, products, sectors and markets – as well as a broader policy agenda that included competition, trade and environmental considerations, trade and labour standards, consumer policy and consumer health, the protection of intellectual property rights, and standardization and certification.

In parallel with the EPA negotiations, the European Commission was actively developing an Africa strategy, with the publication of the EU Strategy for Africa in 2005, followed soon after by the Joint Africa–EU Strategy adopted at the Lisbon summit meeting in December 2007 (European Council 2007).[3] The joint declaration issued in Lisbon referred to the intention 'to build a new strategic political partnership for the future, overcoming the traditional donor–recipient relationship and building on common values and goals in our pursuit of peace and stability, democracy and rule of law, progress and development'. The intention is to develop a long-term strategic partnership, proposing specific strategies in the following areas: peace and security; governance and human rights; trade and regional integration; key development issues.

This joint strategy goes far beyond the parameters of previous EU inter-regional co-operation to propose an expanded institutional framework, with the African Union as the voice of continental issues and the most important institutional partner for the EU. Emanating from this strategy and new institutional framework is an interconnected set of policies and action plans with specified timeframes and indicated outcomes, exemplified in the First Action Plan (2008–2010) which sets out eight lines of action covering areas such as peace and security, trade and regional integration, democratic governance and human rights, the millennium development goals, and migration/mobility/employment.[4]

5. HOW REAL IS THIS POLICY CHANGE – WHAT LEARNING CAN BE IDENTIFIED IN EU–AFRICA CO-OPERATION?

With the Joint Africa–EU Strategy, EU policy appears to have moved away from the policy content and the general approach adopted under the earlier Lomé accords, and even the Cotonou Agreement. Regional integration remains a key component in the new strategy, and is presented as a dual approach: regional integration linking the EU and the African countries through the EPAs, and regional integration among the African countries. How far can we discern policy learning on the part of the EU in the evolving EU–Africa inter-regional policy?

The post-Cotonou regime rests upon the dual strategy of sub-regional integration, and the integration of Africa into the global economy (European Commission 2005b). Development strategy is here based upon the principle that trade, not aid, is the route towards economic and social progress, and the reduction of poverty (European Commission 2005a). Close examination of the discourse suggests that regional integration is here understood as economic/trade liberalization, something that the EPA negotiations have in fact revealed (European Commission 2008a).

How can we explain this shift in EU–Africa relations from the Lomé accords to the post-Cotonou regime using the policy learning analytical framework? Within the historical institutionalist perspective, it is institutions that affect policy outcomes, since they mediate political struggles rather than actually reflecting the distribution of political power and, once in place, can take on a life of their own and determine the scope and pace of political and policy development (Pierson 1998). The European Commission, acting on behalf of the member states to manage EU–ACP relations, presided over a very stable policy regime for several decades until it was eventually forced by external pressures to re-evaluate the nature of this policy and the policy instruments. Historical institutionalism explains this stability in terms of path dependency, where institutional dynamics and preferences 'lock in' policy into a certain framework and direction.

The shift of policy in the post-Cotonou regime, with its emphasis on reciprocal trade relations between Europe and Africa, regional integration among the

African states, and inter-regional integration in the EPAs mark a widening in the range and scope of policy instruments, departing from the earlier policy period with its reliance on aid and technical assistance policy framed by the discourse of the development debate. Forces for change, in the shape of new ideas on development through the market (the trade not aid approach) and the growing public discontent over the 'waste' of public finances allocated to development, combined with the EU concerns to improve the co-ordination and effectiveness of European policy all provided appropriate conditions for the reappraisal of policy.

Post September 11 2001, the European discourse broadened to emphasize security, and the Security Strategy adopted by the EU Council of Ministers in 2003 identified a number of security threats, among which violent conflict in sub-Saharan Africa was included (EU Council 2003; Olsen 2009; Sicurelli 2008). The European Security Strategy emphasized that 'security is a precondition for development', and it advocated regional integration as an important vehicle for promoting both security and development. Meanwhile, responding to the impetus towards improved co-ordination and coherence across the policy spectrum (trade, development, security), the European Commission published the 'European Consensus' on development in 2005 (European Commission 2005a). Against this background, emphasizing the links between security and development, trade and regional integration, and following the consensus among the European actors (the EU institutions and the member states) on development priorities and instruments, the EU Africa Strategy was published in 2005. Amidst a flurry of activity for the EU, and attempting to face down growing criticism of the Commission's negotiating tactics and the general scope and content of these EPAs, the Lisbon EU–Africa summit meeting proposed an even more ambitious programme for a long-term strategic partnership (European Council 2007).

What does this pattern of policy development suggest in terms of policy learning? Can we discern learning in the trajectory of policy development and the instruments adopted by the European authorities? What level of learning is taking place, and what are the conditions that trigger learning in the EU context? According to Ernst Haas, international organizations are important innovators in international life (Haas 1990). The conditions identified by Haas that are conducive to learning include a stable coalition of like-minded states, and sufficient shared consensual knowledge to evaluate beliefs about appropriate causes and solutions to existing problems:

> learning may involve the elaboration of new cause–effect chains more (or less) elaborate than the ones being questioned and replaced. The resulting conceptualization of the world may be more (or less) holistic than the earlier one. It may imply progress or regress, depending on the normative commitment of the observer or the preferred reading of history ... The problem has to be 'taken apart'; its parts have to be identified and sorted into patterns different from the ones that had been featured in an earlier

round. That done, the problem has to be reaggregated into a different nested set, either more complex and comprehensive than the original one or less so.
(Haas 1990: 24)

Both external and internal triggers to learning about the policy towards promoting regional integration can be identified. As lead actor representing the EU, the European Commission was well placed to become a learning organization – it had led the negotiations with the ten accession states for the 2004 enlargement; it has developed a larger role as the external representative of the EU; and it has played the leading role in managing and developing EU–ACP relations for many decades. Moreover, the European Commission is very active in the strategy to enhance the EU as an international actor and global player. In the context of promoting regional integration externally, and inter-regionalism generally, the European Commission is the leading actor in dialogue with other regional groupings. Among the member states, there is broad consensus around the goal of making the EU an international actor, and as the discussion above suggested, the EU member states have come to share consensual knowledge around the appropriate set of development policies, and, more recently, the set of policies around which to conduct EU–Africa relations. This broad consensual knowledge does not preclude differences between the member states – after all, development policy is an area of shared competence where both the member states and the EU conduct development policies, the main requirement being to ensure co-ordination between the national and supranational levels of policy.

What type of learning can be identified in the context of EU–Africa co-operation? And in the promotion of regional integration within Africa? We have seen the policy change in response to external pressures – the growing disillusion with the Lomé approach (the volume of ACP exports to the European Community had halved from the 1970s to the end of the 1990s); criticism of the development assistance on several fronts (the failure to deliver development outcomes, and the misuse of development aid by corrupt governments); and the change in development discourse internationally, led by the international institutions under the so-called Washington Consensus. While the EU showed some flexibility in its dealings with Africa (particularly the recent Joint Africa–EU Strategy), the lessons learned by the EU in general and the European Commission in particular during the course of the enlargement negotiations with the ten accession countries were much in evidence when it came to the EPA negotiations – conditionality clauses included reference to normative principles, and aspects of regional governance.

Using Peter Hall's hierarchy of levels of change consequent upon social learning (referred to earlier in section 2), we can identify both first order and second order learning – changing existing instruments (from Lomé to Cotonou) and the adoption of new instruments (EPAs, regional integration, trade and development assistance, conditionality and the essential elements clauses). The first and second order learning in Hall's analysis has much in common with the 'adaptation' that international organizations make, as described by Ernst Haas:

successful adaptation implies the willingness to reconsider the tie between means and ends, and to reformulate the organization's program accordingly. Successful adaptation may also call for adding new purposes or dropping old ones, without also involving a searching examination of assumptions about cause–effect links.

(Haas 1990: 36)

In fact, Peter Hall's third order change has much in common with the true learning that Haas considers to be fairly rare – for both authors, this type of learning involves a paradigm shift, a re-ordering of priorities and goals, as well as new policy instruments. According to Haas, this type of learning is uncommon, and most of the time organizations engage in adaptation, either in the context of incremental growth, or in a more complex political environment with many actors and unordered policy preferences (which he characterizes as turbulence).

Useful though these categories are, it is difficult to discern higher level learning without looking at the extent of learning and the impact upon actors' belief systems. Following this line of analysis, we can distinguish the three levels: fundamental, core beliefs (normative, and thus impossible to change); policy core beliefs – the cognitive frame of reference shared by policy actors, which can change over a long period of time, or more rapidly in response to external pressures; and secondary beliefs, linked to policy preferences where actors make choices between different policy instruments. In the case study of EU–Africa co-operation, the promotion of regional integration has produced the type of first and second order learning (including the adoption of new policy instruments) but the EU has retained its fundamental core beliefs, notably the values associated with its identity as a normative actor – the promotion of democracy and the rule of law, the protection of human rights, and the pursuit of multilateralism as an appropriate forum for international decision-making (Scheipers and Sicurelli 2008; Laidi, 2007).

6. EXPORTING GOVERNANCE OR NORMS?

Regional integration policy is nested within a broad range of policy instruments, where there is a heavy emphasis on trade, technical assistance, and development aid. Inter-regional institutional ties are much more recent, and the historical colonies links have moved in quite different directions, with the EU gradually picking up a series of external trade links shaped by pragmatic economic considerations and post-colonial ties. Despite a renewal of the EU's engagement in Asia, and a resurgence in the EU's Asia strategy, this has not been accompanied by the type of activity and scope of policy action that we saw in the context of EU–Africa inter-regionalism. Institutional ties are growing in order to support a very broad range of intergovernmental co-operation, without specifically targeting the promotion of regional integration as a policy priority (Balme and Bridges 2008).

The EU's reluctance to give prominence to regional integration as an appropriate policy for the Asian countries to follow can be attributed to several reasons. Power asymmetries between the EU and the Asian region are much less significant than between the EU and Africa, so the EU is unable to make use of the conditionality argument to the same extent. Regional economic integration within Asia is very much driven by the rational calculations made by the states in the region. As the EU is gradually learning, the kind of cost–benefit calculations being made in Brussels of closer European co-operation with emerging Asian powers and fast-growing economies are something which the Asian states have been engaging in for quite some time. However, the Asian states are better able to withstand the pressures of the EU than the African states, and resist any attempt to propose a regional integration model designed by European architects. Even bilateral negotiations can come under criticism where the agenda includes anything other than the strict trade clauses that Asian states expect, as the EU found to its cost when negotiating with India for a free trade agreement which included human rights clauses that India objected to in what it considered a trade agreement.

Regional integration is strengthening in Asia, and in other parts of the world, though its popularity ebbs and flows with the tide of political opportunism and rational calculation among the participating actors, as well as external incentives/pressures (in the wake of the Asian financial crisis of 1997, there was a resurgent interest among states in Asian regionalism). For the EU, the promotion of regional integration is a way to validate its own internal coherence on the international stage, and there is no doubt that the European model retains some attraction. Promoting regional integration allows the EU to pursue the larger goal of influence as an international actor, and is particularly appropriate as a policy instrument for a European political community that has yet to define a common foreign policy. The policy displays the reverse image of the EU, drawing attention to the EU as a value-based political community while at the same time allowing that political community to act as a single actor on the global stage.

There is a learning through socialization embedded in this policy, for the European actors and also for the EU's partners in the dialogue. Until now, learning was largely confined to state actors and to the EU bureaucrats, since non-state actors and civil society were marginalized in the negotiation processes, from the enlargement negotiations through to the EPA negotiations and inter-regional co-operation generally. Indeed, this comparatively narrow set of actors undermines the possibility for higher-level learning, and promotes what Haas described as habit-driven policy learning within a pretty stable context of actors and policy preferences. However, the growing dissatisfaction with the EPAs among European and African non-state actors did result in an international mobilization of critical opposition, though without halting the programme (European Commission 2008b).

There is no indication that the EU is seeking to export the EU model, and such an ambitious agenda would undoubtedly challenge both the political capacity and resources of the EU. The European Commission acknowledges that in a very pragmatic way: 'The EU does not try to impose its system on others, but is not shy about its values ... open markets, economic growth and a political system based on social responsibility and democracy.' In true realist style, the Commission affirms that 'enlightened self-interest just as much as global solidarity' is a cornerstone of EU external relations policy generally, where 'supporting economic development and political stability in the wider world is an investment in one's future' (European Commission 2007).

The promotion of democracy walks a fine line with the imposition of democracy, and the risk of undermining the EU's credibility is high. Moreover, persuading other regional groupings to accept the notion of primacy of the supranational legal order, or the formal equality between member states, is a tall order in a region where a regional hegemon may take a lead role in interstate relations. That leaves the option of promoting regional integration as a way of exporting (European) regional governance, and European norms. These goals were most clearly and effectively realized in the case of European enlargement, where accession states are required to comply with the *acquis communautaire* as well as meeting the Copenhagen criteria. Elsewhere, the export of regional governance standards and European norms can be, at best, partial in so far as the EU is a non-state actor with restricted capacity in the institutions of global governance.

Turning to the identity of the EU as a normative actor, and to its self-portrayal on the international stage, there remain some questions over the political capacity of the EU to transfer norms internationally, notwithstanding the consistent efforts to incorporate normative values in the growing number of international agreements. The success of the strategy of promoting EU norms internationally depends in large measure upon the willingness of the rest of the world to endorse these norms, and this is also linked to the EU's credibility with other international and regional actors. So far, the EU's normative identity tends towards a self-referential identity, and without the recognition of other actors and their endorsement of the normative values to the extent of creating a consensual knowledge shared by all political actors, the goal of norm promotion remains restricted to the EU's immediate sphere of influence, and the areas in which it can exercise authority by virtue of superior power (Mayer 2008). In the present situation, the most likely option for policy learning in this area of EU external relations remains the first or second order learning described by Hall.

7. CONCLUSION

This article sought to apply a policy learning framework to the EU's promotion of regional integration, and to contribute to an understanding of the dynamics of policy learning in the context of the EU's external relations. First, it offered an analytical framework for the adoption of the policy learning approach, identifying the key contributions in the literature with particular relevance for the issue under examination. The different types of learning, and the conditions under which learning take place, are highlighted with a view to considering the learning possibilities in what is arguably a complex area of European external relations. The complexity of this policy area is exemplified in the discussion on the diversity of policy approaches used by the EU (section 3), while the case study of EU–Africa inter-regional policy exemplifies both the possibilities and the limitations of promoting regional integration elsewhere (section 4).

This study has sought to extend the policy learning framework to an analysis of external relations. It highlights the importance of understanding the capacities for learning in the context of external forces and influences, and also the limitations of a policy learning framework that fails to take account of the power dynamics between international political actors. This is a policy issue area where states and the EU are still the primary actors, though the situation is beginning to change with pressures from non-state and civil society actors to be involved in the process – indeed, the EPA negotiations mobilized a large transnational civil society opposition to the European Commission's proposals. As other studies have shown, the possibility for policy learning is greatly enhanced with more diverse political representation. Finally, the study has highlighted the degree to which learning remains limited by the political and institutional capacity of the EU, and to this extent there remains a varied range of constraints on the capacity of the EU as an international actor.

ACKNOWLEDGEMENTS

For constructive and helpful comments I would like to thank Tony Zito, the internal reviewers and two external referees.

NOTES

1 The research for this article is based on a number of interviews conducted with various European Commission officials from DG Relex, Trade, and Development over the period October 2006 to March 2008, and a reading of policy documents and secondary sources. While recognizing the diversity of approaches across the different DGs in the European Commission, this article presents the overall institutional position, and reflects the strong overlapping concerns and positions on development, trade, and security in the evolving European policy after the 1990s.
2 The Cotonou Agreement covers relations between the EU and Sub-Saharan Africa while relations with the countries of North Africa are based on the Euro-Mediterranean

Partnership and Association Agreements, and the European Neighbourhood Policy and ENP Action Plans.
3 The Africa–EU Strategic partnership, however, applies to the whole of the African continent.
4 The eight partnership and priority actions are: Africa–EU partnership on peace and security; Africa–EU partnership on democratic governance and human rights; Africa–EU partnership on trade, regional integration and infrastructure; Africa–EU partnership on the Millennium development goals; Africa–EU partnership on energy; Africa–EU partnership on climate change; Africa–EU partnership on migration, mobility and employment; Africa–EU partnership on science, information society and space.

REFERENCES

Alecu de Flers, N. and Regelsberger, E. (2005) 'The EU and inter-regional cooperation', in C. Hill and M. Smith (eds), *International Relations and the European Union*, Oxford: Oxford University Press.

Argyris, C. and Schön, D.A. (1978) *Organizational Learning. A Theory of Action Perspective*, Reading, MA: Addison-Wesley.

Balme, R. and Bridges, B. (2008) *Europe–Asia Relations: Building Multilateralisms*, Basingstoke: Palgrave.

Bandelow, N.C. (2008) 'Government learning in German and British European policies', *Journal of Common Market Studies* 46(4): 743–64.

Bomberg, E. (2007) 'Policy learning in an enlarged European Union: environmental NGOs and new policy instruments', *Journal of European Public Policy* 14(2): 248–68.

Bretherton, C. and Vogler, J. (2005) *The European Union as a Global Actor*, London: Routledge.

Checkel, J. (2001) 'Why comply? Social learning and European identity change', *International Organisation* 55(3): 553–8.

Conde, C.H. (2007) 'ASEAN pursues EU-style regional integration', *International Herald Tribune*, 15 January.

Dolowitz, S.P. and Marsh, D. (2000) 'Learning from abroad: the role of policy transfer in contemporary policy-making', *Governance* 13: 5–23.

European Commission (1995) *Communication on European Community Support for Regional Economic Integration Efforts among Developing Countries*, COM (1995) 219 final, Brussels, 16 June 1995.

European Commission (2005a) *Proposal for a Joint Declaration by the Council, the European Parliament and the Commission on the European Union Development Policy. 'The European Consensus'*, COM (2005) 311, Brussels: European Commission.

European Commission (2005b) *EU Strategy for Africa: Towards a Euro-African Pact to Accelerate Africa's Development*, COM (2005) 489 final, Brussels: European Commission.

European Commission (2007) *The EU in the World. The Foreign Policy of the European Union*, CEC publications, Brussels (cat. no. NA-AB-07-126-EN-C).

European Commission (2008a) Communication from the Commission to the Council, the European Parliament, the European Economic and Social Committee and the Committee of the Regions. *Regional Integration for Development in ACP Countries*, COM (2008) 604 final/2, 6 October 2008.

European Commission (2008b) Communication from the Commission to the Council and the European Parliament. *One Year after Lisbon: The Africa–EU Partnership at Work*, COM (2008) 617 final, 17 October 2008.

EU Council (2003) *A Secure Europe in a Better World: European Security Strategy*, Brussels, 12 December 2003.
European Council (2007) *The Africa–EU Strategic Partnership, A Joint Africa–EU Strategy*, December 2007.
Farrell, M. (2009) 'The EU and Asia: a move towards hybrid interregionalism', in F. Soderbaum and P. Stalgren (eds), *The EU and the Global South*, Boulder, CO: Lynne Rienner.
Fawcett, L. and Hurrell, A. (eds) (1995) *Regionalism in World Politics: Regional Organization and International Order*, Oxford: Oxford University Press.
Finnemore, M. and Sikkink, K. (1998) 'International norm dynamics and political change', *International Organisation* 52(4): 887–917.
Forster, A. (2000) 'Evaluating the EU–ASEM relationship: a negotiated order approach', *Journal of European Public Policy* 7(5): 787–805.
Gamble, A. and Payne, A. (eds) (1996) *Regionalism and World Order*, London: Macmillan.
Goldstein, J. and Keohane, R. (1993) 'Ideas and foreign policy: an analytical framework', in J. Goldstein and R. Keohane (eds), *Ideas and Foreign Policy: An Analytical Framework*, Ithaca, NY: Cornell University Press, pp. 3–30.
Haas, E. (1990) *When Knowledge is Power: Three Models of Change in International Organizations*, Berkeley, CA: University of California Press.
Hall, P.A. (1993) 'Policy paradigms, social learning, and the state: the case of economic policymaking in Britain', *Comparative Politics* 25(3): 275–96.
Hill, C. and Smith, M. (2005) *International Relations and the European Union*, Oxford: Oxford University Press.
Hurrell, A. (2007) 'One world? Many worlds? The place of regions in the study of international society', *International Affairs* 83(1): 127–46.
Laidi, Z. (2008) 'The normative empire – the unintended consequences of European power', Garnet Policy Brief 6, February 2008, Paris: CERI.
Levy, J. (1994) 'Learning and foreign policy: sweeping a conceptual minefield', *International Organisation* 48(2): 279–312.
Mayer, H. (2008) 'Is it still called "Chinese whispers"? The EU's rhetoric and action as a responsible global institution', *International Affairs* 84(1): 61–79.
Nedergaard, P. (2006) 'Policy learning in the European Union: the case of the European Employment Strategy', *Policy Studies* 27(4): 311–323.
Oliver, M.J. and Pemberton, H. (2001) 'Learning and change in twentieth-century British economic policy', Centre for European Studies Working Paper No. 109.
Olsen, G.R. (2009) 'Africa. Still a secondary security challenge to the European Union', in T. Tardy (ed.), *European Security in a Global Context: Internal and External Dynamics*, London: Routledge.
Pierson, P. (1998) 'The path to European integration: a historical institutionalist analysis', in W. Sandholtz and A. Stone Sweet (eds), *European Integration and Supranational Governance*, Oxford: Oxford University Press.
Pollack, M. (2004) 'The new institutionalisms and European integration', in A. Wiener and T. Diez (eds), *European Integration Theory*, Oxford: Oxford University Press, pp. 137–56.
Radaelli, C. (2004). 'Who learns what? Policy learning and the open method of co-ordination'. Paper prepared for ESRC seminar series 'Implementing the Lisbon Strategy, Policy Learning Inside and Outside the Open Method', European Research Institute, University of Birmingham, 26 November, 2004.
Sbragia, A. (2008) 'Review article: Comparative regionalism: what might it be?', *Journal of Common Market Studies*, Annual Review of the EU in 2007.
Scheipers, S. and Sicurelli, D. (2008) 'Empowering Africa: normative power in EU–Africa relations', *Journal of European Public Policy* 15(4): 607–23.

Sicurelli, D. (2008) 'Framing security and development in the EU pillar structure. How the views of the European Commission affect EU Africa policy', *Journal of European Integration* 30(2): 217–34.
Smith, K. (2008) *European Union Foreign Policy in a Changing World*, Cambridge: Polity Press.
Soderbaum, F. and Shaw, T. (2003) *Theories of New Regionalism: A Palgrave Reader*, Basingstoke: Palgrave.
Telò, M. (ed.) (2007) *European Union and New Regionalism: Regional Actors and Global Governance in a Post-Hegemonic Era*, Aldershot: Ashgate.

Governance and policy learning in the European Union: a comparison with North America

Éric Montpetit

INTRODUCTION

Do actors involved in the policy processes of the European Union (EU) learn more than actors developing and managing policies in nation states, in particular outside of the EU? An important share of the scholarly work on the EU answers this question in the affirmative. It argues that continental integration has given shape to a unique governance structure, in which authority is no longer the purview of nation states. Delegated to various non-governmental actors or shared between public and private actors, authority in this governance structure does not depend on hierarchy so much as it rests on persuasion. Unlike conventional nation states in which actors at the top of hierarchies can make decisions alone, the horizontal governance structure of the EU requires diverse actors to discuss with each other and learn from each other to reach a consensus before any decision can be made. Several Europeans take pride in this governance structure,[1] which places deliberation, dialogue, reasoned argumentation and soft power[2] above the coercive means and the discretionary authority of top officials. To my knowledge, however, no empirical study offers a comparison of the learning propensity of policy actors in the EU and nation states, particularly outside Europe. The purpose of this article is to provide such a comparison, which includes two North American countries: the United States and Canada.

Specifically, the article proposes three tests of the propensity of EU policy actors to learn. These tests rest on a comparative survey of actors involved in the development of biotechnology policy in Europe and North America. These actors were involved in policy development for either human genetics or agri-food biotechnology. The survey was conducted twice, once in the summer of 2006 and once in the summer of 2008. It yielded 666 useable questionnaires. The involvement of respondents in two biotechnology subsystems adds comparative possibilities, as the degree of involvement of the EU differs significantly between these subsystems – it is lower in human genetics than in agri-food biotechnology (Abels 2007). The survey enables the construction of three distinctive measures of policy learning: one centered on intensity, one on consensus formation and one on policy transfers. These three measures form the basis of the three tests, each failing to find a larger inclination to learn in the EU. These results cast a shadow on theories suggesting that European integration has produced a unique governance structure, featuring learning as its main mechanism for decision-making.

The article is divided in five sections. First, I review the literature suggesting that European governance promotes learning. Second, I introduce the biotechnology actor survey. Third, I present the three tests. Fourth, I summarize the results of the tests. Lastly, I revisit the literature in light of the results.

POLICY LEARNING IN THE EU

Policy learning occurs through persuasion, deliberation, or similar soft power processes. Organizations and individuals can learn and learning may be about opinions on technical objects, political ideas and strategies (Bennett and Howlett 1992; Zarkin 2008). In this article, I adopt Sabatier and Zafonte's (2001: 11566) definition of policy learning as 'relatively enduring alterations of thought or behavioral intentions'. Sabatier and Zafonte (2001: 11566) add that learning normally 'result[s] from experience and/or the assessment of new information involving the precepts of belief systems'. The change of thought involved in learning, therefore, does not come lightly, without some form of confrontation between external information or experience challenging opinions and beliefs held for some time. The focus of my empirical investigation is on learning by individuals about relatively technical policy issues, rather than learning about ideas or strategies at the level of organization or entire policy subsystem. I assume that learning at system level starts with individuals willing to alter their thoughts when they are faced with challenging opinions.

Sabatier's advocacy coalition framework provides one of the most influential understandings of policy learning (Jenkins-Smith and Sabatier 1993). The framework suggests that actors choose their coalition allies based on the proximity of core policy beliefs (Leach and Sabatier 2005). In any issue area – a subsystem in the framework's terminology – actors should divide themselves in at least two adversarial advocacy coalitions competing for the realization of conflicting core beliefs. The framework hypothesizes that members of competing advocacy coalitions rarely interact with each other and carefully filter incoming information and evidence: 'The result is a "dialogue of the deaf" in which members of different coalitions talk past each other' (Sabatier and Zafonte 2001: 11566). As underlined by critics, Sabatier's advocacy coalition framework is closer to a non-learning model (Fisher 2003). In fact, the framework's prediction regarding policy learning is consistent with recent research suggesting that people dislike political debates (Hibbing and Theiss-Morse 2002). According to Mutz (2006), citizens prefer avoiding politics rather than advocating ideas fellow citizens might dislike. Therefore, face-to-face deliberations among people who hold different views would occur rarely. However, Mutz (2006: 49–54) argues, Europeans engage in deliberation – accepting to hear views different from their own – more frequently than Americans.

Sabatier (1998) acknowledges that his framework was developed with the adversarial American political system in mind. Thanks to the separation of powers, the fragmentation of governance and ensuing venue shopping strategies, the American political system might not encourage policy learning to the same extent as more consensual systems. However, Sabatier (1998) argues, European integration increases the complexity of policy relevant relationships and opens up policy-making to new actors, bringing Europe closer to the United States. Likewise, Kelemen (2006) argues that the vertical rivalry between the EU and member states, on the one hand, and the horizontal rivalry between the Commission, the Council of Ministers and the European Parliament, on the other hand, have encouraged the production of detailed laws and regulations, which are key features of adversarial systems. In fact, these detailed laws and regulations have strengthened the European Court of Justice, solicited regularly to resolve litigations over their enforcement. A number of years ago, Streeck (1992) had already noted that continental integration had moved Europe away from corporatism and closer to American pluralism. In the EU of the Single European Act, he argued, state and key civil society actors no longer cooperate in stable relationships based on trust. National peak associations, once partners of nation states in these relationships, face the challenge of coordinating their efforts at the European level without eroding their internal cohesion. The challenge is surmounted rarely and the result often is increased fragmentation in interest systems. In contrast with corporatist environments, interest groups and other private actors in this new environment become adversaries in competitions for access to policy-makers and influence, both at the member state and EU levels. Recent accounts of interest group politics in Europe support this perspective (Coen 1998). In short, stable relationships based on trust are slowly replaced by formal rules governing actor competition and dispute resolution. Thanks to changes engendered by European integration, policy-making in Europe would become increasingly indistinguishable from policy-making in the United States, where policy learning is limited by adversarial attitudes.

Not all analysts agree, however, that the EU is evolving in the direction of the American political system. Surely, European integration has transformed the corporatist arrangements of several member states, notably by dispersing power within networks, which are inclusive to some of the actors excluded by former territorially bounded arrangements (Héritier and Lehmkuhl 2008). However, some analysts suggest that the consensual policy style associated with several member states proved resilient despite the network changes engendered by continental integration (Risse-Kappen 1996; Peterson 1997; Skogstad 2003).[3]

From these observations, EU scholars have drawn implications for policy learning. Large horizontal networks, in which actors seek a consensus, encourage face-to-face discussions between actors who have different policy views. Thanks to inclusiveness, actors cannot filter out inconvenient views or associate themselves exclusively with actors who share similar beliefs. Moreover, consensus building requires actors willing to hear what the other side has to say and change their opinion when faced with convincing arguments. In other words, European consensus-oriented networks encourage policy learning (Börzel 1998: 264; Kohler-Koch 1996). Several analysts agree that the EU fosters policy learning intensity, in comparison with adversarial American institutions in particular (Lijphart 1999). Summarizing this literature, Pollack (2005) writes:

> students of EU governance often (although not always) emphasize the capacity of the EU to foster 'deliberation' and 'persuasion' – a model of policy-making in which actors are open to changing their beliefs and their preferences, and in which good arguments can matter as much as, or more than, bargaining power.
>
> (Pollack 2005: 36)

Consensus in the literature on EU governance is not only related to a historically inherited policy style. It stems also from actors' alleged concerns about legitimacy deficits. Analysts of the EU have complained that the limited power of the European Parliament, the exercise of quasi-legislative functions by member states' executive officials through the Council of Ministers and the key role played by the bureaucrats of the Commission in policy development leave the EU with a large democratic deficit (Risse-Kappen 1996). In contrast, the institutions of nation states were designed to produce democratic legitimacy. American political institutions emphasize, in particular, democratic accountability, thanks to the direct election of the chief executive every four years as well as regular congressional, state and local elections. Unlike American officials, therefore, EU officials have to be on the lookout for sources of legitimacy (Skogstad 2003).

Students of the EU argue that European officials frequently resort to expertise to legitimize decisions (Verdun 1999; Haas 1998). This expertise is provided by committees of experts and administrators, drawn from various member states, rather than being centrally located within the limited bureaucracy of the European Commission (Peterson 1997; Risse-Kappen 1996; Marks *et al.* 1996; Paré and Montpetit, forthcoming). This pooling of expertise at the supranational level improves problem-solving, while preserving some of the *de jure* legitimacy associated with member states (Wessels 1998). More importantly, these committees do not reproduce conflicts among member states, but function in a consensual manner. In fact, Wessels (1998: 225) observes 'a clear propensity within the committees to stress technical expertise and consensus'. Consensus, he argues, makes it more difficult for European officials, whose legitimacy is contested, to bypass committees. In other words, expert consensus confers onto decisions a legitimacy that the formal EU institutions fail to produce.

While noting that EU networks are not exclusively oriented on the provision of expertise, Skogstad (2003) agrees with this reasoning. She argues that the legitimation imperatives of the EU encourage consensus formation. Lacking proper accountability structure, the democratic legitimacy of the EU would rest on networks. In turn, networks are sources of legitimacy when they function according to an integrative logic, favorable to consensus formation. An integrative logic encourages participation and the formation of a shared understanding of the public interest, as opposed to the aggregative logic of conventional political institutions, which features negotiation, compromise and arbitration. For Skogstad (2003: 335), the legitimation imperatives of the EU create a pressure for consensus unparalleled in nation states: 'To date, nation states like the USA and Canada have not encountered the same imperative for democratizing regulatory procedures. Because their independent regulators can, at least in theory, be reined in by directly accountable politicians.' It follows that the EU should produce its policies through consensus-oriented networks more frequently than nation states.

Radaelli (2000) provides additional details on the nature of the consensus arising in the EU as a result of the legitimacy deficit. He argues that consensus in the EU is akin to isomorphism, a process whereby imitation in itself is a source of legitimacy. In such a process, actors are less concerned about improving policy efficiency with lessons from valuable foreign experiences than they are preoccupied with their capacity to claim that their policy choices were borrowed from reputed places. It would be prominent in the EU as it would prevent citizens from complaining that policy choices are the imposed views of Brussels' unaccountable appointees (Radaelli 2000: 38). Thanks to this dynamic, EU officials can claim that their policy decisions are transfers of best practices. Paré and Montpetit (forthcoming) add that EU policy development by committees, comprising participants with direct knowledge of member state policy experiences, further encourage policy transfers. Bulmer and Padgett (2005), however, dissociate transfers from the soft power logic of Radaelli's isomorphism, arguing that transfers are strongest in sectors where EU institutions are legitimate enough to impose them coercively. The comparison between the agri-food and human genetics subsystems, presented below, will shed light on these differences of perspective on policy transfers.

The above review of the literature on EU governance can be summed up with three hypotheses. First, the consensual policy style characterizing Europe increases the intensity of policy learning, while the adversarial North American style constrains it. Second, the legitimacy deficit associated with EU institutions encourages consensus formation, while the accountability procedures associated with nation states reduce its frequency. Third, the EU's legitimacy deficit or/and structure increases reliance on policy transfers, in comparison with nation states. The data used to test these hypotheses come from a survey of policy actors, presented in the next section.

THE BIOTECHNOLOGY ACTOR SURVEY

The Biotechnology Actor Survey (BAS) is a comparative survey of actors involved in human genetics and agri-food biotechnology policy development in Brussels, France, the United Kingdom, Canada and the United States. Respondents are civil servants, independent experts, with a university affiliation, representatives of industry and advocacy organizations. The survey was conducted twice, once in 2006 and once in 2008. Respondents from Brussels were sought only in 2008 (89 people responded to both surveys). The sector of biotechnology is appropriate in light of Sabatier and Zafonte's (2001) argument suggesting that policy learning is easier in natural rather than social systems. Moreover, biotechnology knowledge evolves at a fast pace with several applications being accepted in the western world in the last 20 years.

The survey was hosted on a website accessible only through a link on email invitations, sent in June of each of the years of the two waves. To obtain the names and contact information of potential respondents, newspaper articles, parliamentary hearings and scholarly work on biotechnology were examined. This examination was followed by a web search for these individuals and their organizations. The first emails were used to multiply invitations, following the snow ball method, until saturation. In 2006, 1,273 potential respondents with valid contact information were identified through this method and in 2008 the list comprised 1,927 names. The figure for 2006 is lower mostly because respondents from Brussels were included only in 2008. Out of the 1,273 potential respondents contacted in 2006, 270 returned useable questionnaires. The proportion was 396 out of 1,927 in 2008. Therefore, both waves yielded response rates around 21 per cent. In addition, the distribution of respondents along subsystems, categories of actor and countries is consistent between the two surveys (see Table 1). More importantly, there is no discrepancy between the proportion of invitations sent to different actor categories, countries or subsystems and the proportion of respondents presented in Table 1. The only comparable survey of which I am aware, a mail survey, has a better response rate, but fewer respondents and a comparable distribution of respondents (Aerni and Bernauer 2005).

Table 1 Distribution of respondents by survey

		2006	2008
Subsystems	Agri-food	153	254
	Human genetics	117	139
Actor functions	Government	77	113
	Industry	38	72
	Advocacy	38	52
	Independent experts	107	158
	Other	9	1
Geographical locations	Canada	143	168
	United States	54	75
	France	42	67
	United Kingdom	31	55
	Brussels	0	31
Total		270	396

The survey was designed to test hypotheses about policy learning, with questions on thought alteration about 16 policy-relevant biotechnology applications in 2006 and 20 in 2008. In each wave, half of the applications were relevant to agri-food biotechnology and the other half to human genetics. Each respondent was directed to the applications related to the subsystem with which she or he identified and was asked whether her or his opinion had become more favorable, less favorable or had remained unchanged in the last year. Examples of the applications are provided below.

Learning intensity is the percentage of applications on which a respondent indicated having become more or less favorable, as opposed to having an unchanged opinion. I consider that respondents who have an unchanged opinion on all or several applications do not learn or learn less intensively than those admitting having altered their thoughts on a large percentage of applications. On average, learning intensity was 30 per cent in 2006 and 35 per cent in 2008. In tests of means differences, Europeans did not display any higher intensity than North Americans.[4]

Unlike learning intensity, consensus is not the propriety of an individual, but of a group of individuals. Therefore, consensus is the movement of opinions of respondents on each of the policy-relevant applications. Consensus formation is strongest on genetically modified (GM) animals, GM modifications associated with economic risks, plants genetically modified to improve health, tissue typing and pre-implantation genetic tests. Consensus formation is weakest on plants genetically modified to resist herbicides, on stack traits varieties, on genetic modification inducing plant sterility and on gamete donation. To realize statistical analyses on the overall movement of opinions, I stacked the data along each of the applications. This enables me to observe European respondents becoming less favorable, on average for all applications, but a larger movement of North

Americans, generally becoming more favorable.[5] Surprisingly then, the data suggest more consensus on the former continent than on the latter.

Lastly, information on policy transfers was collected through a question on the factors which influenced the opinion of respondents most. The policy experience of foreign countries was one of the options. Respondents were also asked to list the countries whose policy experience was worth drawing from. Unfortunately, questions relevant to policy transfers were included in the 2006 wave only. In 2006, 18 per cent of the respondents said their opinion was inspired by foreign experiences. No significant differences were found between Europeans and North Americans. Therefore, descriptive statistics infirm the hypotheses suggesting that learning is a distinctive feature of European governance. I now move to more sophisticated statistical tests.

THE TESTS

The three tests are regressions using, in turn, learning intensity, reliance on policy transfers and consensus formation as dependent variables. All three tests include the same independent variables. Besides the country of origin of the respondent (including Brussels for EU respondents in 2008), the survey provides information on the biotechnology subsystem of the respondent and the actor category to which she or he belongs. Countries of origin are the key variables, as our three hypotheses suggest that policy learning should differ along institutional/stylistic lines, which are geographically dependent. The second and third hypotheses insist, in particular, on contrasts between nation states and the EU. Conveniently, the 2008 wave of the survey includes respondents from Brussels, along with respondents from the four nation states of the first wave. Subsystem difference may also be useful to test the second and third hypotheses. Indeed, when asked how much of their professional time is spent on EU committees or other EU institutions, European respondents in the agri-food subsystem respond a little under 25 per cent. Unsurprisingly, the response is under 10 per cent for European respondents in human genetics. In other words, if EU institutions encourage learning to a larger extent than institutions of nation states, including European nation states, European respondents in the agri-food subsystem should learn more than those in human genetics.

The second and third hypotheses also insist on the role of legitimacy deficits in learning processes. In 2006, a question asked respondents whether they believe the biotechnology policy decisions of their country serve the public interest. In 2008, the question clearly asked whether biotechnology policy decisions in their country (or the EU for Brussels respondents) enjoy democratic legitimacy. From these questions, I created a dummy variable identifying those respondents whose perception indicates a deficit of legitimacy.[6] In 2008, respondents from Brussels were no more or less likely to consider illegitimate decisions made by EU institutions than other respondents were to view the decisions of their respective country as illegitimate.

To measure adequately the possibility of geography-specific institutional influences on policy learning, it would be useful to compare it with an alternative source of learning. The survey allows a comparison with the potential influence of the policy functions of respondents. Scholars argue that civil servants, for example, have policy functions sufficiently distinct from interest groups and independent experts to learn in a distinctive manner, independently of the country in which they work (Heclo 1977; Aberbach and Rockman 1997). I use variables identifying government, industry, advocacy and experts to make this comparison between hypothesized geography-specific institutional influences and function-specific institutional influences on learning. The gender of the respondent and the number of years of involvement in biotechnology are also included as standard control variables.

In the first test, geographical variables should be correlated with learning intensity. Again, the first hypothesis insists on the contrast between the North American and the European policy styles. Using Canada as the reference, I expect significant positive coefficients for Brussels, France and perhaps the United Kingdom. The United States should not be significantly different from Canada, which I assume has an adversarial style. Should the first hypothesis be right, the dummy identifying Europeans in the agri-food subsystem should also be significant and positive. Naturally, the coefficients and significance of the variables associated with each actor category should not be as large as those associated with geographical variables, indicating that policy functions have less influence than geography-specific institutions. The same logic applies to the test on policy transfers. In this latter test, however, I expect actors who agree that decisions suffer from a legitimacy deficit to be particularly influenced by the policy experience of foreign countries.

The third test is on consensus formation. Again, I expect the regression to show that convergence of opinions is associated with geography and legitimacy rather than actor categories. Movements of opinion can occur in the directions of less or more favorable. Opinion can also be stable.[7] Using stable opinion as the base outcome in multinomial logistic regressions, I expect significant positive coefficients for geographic and legitimacy variables for either of more or less favorable, but not for both. Positive significant coefficients for both, more and less favorable, indicate opinion divergence, not convergence. Negative coefficients indicate the absence of movement and therefore the absence of learning. Insignificant coefficients indicate the absence of a particular inclination toward learning associated with the variable.

THE RESULTS

The results are presented in Table 2. The findings for learning intensity (the first two columns of Table 2) do not match the expectations related to the first test. In general, European respondents do not learn more intensively than North American actors. European respondents who belong to the agri-food subsystem do not learn anymore intensively either. Even respondents who work in Brussels,

Table 2 Results for learning intensity, policy transfers and consensus formation

	Tobit		Logit	Multinomial Logistic			
	2006	2008	2006	2006		2008	
	Intensity	Intensity	Transfer	Less	More	Less	More
Gender	−13.03**	−7.61	0.20	−0.45**	−0.45***	−0.14	−0.32***
	(5.93)	(4.96)	(0.41)	(0.19)	(0.10)	(0.10)	(0.12)
Years	−1.45***	−0.09	−0.04	−0.05***	−0.04***	−0.02***	0.00
	(0.42)	(0.26)	(0.03)	(0.01)	(0.01)	(0.01)	(0.00)
Subsystem	−1.86	11.63*	−1.39***	0.57**	−0.57***	0.53**	0.25
	(7.15)	(4.98)	(0.51)	(0.23)	(0.22)	(0.26)	(0.29)
Industry	13.63*	16.12**	−0.10	0.05	0.76***	−0.00	0.80***
	(8.67)	(6.27)	(0.61)	(0.24)	(0.17)	(0.18)	(0.09)
Advocacy	10.47	8.46	−0.32	0.44**	0.10	0.50***	−0.52*
	(9.15)	(7.14)	(0.61)	(0.21)	(0.30)	(0.19)	(0.30)
Government	−3.57	5.15	−0.20	−0.08	0.05	0.14	0.23***
	(7.26)	(5.95)	(0.55)	(0.16)	(0.12)	(0.12)	(0.08)
USA	−2.19	−2.98	−1.28**	−0.15	0.08	−0.44***	−0.02
	(7.34)	(5.91)	(0.64)	(0.22)	(0.14)	(0.16)	(0.19)
UK	3.73	4.45	−0.80	0.61***	−0.15	0.44**	−0.03
	(9.72)	(8.46)	(0.61)	(0.23)	(0.21)	(0.20)	(0.11)
France	13.39	12.00	0.11	0.56**	0.32	0.45**	0.35***
	(12.08)	(8.97)	(0.77)	(0.28)	(0.20)	(0.19)	(0.13)
Brussels	—	9.40	—	—	—	0.39	0.27
		(11.26)				(0.29)	(0.22)
Europe agriculture	−17.89	−4.74	−1.39	−0.98***	−0.32**	−0.03	−0.17
	(12.93)	(9.86)	(1.29)	(0.30)	(0.13)	(0.20)	(0.12)
Legitimacy deficit	9.10	6.80	0.99**	1.18***	−0.54***	0.77***	−0.33**
	(7.02)	(5.23)	(0.48)	(0.15)	(0.15)	(0.09)	(0.14)
Constant	38.25***	15.47**	−0.52	−1.89***	−0.66***	−2.01***	−1.44***
	(8.10)	(7.13)	(0.51)	(0.14)	(0.13)	(0.21)	(0.19)
N	236	307	219	1887		3106	
Pseudo R2	0.02	0.01	0.14	0.07		0.06	

Notes: *** p ≤ 0.01; ** p ≤ 0.05; * p ≤ 0.1. Standard errors are indicated in parentheses and they are cluster robust in the multinomial logistic regressions, each cluster corresponding to a stack. Opinion stability is the base outcome in the multinomial logistic regressions. 40 per cent of the distribution for learning intensity is left-censored at 0, justifying the use of tobit rather than standard OLS estimates.

and who are therefore involved with EU institutions daily, do not display any larger inclination to learn than respondents associated with nation states (Canada is the reference category). The only significant predictor of learning intensity, across both waves of the survey, is the actor category. In fact, respondents belonging to industry learn more intensively than respondents who are independent experts (the reference category). Respondents belonging to the other categories, however, are no more no less likely to learn intensively than independent experts. Nevertheless, the results for learning intensity show that the policy function of the actors is more important than the geography-specific institutions in which they are involved.

Results for policy transfers, the third column of Table 2, also fail to produce significant coefficients for Brussels, Europe agriculture and the two European nation states. First, European respondents, no matter how involved they are in EU institutions, are not any more inspired by the policy experience of foreign countries than Canadian respondents. However, American respondents are less likely than Canadian respondents to be inspired by the policy experience of foreign countries. Second, respondents who are involved in the human genetics subsystem are more likely to be inspired by foreign policy experiences than respondents who are involved in agri-food biotechnology, independently of their country of origin. Lastly, the perception of a legitimacy deficit is a key variable explaining policy transfers, whether or not respondents are involved in EU institutions. Knowing legitimacy concerns are not any more pronounced among Brussels respondents, involvement in EU governance fails clearly to predispose to policy transfers. A model specification testing interactions between EU involvement and perception of legitimacy deficit was also estimated and yielded similar results. Likewise, Americans' disinclination to be influenced by foreign experiences is unrelated to a perception of legitimacy deficit.

Figure 1 adds information on policy transfers. The figure presents the percentage of times a country was identified by respondents as a source of influence for

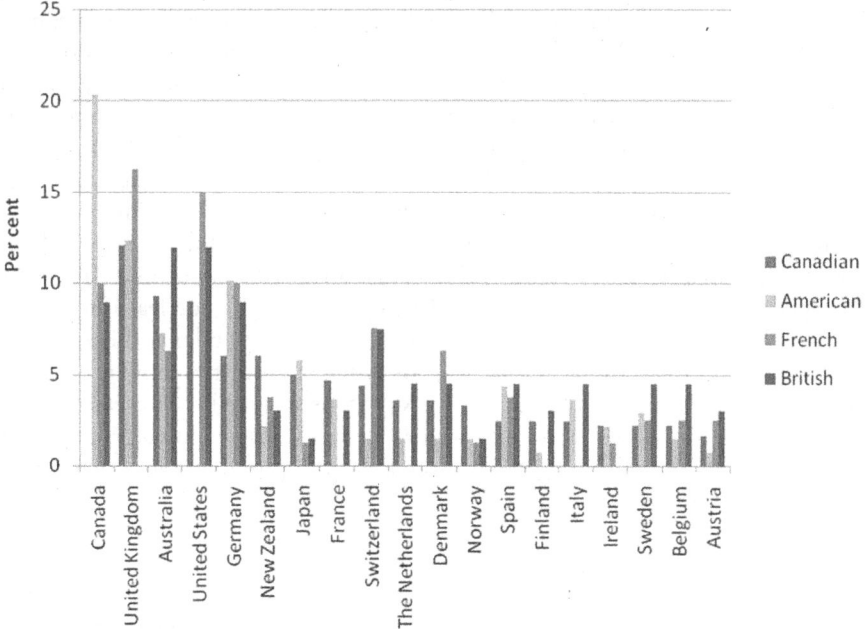

Figure 1 Countries, beside their own; Canadian, American, French and British respondents consider sources of policy inspiration

policy development in their country. If the committee system of the EU were to predispose transfers from member states, European respondents should indicate European countries far more frequently than North American respondents. Judging by Figure 1, the difference is not clear. France is cited more frequently by North Americans than by British respondents, even though French respondents cite the United Kingdom more frequently than North Americans. Canada and the United States, as well as Australia, are cited as exemplars by Europeans far more frequently than several European member states. If Canadians do not cite Germany frequently, Americans do so more often than British and French respondents. In short, the structure of the EU does not seem to encourage member states to perform policy transfers among themselves any more frequently than countries outside the EU do.

The last four columns of Table 2 present results for consensus formation. Here again, results are relatively consistent between the two waves of the survey. Respondents in the agri-food subsystem are more likely to have become less favorable than respondents in human genetics. Consensus is particularly apparent among respondents belonging to the same actor category. In comparison with independent experts, industry moves toward becoming more favorable and advocacy toward less favorable. Moreover, in 2008, the move toward more favorable among government actors is more decisive than among independent experts. In contrast, the multinomial logistic regressions point at weak geographical consensus. In fact, only the UK distinguishes itself from Canada, the reference category, with movement toward becoming less favorable. France is also different from Canada, but far from developing a consensus the European country displays growing divisions. It is noteworthy that there is no more consensus in Brussels than in Canada, nor is there more consensus in the European agri-food subsystem than elsewhere. Interestingly, respondents who perceive a lack of legitimacy behind the decisions made in their country also tend to become less favorable to biotechnology applications. Again, however, legitimacy concerns are not any larger in Brussels than in North America.

In short, none of the three tests yield results supporting the three hypotheses establishing a relationship between European governance and policy learning. European actors in the area of biotechnology policy do not learn any more intensively than North American actors. European respondents do not claim to learn from the policy experiences of foreign countries any more than North Americans, even though results are consistent with suggestions that policy transfers are driven by legitimacy concerns. Lastly, involvement with EU institutions does not encourage consensus formation any more than involvement with nation states.

DISCUSSION

Comparative policy research has emphasized the role of geography-specific variables such as institutions and policy styles in explanations of policy development. This trend was encouraged by students of the EU who have treated its system of governance as unique; not quite a state, nor an international organization. The structure of governance gradually constructed with European integration would have given form to distinctive ways of making public policy. Policy development in the EU would occur in networks, in which government actors often take a back seat (Peterson 1997; Marks *et al.* 1996; Héritier and Lehmkuhl 2008). Power in these networks would be exercised softly, that is through persuasion, rather than through coercion (Kohler-Koch 1996; Risse-Kappen 1996; Skogstad 2003). Expert knowledge would play a key role in decision-making (Verdun 1999; Haas 1998; Wessels 1998). Authors who have argued that EU institutions create distinctive patterns of policy development have not always referred directly to the concept of policy learning; however, most of them suggest clearly that policy learning is a by-product of several of the Union's policy processes. Risse-Kappen (1996: 73) speaks about the 'deliberative' and 'communicative' processes of the EU, capable of 'opening space for new and innovative solutions'. Kohler-Koch (1996: 372–3) insists on the role of the EU in processes of 'social learning' to 'propagate the idea of co-operative problem-solving', which itself is an idea concerning governance structure conducive to 'joint learning'. In other words, several analysts have insisted, since the 1990s, that the governance in the EU promotes policy learning, often in a consensual direction.

To my knowledge, this distinctive policy-making feature of the EU has not been empirically examined through comparison with countries from other continents. This article fills this gap by providing such a comparison. Specifically, the article examines the propensity of European actors from both Brussels and member states to learn in comparison with North American actors. In addition, it compares two distinctive policy subsystems, one in which the EU is highly involved and one in which it intervenes moderately, at best. The comparison fails to confirm that policy learning is more prevalent in Europe and that EU institutions/style promote it to a larger extent than the institutions/style of nation states. Interestingly enough, more support was found for differences in learning capacity between categories of actors, having distinctive policy functions, than for geographical differences. Interest group leaders and government employees from both continents were found to learn in a consensual manner more frequently than independent experts. This finding suggests that studying actors' policy function is at least as important as studying the distinctiveness of geography-specific institutions and related policy styles.

Policy transfers, the results also suggest, are more frequent in human genetics than in the agri-food subsystem. This latter finding runs against Bulmer and Padgett's (2005) suggestions that policy transfers are more significant in sectors, such as agri-food biotechnology, where EU institutions are strongest. However, the finding makes sense for anyone with in-depth knowledge of the two subsystems. The regulation of risks related to agri-food biotechnology is an internationally contested issue, several countries claiming to have the best system.[8] In contrast, the regulation of human genetics, outside of the United States, was inspired by the early model provided by the United Kingdom. In

1990, British policy-makers adopted a law to enable the creation of an autonomous governmental agency to regulate this sector at arm's length. The British experience with this agency was seen as sufficiently positive by French and Canadian policy-makers to design legislations enabling the creation of similar agencies in 2004 (Montpetit *et al.* 2007). When asked which country has a lesson-inspiring policy experience, 61 out of the 117 respondents in the human genetics subsystem mentioned the United Kingdom. In short, the British experience inspired policy-makers abroad, but without any help from the EU.

Nevertheless, Radaelli (2000) has a point when arguing that policy transfers are driven by legitimacy concerns. The results show clearly that perception of a legitimacy deficit encourages policy actors to look at foreign experiences as sources of inspiration. In addition, legitimacy concerns appeared as an important predictor of consensus. When respondents perceive a legitimacy deficit, on average, they become less favorable to biotechnology applications. Legitimacy concerns were expressed by 27 per cent of all respondents, a score, however, which is not any higher among Brussels respondents. In short, legitimacy concerns play a significant role in policy development, thereby deserving attention in policy studies, but not any more in Europe than in North America.

Does this mean that the EU is moving in the American adversarial direction (Kelemen 2006), that European consensual interest systems are being replaced by pluralist systems (Coen 1998), that EU policy processes are increasingly matching American processes in terms of the complexity of policy relationships (Sabatier 1998)? In short, does this mean that actors involved in policy development in the EU are just as reluctant to learn from actors whose views differ as are American actors?

As far as learning inclination goes, respondents involved in EU institutions are not much different from American respondents. However, one should avoid interpreting this observation as evidence of a disinclination of American respondents to learn. The only evidence of a disinclination to learn on the part of American respondents is in the results regarding policy transfers. Of all respondents, those from the United States are least likely to be inspired by the experience of a foreign country. The United States is a large federal country, which understandably is inward rather than outward looking when it comes to drawing policy lessons (Shipan and Volden 2008). Beside results on transfer, nothing in the tests points at a disinclination to learn. Therefore, it is just as plausible that inclination to learn in North America has been underestimated, most notably by the advocacy coalition framework (Jenkins-Smith and Sabatier 1993; Sabatier and Zafonte 2001). In fact, the analysis indicates that North American policy actors, just like European actors, are capable and inclined to learn and form consensus. Moreover, several scholars disagree with the argument that policy actors in adversarial systems, the United States in particular, are dissuaded from learning (Innes and Booher 2003; Fisher 2003; Schön and Rein 1994; Schneider and Ingram 2007; Mansbridge 1992).

Studies of European governance point out that in the absence of a vertical authority to arbitrate between competing policy preferences, EU actors must allow their preferences to converge to enable decision-making. In the EU, policy learning would substitute authoritative arbitration by accountable elected officials, the typical mechanisms of dispute resolution in adversarial systems. These studies, however, might misrepresent the effect of vertical authority. Even where authoritative arbitration by accountable officials can be counted on to make decisions, several actors still prefer learning. Scharpf (1994) puts it clearly when he observes that policy actors in hierarchies work hard to agree among themselves before resort to authority becomes necessary. Authority, he argues, acts as a 'shadow' hanging over networks of policy actors more frequently than it provides actual mechanisms of dispute resolution. Actors cooperate and presumably learn from each other to avoid authority, whichs tend to be discretionary and unpredictable. In short, learning may be necessary for decisions in the EU, but it is preferred over authority in hierarchical nation states, including the United States. Therefore, policy actors are inclined to learn, whether they belong to the EU or not.

The results of the three tests presented in this article call for a significant revision of the theories suggesting that governance in the EU is particularly conducive to policy learning. In fact, policy development in nation states, including North American states, features policy learning in much the same way as in the institutions of the EU.

CONCLUSION

The objective of this article was to assess the extent to which policy development in Europe involves learning to a larger extent than it does in North America. While several scholars claim that European integration moves policy processes closer to what they are in North America, the United States in particular, several students of the EU have insisted alternatively on a distinctive policy style, on consensus-oriented networks and on policy transfers driven by concerns over a legitimacy deficit afflicting EU institutions. If students of the EU are right, distinctive manifestations of policy learning between the EU and nation states, especially nation states outside Europe, should occur. Using a survey of biotechnology policy actors, this article proposes three tests comparing learning intensity, consensus formation and propensity to resort to policy transfers between Brussels and four countries. All three tests failed at finding differences suggesting that actors involved in EU institutions display a greater inclination to learn, in particular in comparison with North American actors.

The results suggest that differences in attitude toward learning are better explained by actors' respective policy function than they are by their association with geography-specific institutions/styles. In other words, actors act less according to the constraints, the opportunities and the norms arising from EU institutions or nation states than they act according to the constraints, the opportunities and the norms arising from the policy function associated with their category of actor (industry, advocacy, civil servant or independent expert). And interestingly, these policy functions do not vary to a large extent between Europe and North America, as far as one can judge from the attitudes of survey respondents toward learning. For example, industry representatives in Europe share the same understanding of their policy function and adopt attitudes which are similar to those of industry representatives in North America. This observation calls for more attention to function-specific rather than to geography-specific institutions in studies of policy development. It also suggests that studies of EU governance have put too much emphasis on the uniqueness of EU institutions.

Studies of the EU have notably insisted on the severity of the legitimacy deficit arising from EU institutions. I have shown that concerns about legitimacy deficits influence policy development to a large extent and therefore they should be accounted for more frequently in policy studies. I have also shown that legitimacy concerns are not any less or any more pronounced outside of the EU. Therefore, accounts of legitimacy deficits are useful in EU policy studies, but they would be just as useful in non-European policy studies. And policy scholars might find inspiration in EU studies, which devote significant space to this theme.

I end this article on two potential limitations of the tests presented in this article. First, the tests focus on learning, leaving aside policy outcomes and output. European and North American biotechnology policies differ sharply and the explanation of this difference may rest in geography-specific institutions. This observation suggests caution before dropping geography-specific variables. Second, the comparison of two contrasting subsystems, human genetics and agri-food biotechnology, contributes undoubtedly to the robustness of the results. However, the two subsystems deal with natural rather than social systems and therefore enjoy some proximity. Multiplying studies of policy learning and ensuring a wider coverage of policy subsystems would provide some reassurance about the generalization potential of the results presented in this article.

ACKNOWLEDGEMENTS

The author acknowledges the financial support of the Social Science Research Council of Canada and thanks Rukmini Canape-Brunet and Catherine Pelletier for excellent research assistance as well as David Aubin, Peter Loewen, Nathalie Schiffino, Frédéric Varone and Karin Ingold for their comments and suggestions. I would also like to thank those who attended presentations of this paper at the Université de Genève and the Facultés universitaires catholiques de Mons.

NOTES

1 Kelemen (2006) makes this argument, suggesting that Europeans will sometimes even look down on American politics, which they view as too adversarial.
2 I use these concepts interchangeably in this article. The type of interaction they all describe is necessary for policy learning.
3 On consensual policy styles, see Richardson (1982); Katzenstein (1985); Lijphart (1999).
4 Similarities and differences calculated in tests of group means differences were $p < 0.1$.
5 The full list of applications and the calculation of opinion movements can be found at <ericmontpetit.com>.
6 Respondents who totally disagreed that decisions in their country (or EU for EU respondents) enjoy democratic legitimacy.
7 Respondents could also answer that they do not know whether their opinion has changed. This option was rarely selected and therefore I do not present results for it, although it was included as a category in the multinomial logistic regression.
8 Even Canada and the United States disagree on which country has the best system. See Montpetit (2005).

REFERENCES

Abels, G. (2007) 'Trade and human rights: inter- and supranational regulation of ART and GM food', in É. Montpetit, C. Rothmayr and F. Varone (eds), *The Politics of Biotechnology in North America and Europe: Policy Networks, Institutions, and Internationalization*, Lanham, MD: Lexington Books.
Aberbach, J.D. and Rockman, B.A. (1997) 'Back to the future? Senior federal executives in the United States', *Governance* 10(4): 323–49.
Aerni, P. and Bernauer, T. (2005) 'Stakeholder attitudes toward GMOs in the Philippines, Mexico, and South Africa: the issue of public trust', *World Development* 34(3): 557–75.
Bennett, C.J. and Howlett, M. (1992) 'The lessons of learning: reconciling theories of policy learning and policy change', *Policy Sciences* 25: 275–94.
Börzel, T.A. (1998) 'Organizing Babylon: on different conceptions of policy networks', *Public Administration* 76: 253–73.
Bulmer, S. and Padgett, S. (2005) 'Policy transfer in the European Union: an institutionalist perspective', *British Journal of Political Science* 35: 103–26.
Coen, D. (1998) 'The European business interest and the nation state: large firm lobbying in the European Union and member states', *Journal of Public Policy* 18: 75–100.
Fisher, F. (2003) *Reframing Public Policy: Discursive Politics and Deliberative Practices*, Oxford: Oxford University Press.
Haas, P.M. (1998) 'Compliance with EU directives: insights from international relations and comparative politics', *Journal of European Public Policy* 5(1): 17–37.
Heclo, H. (1977) *A Government of Strangers: Executive Politics in Washington*, Washington, DC: Brookings Institution.
Héritier, A. and Lehmkuhl, D. (2008) 'Introduction: the shadow of hierarchy and new modes of governance', *Journal of Public Policy* 28: 1–17.
Hibbing, J.R. and Theiss-Morse, E. (2002) *Stealth Democracy: Americans' Beliefs about How Government Should Work*, Cambridge: Cambridge University Press.

Innes, J.E. and Booher, D.E. (2003) 'Collaborative policymaking: governance through dialogue', in M.A. Hajer and H. Wagenaar (eds), *Deliberative Policy Analysis: Understanding Governance in the Network Society*, Cambridge: Cambridge University Press.

Jenkins-Smith, H.C. and Sabatier, P.A. (1993) 'The dynamics of policy-oriented learning', in P.A. Sabatier and H. Jenkins-Smith (eds), *Policy Change and Learning: An Advocacy Coalition Approach*, Boulder, CO: Westview Press.

Katzenstein, P.J. (1985) *Small States in World Markets: Industrial Policy in Europe*, Ithaca, NY: Cornell University Press.

Kelemen, D.R. (2006) 'Suing for Europe: adversarial legalism and European governance', *Comparative Political Studies* 39: 101–27.

Kohler-Koch, B. (1996) 'Catching up with change: the transformation of governance in the European Union', *Journal of European Public Policy* 3(3): 359–80.

Leach, W.D. and Sabatier, P.A. (2005) 'To trust an adversary: integrating rational and psychological models in collaborative policymaking', *American Political Science Review* 99(4): 491–504.

Lijphart, A. (1999) *Patterns of Democracy: Government Forms and Performance in Thirty-Six Countries*, New Haven, CT: Yale University Press.

Mansbridge, J.J. (1992) 'A deliberative theory of interest representation', in M. Petracca (ed.), *The Politics of Interest: Interest Groups Transformed*, Boulder, CO: Westview Press.

Marks, G., Hooghe, L. and Blank, K. (1996) 'European integration from the 1980s: state-centric v. multi-level governance', *Journal of Common Market Studies* 34(3): 341–78.

Montpetit, É. (2005) 'A policy network explanation of biotechnology policy differences between the United States and Canada', *Journal of Public Policy* 25(3): 339–66.

Montpetit, É., Rothmayr, C. and Varone, F. (eds) (2007) *The Politics of Biotechnology in North America and Europe: Policy Networks, Institutions, and Internationalization*, Lanham, MD: Lexington Books.

Mutz, D.C. (2006) *Hearing the Other Side: Deliberative versus Participatory Democracy*, Cambridge: Cambridge University Press.

Paré, I. and Montpetit, É. (forthcoming) 'Network deliberation and policy transfer in the development of a European genome policy', *Journal of Comparative Policy Analysis*.

Peterson, J. (1997) 'States, societies and the European Union', *West European Politics* 20(4): 1–23.

Pollack, M.A. (2005) 'Theorizing EU policy-making', in H. Wallace, W. Wallace and M.A. Pollack (eds), *Policy-making in the European Union*, 5th edn, Oxford: Oxford University Press.

Radaelli, C. (2000) 'Policy transfer in the European Union: institutional isomorphism as a source of legitimacy', *Governance* 13(1): 25–43.

Richardson, J. (ed.) (1982) *Policy Styles in Western Europe*, London: Allen & Unwin.

Risse-Kappen, T. (1996) 'Exploring the nature of the beast: international relations theory and comparative policy analysis meet the European Union', *Journal of Common Market Studies* 34(1): 53–80.

Sabatier, P.A. (1998) 'The advocacy coalition framework: revisions and relevance for Europe', *Journal of European Public Policy* 5(1): 98–130.

Sabatier, P.A. and Zafonte, M.A. (2001) 'Policy knowledge: advocacy organizations', in N.J. Smelser and P.B. Baltes (eds), *International Encyclopedia of the Social & Behavioral Sciences, Volume 17*, Amsterdam: Elsevier.

Scharpf, F.W. (1994) 'Games real actors could play: positive and negative coordination in embedded negotiations', *Journal of Theoretical Politics* 6: 27–53.

Schneider, A. and Ingram, H. (2007). 'Ways of knowing: implications for public policy'. Paper prepared for the annual meeting of the American Political Science Association, Chicago.

Schön, D.A. and Rein, M. (1994) *Frame Reflection: Toward the Resolution of Intractable Policy Controversy*, New York: Basic Books.

Shipan, C.R. and Volden, C. (2008) 'The mechanisms of policy diffusion', *American Journal of Political Science* 52: 840–57.

Skogstad, G. (2003) 'Legitimacy and/or policy effectiveness? Network governance and GMO regulation in the European Union', *Journal of European Public Policy* 10(3): 321–38.

Streeck, W. (1992) 'From national corporatism to transnational pluralism: European interest politics and the single market', in T. Treu (ed.), *Participation in Public Policy-making: The Role of Trade Unions and Employers' Associations*, Berlin: Walter de Gruyter.

Verdun, A. (1999) 'The role of the Delors Committee in the creation of EMU: an epistemic community?', *Journal of European Public Policy* 6(2): 308–28.

Wessels, W. (1998) 'Comitology: fusion in action. politico-administrative trends in the EU system', *Journal of European Public Policy* 5(2): 209–34.

Zarkin, M.J. (2008) 'Organizational learning in novel policy situations: two cases of United States communication regulation', *Policy Studies* 29(1): 87–100.

The power of institutionalized learning: the uses and practices of commissions to generate policy change

Patrik Marier

INTRODUCTION

Compared to the other articles in this special issue, which emphasize learning at the European Union (EU) level, this contribution analyzes how the creation of commissions at the member state level can improve learning capacities and, as importantly, facilitate the adoption of new programs. This level of analysis is chosen because empirical evidence suggests a very limited influence on the part of the EU and EU learning processes when it comes to pension reform (see, for example, de la Porte and Nanz 2004). While acknowledging that the EU has increased knowledge of pension systems in other member states, the individuals interviewed for this project emphasized that the policy process on which pension reforms have been enacted remains strongly embedded within national settings. This echoes a recent study of pension reform in Greece where Featherstone (2005: 734) concludes that 'the EU stimuli are in fact limited in their nature and that entrenched institutional obstacles in domestic systems can readily thwart their potency'.

The key aim of this article is to study the conditions under which pension commissions influence policy change. Studying commissions enriches the discussion on policy learning for three key reasons. First, learning does not occur without intent and requires dissatisfaction with current programs and policies (Rose 1991: 10). The creation of a commission sends a strong signal that authorities are not satisfied with various aspects of a program or policy and provides additional resources to learn. Second, some commissions have a specific mandate to provide a detailed evaluation of a current program alongside a detailed analysis of what is being done abroad. As a result, commissions often include learning from within and learning from abroad and retrospective and prospective analyses. Finally, the workings of commissions provide important information on how states actually learn.

Whereas pension policy for an article on learning may seem odd, there are merits to this focus. Pensions represent a policy area where past policies strongly influence the (future) options available to policy-makers (Hogwood and Peters 1982; Pierson 2000). As stressed by the literature on welfare state retrenchment, reforming public pensions can have high political costs and few rewards (Pierson 1996). Nonetheless, in the past 25 years, multiple pension reforms have been introduced across Organization for Economic Co-operation and Development (OECD) countries to tackle numerous policy objectives such as increasing private savings, reducing future public pension liabilities, and adapting public schemes to new socio-economic realities (OECD 2005). Interestingly, in spite of the increasing use of commissions to alter social policies, their importance is usually ignored in the retrenchment literature in favour of more traditional actors such as political parties, institutions, and interest groups. Thus, a closer inspection is warranted.

In terms of method, this contribution focuses on the importance of commissions by comparing public pension reforms in France, Sweden, and the UK. They were selected based on their different national traditions regarding the use of commissions. Sweden has a long-standing tradition of influential parliamentary committees whose outputs often result in legislation (Heclo 1974; Premfors 1983). In the UK, commissions are usually appointed by government officials to address a particular problem and rarely include Members of Parliament (MPs) (Bulmer 1993). France relies on various forms of consultative bodies. As in the UK, it is not uncommon for a minister or the Prime Minister to appoint a commission or for a member of the cabinet to conduct an investigation. Also, some institutionalized forms of inquiry, such as the *conseil économique et social*, provide a forum for state-recognized interest groups to voice their preferences and seek consensus on public policy matters (Wilson 1987).

France, Sweden, and the UK have established various commissions in the past 25 years to reform their pension systems. Interestingly, national traditions cannot explain the policy influence of commissions on recent pension reforms. On the one hand, in two cases, Sweden and the UK, recent reforms originated from commission proposals. France, on the other hand, has instituted at least 13 inquiries during this time period to alter just a few parameters and to harmonize key elements of its pension system. A thorough analysis of all commissions related to pension policy launched in the three countries would be too lengthy for a journal article. This contribution focuses on recent commissions that have influenced the latest pension reforms in each country. Relying on government documents, opinions published by interested parties, and over 30 interviews with ministers and/or ministerial staff, Prime Minister's staff, members of commissions, interest group representatives, and civil servants, this contribution tackles three questions: What do governments gain by establishing pension commissions? What are the tools employed by commissions to make recommendations and ensure that their output will have political significance? And how do commissions influence policy outcomes?

To answer these questions, this paper is divided into four sections. The first presents a theoretical analysis of the role and importance of commissions within the policy process and discusses how it applies to reforming public pensions. The second part involves a brief summary of the reforms introduced in each of the three countries. This is followed by a study of pension commissions using the theoretical elements introduced in the first section. An evaluation of the theoretical framework and its potential applicability to other policy sectors and countries is provided in the conclusion.

THE ROLE AND IMPORTANCE OF COMMISSIONS WITHIN THE POLICY PROCESS

Defining commissions

Defining what a commission is represents a difficult task because of its various institutionalizations and its multiple functions. For the purpose of this paper a commission refers to any working group created and mandated by a government to study a particular policy and/or program. This implies that a commission is subordinate to the government. Consequently, its report is non-binding and the government has the authority to accept, alter, or reject its findings. However, this definition excludes agencies and/or departments mandated to manage and/or supervise pensions. Final reports are published by these organizations; however, their functions are clearly procedural providing basic information related to the ongoing management of pensions. This definition includes key tasks associated with commissions such as inquiring, advising, negotiating, and, under some circumstances, legislating.

Learning, delaying, framing? Why do governments rely on commissions?

There are at least six key reasons behind the creation of commissions. While all six contain political elements, the first three (enhancing knowledge, facilitating political compromise, and educating the general population) are primarily learning functions and involve mostly non-partisan conflicts. The last three (delaying, avoiding blame, and increasing support for a proposition) have clear partisan motives, with investigative efforts being less substantial than in the first three. As governments may have multiple reasons for the creation of a commission, these motives are not necessarily independent. Political motives persist even when commissions are given autonomy to inquire and learn about a policy problem since governments set up commissions with an outcome in mind (Bulmer 1983: 659).

A primary reason why a government appoints a commission is to enhance its knowledge capacity to deal with a particular issue. A commission is thus created to facilitate learning, which faces multiple hurdles within organizations. Organizational learning usually comes from well-established routines on which organizations function, such as practices, forms, rules, strategies, and conventions. Bureaucrats learn from the policy itself and make incremental adjustments to improve it (Heclo 1974; Lindblom 1959). The long-term effects of 'learning by doing' may result in a 'competency trap' where most learning happens while exploiting current practices, which occurs at the expense of exploring better or more efficient alternatives (March 1991). It is far easier to improve on what has been used rather than assimilate new learning. As stressed in the literature, learning by practice generates improvements. However, the more one invests in these improvements, the less likely it is for an organization to be willing to adopt better alternatives, especially if the implementation costs are substantial. This results in the persistent use of sub-optimal procedures (Levitt and March 1988). An in-depth assessment of a policy or program often requires scrutiny beyond the traditional legislative process (Salter 2003) and resources beyond those available within ministries (Bradford 1998; Inwood 2005; Premfors 1983).

The organizational structure of government also impedes the learning process. Public administration is not a monolithic institution but rather a collection of various agencies and departments with their own organizational culture and operating procedures. Once a practice has been adopted to handle a specific policy issue, exceptional circumstances are necessary to alter it. This point is underlined clearly by Zito (2001: 600), who stresses that epistemic communities are more likely to succeed in the EU 'where the policy costs are obscure or where a crisis has challenged fundamentally the traditional assumptions held by a wide range of EU actors'.

In the cases under study, references are made to reforms in various countries. For example, the British Pensions Commission's second report has multiple references to pension reforms in Sweden and the United States. Both France's Charpin Report and the Conseil d'orientation des retraites have a section devoted to pension reforms abroad. However, all members of commissions interviewed downplayed the importance of these experiences in their learning process. To put it succinctly, reforms must build on the current pension infrastructure and thus introducing measures from abroad is extremely difficult. This does not prevent members of a commission from analysing the introduction of an idea originating from abroad in order to tackle a particular issue. For example, in the context of the latest British reform, the adoption of automatic enrolment as a compromise between mandatory and voluntary options stems from American studies and the introduction of a similar measure in New Zealand.

To move beyond these obstacles, a government may stimulate exploration and innovation. Creating a commission allows an independent body to analyze various viewpoints and proposals, gather substantial information, and effectively increase pressure on the government to act (Bulmer 1983: 663). Commissions operate under exceptional circumstances, away from regular bureaucratic activity, taking on 'supernonroutine' tasks (Sheriff 1983). Commissions are also set up to provide detailed analysis of complex issues, pooling the best minds to provide governments with the proper knowledge to resolve the problem (Bulmer 1993).

The second reason for creating a commission is to appease interested parties and to establish the basis for political compromise. Commissions are notorious for giving a voice to groups and organizations with stakes in the policy area being studied. A government might actually hope that a commission can generate compromise among divided opinions (Long 1994), in which case it becomes extremely difficult for a government to ignore or sidestep the compromise solution (Park 1972). Beyond providing additional expertise on policy issues, Swedish commissions have long been recognized as a fruitful arena for political negotiations among the various political parties (Heclo 1974; Premfors 1983: 628). As such, a government may want to test the political waters by referring a policy idea to a commission for further analysis and to see whether the idea has strong support across a wide range of interested parties (Bulmer 1983: 661). Even in a strongly centralized government, a commission can pacify the members of its own cabinet and forge a uniting vision for a particular policy (Wheare 1955).

Educating the public on a controversial issue is the third reason behind the creation of commissions. Commissions clarify issues surrounding a particular policy and publicize research conducted in the area (Chapman 1973: 184). As such, commissions have the capacity to create policy discourse favorable to alternative solutions by changing long-held beliefs, and by recasting problems and solutions in a new light (Inwood 2005: 52–3).

Partisan motives also play an important role in the creation of commissions and are the primary motivation for the next three reasons. The fourth purpose in establishing a commission is that a government may simply want to delay deciding on a policy concern (Bulmer 1983; Long 1994; Park 1972; Wheare 1955) or remove politically harmful issues from the public arena. Fifth, a government may set up commissions in order to obtain additional support for its own policy (Bulmer 1983) or, alternatively, lessen support for a popular idea it disapproves of. Wheare (1955: 91–2) calls the latter a 'committee to nullify' since the objective is to kill a proposal by underscoring its weaknesses or stirring up divergence of opinion. Finally, another reason to create a commission is to avoid blame for introducing unpopular measures. A government may feel that substantial policy changes are necessary, but be wary of their implementation since they can result in a political backlash.

COMMISSIONS AND WELFARE STATE REFORM

Slower economic growth, population ageing, and a questioning of the role of the state in the economy have led numerous governments to appoint commissions to seek alternatives to current social policies. While the recent literature on the welfare state has focused mostly on retrenchment (Pierson 1996), governments have resorted to commissions for multiple reasons beyond avoiding blame, as stated in the previous section. The cases analyzed in this paper support the claims that commissions have been instituted to enhance knowledge of pension policies, appease policy actors, educate the public on pensions, and, in some cases, delay making a decision.

Theoretical propositions

Generalizing the policy influences of commissions is a challenge for at least three reasons. First, diverse institutional set-ups have been utilized within countries; even more so across countries. Even if a formal setting is exactly reproduced, numerous elements will vary, including the terms of reference, the membership, and the way expertise is used. Second, depending on the nature of the actors, the dynamics surrounding the commission will differ. For example, the deliberations of a group of experts will be very different from deliberations consisting exclusively of politicians. Third, the type of policy and its history can vary sharply from one area to another. For example, while the development of pension policies has been fairly consensual in Canada, they were the source of tremendous political conflicts in the 1950s in Sweden. Fourth, external elements, such as the election of a new government, can shatter the importance of a commission and its conclusions. It is with these caveats in mind that an attempt is made to generalize the causal factors behind the type of policy influence of commissions. As such, it is preferable to interpret the theoretical propositions in terms of likelihood rather than universal laws.

Based on various outcomes described in the literature, commissions tend to have at least five different types of influence on policy outcomes, ranging from counteraction to full endorsement. This list is not exhaustive and a combination of outcomes may occur depending on the number of programs and/or policies studied by a commission. First, the reforms introduced by a government can be opposite to those proposed by a commission. The commission may have a very positive impact in identifying policy challenges which were unforeseen or neglected by the government, with the latter opting to address them by adopting a different set of policies from those recommended by the commission (*alarm raiser*). This outcome is most likely to occur if members of a commission are given a vague mandate or if they go beyond it.

Second, the conclusions of a commission may have little content or no effect; the report simply gathers dust in a parliamentary library without further consideration from the main political actors (*status quo*). The commissioners may have been so divided that the report fails to provide a coherent solution to the policy problem in question or the government opted to ignore the commission's findings, as in the case of the inquiry into the value of pensions, where Thatcher dismissed the goal that efforts should be made to make private occupational pensions as generous as those found in the public sector. Third, a government can ignore numerous recommendations of a commission, choosing to implement only a few. Consequently, the government continues to endorse the existing policy structure and simply reforms some elements without altering the core (*incrementalism*). The influence of a commission headed by Laraque in France to institute a universal French pension system is reflective of this type of control. While the proposal to create a unique pension scheme for workers failed, multiple elements, such as the creation of a pay-as-you-go system, were enacted (Guillemard 1986; Ashford 1986).

Fourth, a commission may have a tremendous long-term impact by transforming the fundamental ideas surrounding a policy. As stressed by Cox (2001), a commission can transform the language traditionally associated with important symbols such as the constitution. This, in turn, facilitates the introduction of reform. As such, the impact of the commission is not a direct one but it can assist in developing conditions conducive to reform at a later date (*idea shaker*). A clear idea shaker was the Macdonald Commission in Canada, which set the stage for the adoption of free trade with the United States (Inwood 2005).

Finally, a commission can be highly influential if a government opts to endorse the major elements of its report and act accordingly (*policy engineer*). A good example of this type of outcome would be the influential role played by the Committee on Economic Security established by Roosevelt, which led to the creation of social security (see, for example, Béland 2005: 74–94).

Five key variables impact the likelihood of a commission having substantial policy influence. The first, and probably the easiest, element to explain is the importance of membership. Inspired by the literature on veto players (Tsebelis 2002), the higher the number of diversified interests and their ideological distance from one another, the less likely that changes to the status quo will emerge from a commission. A commission with a very large membership is unlikely to succeed in proposing substantial changes to a program or policy. If a government creates a panel of experts, it is imperative that the members selected have the political support of most interested parties, such as key members of government and social partners, if they want to have a substantial influence. Although the support of opposition parties may not be a prerequisite, having their support can facilitate the long-term adoption of a commission's proposal. The inclusion of civil servants within a commission may also prove to be an asset since they are likely to be involved in the implementation of any proposal adopted by the government. This can prove to be effective against potential claims that unfeasible proposals have been adopted (see Peters 2001). A similar argument can be made for the inclusion of social partners in continental Europe owing to their formal role in the management of pensions (Béland 2001; Marier 2008). However, based on Tsebelis (2002), their inclusion increases significantly the number of members within a commission and the disparity of ideological preferences, making a status quo outcome more likely.

The second important variable is the terms of reference. It is more difficult for a government to dismiss a commission with a clear mandate, and sufficient time and resources. Thus, a clear directive to reform the pension system is more likely to generate propositions that are considered seriously by a government (*incrementalism to policy engineer*) than a restricted mandate, where the government simply asks for a diagnosis of the pension system (*alarm raiser to incrementalism*). In the latter case, recommendations beyond the mandate prescribed can be easily brushed off by the government because it can claim that the commission went beyond its mandate.

The selection of members and the mandate are two important tools for any government to steer the activities of the commission and dictate the terms of what is being learnt. This can have a significant impact on what is being learnt and on the type of influence a commission can potentially have. The creation of a commission with a large and diversified membership, a vague mandate, and a short time period is unlikely to yield any substantive results both in learning and policy output. As a result, *status quo or incrementalist policy outcomes* would be expected. In contrast, the creation of a commission with a limited membership, consisting mostly of a small group of experts with substantial resources and time to conduct their analysis, is far more likely to generate *idea shaker or policy engineer policy outcomes*.

The level of independence and support experienced by the commission represents the third variable. Can the commission perform its research tasks without the interference of the government and the participation of other stakeholders such as the civil service? Does the commission have strong support from the legislature and the executive, interested parties, and the civil service? If it does, its prestige is likely to be enhanced and it will have a captive audience. All experts interviewed for this research stressed that they work with the objective that their recommendations will be seriously considered by governments and subsequently result in policy change reflecting their findings.

The fourth variable is the institutional environment surrounding the commission. It is far easier for a highly centralized executive with a single party government to dismiss outright the work of a commission (especially if it was established by the former government).[1] On the contrary, it will be more difficult to dismiss this work where there is a highly fragmented legislature relying on commissions to learn about policy options and build a political consensus.

The last variable concerns the political, economic and administrative viability of a commission's output (Bradford 1998). A report is much more likely to have a strong political impact if its solution fits with the political, economic, and administrative actors. Moreover, is it a unanimous report or one with a substantial majority? If the members of the commission are unanimous in their support, the commission can act as an additional pressure group to encourage change and gather strong public sympathy, forcing the government to address its recommendations very seriously (Park 1972: 460). In sum, it is important to note that these elements are not requisites but rather variables that help to identify the likelihood of a commission having any influential output.

ROLE OF COMMISSIONS IN PENSION REFORMS IN FRANCE, SWEDEN, AND THE UK

This section is divided into two parts. A brief description of pension reforms introduced in each country is presented (see also Table 1). This is followed by a comparative analysis of the influence of commissions in achieving the respective policy outcomes. To facilitate the evaluation of the theoretical elements presented above, the discussion is organized and analyzed by outcome groupings (policy engineer, idea breaker, incrementalism, status quo, and alarm raiser) and focuses solely on most recent reform activities.

Pension reform in France, Sweden and the UK

The French pension system is highly fragmented along occupational lines consisting of more than 100 schemes (Charpin 1999). Convergence has, however, occurred in terms of rules and benefits. As such, most private sector workers find themselves in the general scheme (*régime general*), and civil servants are enrolled in either the civil service scheme (*régime des fonctionnaires*) or in one of the so-called special schemes (*régimes spéciaux* – mostly confined to state employees in organizations such as the *Régie autonome des transports parisiens*). Three major reforms have occurred in the past 20 years. In 1993, the Balladur government focused on the general scheme and transformed few parameters lengthening the contribution period required for a full-term pension from 37.5 years to 40, altering the base wage utilized to calculate a pension by using the best 25 years instead of the best 10, and indexing pension benefits on prices as opposed to wages.

In 2003, the Raffarin government succeeded in imposing changes similar to those presented by Balladur on those enrolled in the civil service regime. Even though the contribution periods were extended, the formulas to calculate full-term pensions were not altered significantly beyond penalizing early retirement. Moreover, both civil service and general schemes were faced with additional increases in the contribution period to be implemented in 2012. The Fillon government introduced similar measures for workers in the special schemes in 2007.

The history of pension policy in Sweden had been marked by stark ideological and political conflicts culminating in a referendum and two elections on the subject in the late 1950s (Molin 1965). Following the adoption of the Social Democratic proposals in 1958, pension reform was left off the political agenda until the late 1980s. Following the conclusion of a public inquiry into the pension system in 1990, a consensus emerged on the need to reform the pension system.

In the aftermath of the 1991 election a pension working group was instituted by Bo Könberg, the new Minister for Health and Social Affairs. As a result of his previous experience in the Pension Commission (1984–90) which had a large membership, Könberg created a small working group including experts and

Table 1 Pension reforms in France, Sweden and the UK

	France	Sweden	UK
Pension reform (name)	1993 – Balladur reform. 1995 – Juppé plan 2003 – Raffarin reform (Fillon plan). 2007 – Fillon reform	1998 – New pension system	2007 – The Pensions Act
Pension reform (content – main elements) highest-earning	1993 – Increase in the length of contribution (37.5 to 40 years); benefits based on the best 25 years of contribution instead of 10; price indexation instead of wage indexation; creation of a retirement fund. 1995 – Increased managerial powers granted to the parliament. 2003 – Increase in the length of contribution for the public scheme (up to 40 years in 2008); increase for both schemes (41 years in 2012 and 42 in 2020); penalty for early retirement; price indexation for the public scheme; possibility of retiring before 60 for those who started work between the ages of 14 and 16; 2007 – Measures similar to those introduced in 2003 for workers in the special schemes.	1998 – Whole new system. Increase in the length of contribution (from 30 years using the 15 for life income); compensatory measures introduced for childcare, study and military service; new indexation mechanism based on economic growth, prices and population ageing; 2.5 per cent of the contributions to be invested in the private sector; installation of a means-test for the guaranteed pension; flexible retirement age.	Creation of a National Pension Savings Scheme (NPSS) based on automatic enrolment with the possibility to opt out into an employer's scheme. The 8 per cent contribution rate is financed by employees (4 per cent), employer (3 per cent) and the state (1 per cent). Re-establish the indexation of the basic state pension and transform the previous state second pension (an earnings-related scheme) into a flat rate pension. Full pension rights are obtained after a minimum of 30 years of work (full- and part-time) instead of 39 for women and 44 for men. Increase in the retirement age for both men and women. The retirement age will be 65 in 2020, 66 in 2026, 67 in 2036, and 68 in 2046.

Note: Adapted from Marier (2008).

politicians to achieve a consensual decision. The outline of a new system was elaborated by early 1994 (SOU 1994), leading to an agreement in principle adopted by the Riksdag in June. An implementation committee was created soon after the 1994 elections to continue the work of the previous committee. The key players remained the same, resulting in a new reformed system in 1998. The key elements of the new system included: the adoption of the 'life income principle' based on the notion that all earnings count; pension points for childcare, study and military service; and a portion of contributions to be invested in private individual accounts. Furthermore, pension benefits were adjusted according to inflation, the state of the economy, and demographic changes.

In the UK, the long-term effects of the pension reforms under the Thatcher government have led to increasing pressure to introduce new reforms in light of the inadequacies of the private sector in providing safe and guaranteed pensions – with close to a third of workers not contributing to a pension plan – and the failure of the current public system to provide sufficient basic income. With more than 100 parameters involved in estimating a pension, the UK system earned the dubious distinction of having the most complex pension system in the world (Pensions Commission 2004). Early in its mandate, the Blair government introduced changes that sought to improve on the policy structure left over from the Thatcher government. However, it soon became clear that more substantial measures would be needed.

The Pensions Act of 2007 introduced numerous measures inspired by the work of the Pensions Commission which had been created in 2002. It included the introduction of personal accounts by 2012, a decrease in the contribution period required to obtain the basic state pension (now set at 30 years) and a change in its indexation mechanism to make it more generous, and a rise in the retirement age to 68 between 2024 and 2046.

In light of the pension reforms introduced in France, Sweden and the UK, two commissions were particularly influential and can be considered to have been policy engineers, a third led to the status quo, a fourth was both an alarm raiser and a source of the status quo, and a fifth qualifies as an alarm raiser, a source of the status quo and an idea shaker (see Table 2).

Policy engineers

The British Pensions Commission and the Swedish Working Group on Pensions were extremely influential in reforming their respective pension systems. In fact, their proposals served as a blueprint for the actual reforms, thus making them policy engineers. They shared important similarities. First, both commissions were successful in engaging and integrating key experts from the civil service. In both cases, the civil servants involved stressed that they had had a highly rewarding and challenging experience. They also had the sense that their work was not going to be in vain. This generated a stimulating learning environment. Second, the commissions had the explicit support of the government executive. Third, the number of members was restricted to

Table 2 Variables affecting the likelihood of having an influential commission

	Membership	Mandate	Support	Institutional environment	Viability of the final report(s)	Type of Influence
Working Group on Pensions* 1991–2002 (Sweden)	Restricted/diverse	Clear	Very strong	Coalition government in the midst of an economic crisis	Strong	Policy engineer
Pensions Commission 2002–2006 (UK)	Extremely limited (3)/diverse	Clear – but limited	Very strong	Majoritarian	Strong	Policy engineer
Charpin 1998–1999 (France)	Extremely limited (1) with a consultation commission	Clear – but limited to a diagnostic; however, hopes of another Livre Blanc	Medium (strong from the civil service; neutral from government).	Centralized executive responsible for pensions	Weak – minority report by Charpin	Alarm raiser/status quo/idea shaker
Conseil d'orientation des retraites 2000 – present (France)	High/diverse (experts + social partners)	Vague	Weak	Centralised executive responsible for pensions	Acceptable – propose many adjustments to existing policies	Alarm raiser/ incrementalism
Pension Commission 1984–1990 (Sweden)	High/diverse (experts, interested parties, civil servants, politicians)	Clear – but very limited	Average	Coalition government	Weak – strong opposition	Status quo (incrementalism with elimination of survivor's pension)

Note: * This actually consists of two working groups (the Working Group on Pensions and the Implementation Group). Owing to the similarities with regard to the actors and deliberations involved, they are treated as the same in this contribution.

three in the UK and to roughly ten in Sweden. Fourth, efforts were made to ensure that the commissions included a broad ideological representation. Fifth, the mandates were clear in both cases. Finally, the members of both commissions stressed that there was a high degree of trust and chemistry between them. This was confirmed by individuals who had dealings with the commissions.

It is important to emphasize that there were a few substantial elements that differed between the two commissions. First, the Swedish Working Group was composed mostly of politicians, many of whom had experience of dealing with pension policy. Experts from the civil service were also involved. The group consulted, but did not include, social partners and other parties interested in their deliberations.

The membership of the British Pensions Commission was composed largely of experts and did not include any politicians. It also sought to achieve a broad representation of employers' and employees' interests. As a result, it included the former Director General of the Confederation of British Industry (CBI) (Adair Turner), a former President of the Trade Union Confederation (TUC) (Jeannie Drake), and a well-known social policy professor (John Hills). Compared to members of the Swedish Working Group on Pensions, none of the Pensions Commission members were affiliated to political parties; as a whole, the commission was non-partisan. However, the members all understood that their proposal had to be politically acceptable and kept in touch regularly with government officials and interested parties (political parties, unions, employers, the pension industry, and pensioner associations).

Second, as a result of the first difference, the ensuing debates following the submission of the commissions' reports were drastically different. In the Swedish case, the proposed pension reform was *de facto* a compromise between five political parties. Any substantial changes would have required a new round of negotiations among the members of the group, making it difficult for other interested parties to influence the plan once the government had agreed to proceed with it. This stands in stark contrast to the reaction to the UK Pensions Commission report. Since the government did not have to negotiate with other parties to make changes (unless it opted to confine managerial responsibilities to private actors), it was in a position either to walk away from the report's conclusions or alter them drastically. Indeed, various criticisms had already emerged, such as the cost of proposed reforms (a failed strategy first utilized by the Treasury) and the difficulty of creating an agency to manage contributions into the National Pension Savings Scheme (NPSS). Nevertheless, most of the elements proposed by the Pensions Commission were adopted in the final legislation. The key reason was that the members of the commission were able to come to a broad consensus. There was substantial support for the two key recommendations. First, the creation of a NPSS had broad support; the only point of contention concerned how and by whom it was going to be managed. Second, the Pensions Commission recommendation to build on the actual public scheme by creating a generous non-means tested flat rate pension plan was well received. In order to achieve this objective, the commission proposed to index the basic state pension with earnings (rather than price). This measure already had the explicit support of numerous policy actors such as the CBI, the TUC, the Pensions Policy Institute, the National Association of Pension Funds, and the Association of British Insurers. Whatever the means used, the commission deemed it imperative to provide a generous flat rate system and improve the treatment of workers facing career interruptions.

Another substantial difference lies in the amount of research done prior to the creation of both groups. Many members of the Swedish Working Group on Pensions had been actively involved in a previous lengthy inquiry (1984–90) into the pension system. Thus, when the working group was created, the group acted quickly, seeking agreement on reforms. The Swedish commission was also able to justify a restricted membership on the basis that multiple actors had been consulted in the previous commission (1984–90). In contrast, the British Pensions Commission originally had very limited information about and research on the British pension system. Consequently, the members decided to first present a detailed analysis of the actual state of pension policy without any recommendations (Pensions Commission 2004). This gathered substantial media coverage and increased the visibility and credibility of the Pensions Commission. It also forced the members of the Pensions Commission to engage with the plethora of actors involved in British pensions. The second report dealt mostly with recommendations (Pensions Commission 2005), which formed the basis of the subsequent White Paper (Department for Work and Pensions 2006).

Status quo and idea shaker

In the aftermath of the Juppé plan and the strikes of 1995, pension politics became even more polarized in France. In the hope of finding a solution to the pension problem, the newly elected Jospin decided to commission a report on the future of the whole pension system in 1998. The mandate was given to the Director of the Forecasting Agency (*Bureau Général du Plan*), Charpin, in consultation with the social partners and the managers of the various pension schemes. The mandate emphasized the necessity of making adjustments to the pension system.

L'avenir de nos retraites, also known as the Charpin report, presented a bleak future for the French pension system and advocated proposals similar to the ones unsuccessfully implemented by Juppé, concluding that 'the diagnoses found in this report demonstrate that a global reform of the retirement system is necessary' (Charpin 1999: 144). To this effect, the report advocated many controversial policy options. First, it proposed increasing the length of the contribution period to 42.5 years to obtain a full-term pension prior to age 65. Charpin emphasized that this change should apply to both the private and public sectors. Second, he rejected the unification of the eclectic

French pension schemes, but maintained that it was imperative to adopt common principles and that 'unjustified' differences were to be avoided; Charpin was quite critical of the lack of reforms to the public sector schemes, and emphasized that these schemes needed to be reformed as well (Charpin 1999: 15).

The conclusions of the report did not receive strong support. The employers' association claimed that it did not go far enough while the unions stressed that lengthening the contribution period to 42.5 years was too drastic. Counter-publications emerged (see, for example, Teulade 2000) and served as a rallying point against Charpin's report. The lack of support for the recommendations proposed by Charpin cemented the status quo. Jospin ended his term without proposing any reform. However, the main elements of the Charpin report did not go unnoticed. The subsequent right-wing government espoused many of the ideas contained in the Charpin report and introduced a reform following its broad lines in 2003; however, politicians avoided any reference to the controversial report.

Status quo

The only point of agreement within the Swedish Pension Commission (1984–90) concerned an adjustment to the survivor's pension. The Commission lasted six years and resulted in dissenting reports with divisions reminiscent of the debates surrounding the creation of the earnings-related pension scheme of the 1950s. These sharp cleavages ensured that the conclusion of the report would not be the starting point of any negotiation on pensions. The mandate of the commission was strictly defined, thus limiting discussion to the pension system's existing parameters. It also included numerous interested parties (unions, employers, pensioner associations, disability groups to mention a few) resulting in meetings with more than 30 individuals. This combination of a restrictive mandate and a large diverse membership made it extremely difficult for the commission to make viable recommendations. The solution of the committee to alter few parameters in the current pension system was soon dismissed since most parties involved judged them as inadequate. The committee established after the 1991 election never really considered the recommendations made by the Pension Commission.

Alarm raiser and status quo

In France, counter publications undermined the credibility of the Charpin report immediately after its release, and made it difficult to conceive that the unions (particularly strong in the public sector where reform was most advocated) would provide sufficient support for Jospin to move forward with pension reform. For example, the publication of a document written by Teulade and endorsed by the *Conseil économique et social* stressed that emphasis should be placed on economic growth, which would on its own resolve most problems relating to the pension system. Thus, instead of presenting a reform proposal, Jospin opted to create the *Conseil d'orientation des retraites* (COR) in 2000 in the hope of creating a consensus on the issue. Comprised of 32 members, including deputies, senators, union and employer representatives, pensioner group representatives, experts, and directors of the various pension schemes, the COR had an original mandate to re-visit a diagnosis of the current pension system in light of the demographic and socio-economic conditions, to describe the conditions required to maintain such regimes, and to maintain the cohesiveness of the regime while ensuring fairness across generations (Conseil d'orientation des retraites 2001). Its creation was criticized strongly by both right-wing parties and the employers' association, the latter refusing to participate in the forum claiming that Charpin had already performed this task. The report was further criticized for its descriptive rather than prescriptive outlook, resulting in a lack of any clear reform propositions. In regard to long-term impact, the COR re-established the credibility of the projections included in the Charpin report, but did not embrace its recommendations. For example, the members could not come to an agreement on the necessity to coordinate the pension schemes of private and public workers (COR 2001: 287). Following the election of a right-wing government, its future seemed uncertain when the government announced its project to reform the civil service regime to coordinate the length of the contribution period necessary to obtain a full pension. However, in the aftermath of the 2003 reform, the government opted to make the COR permanent, monitoring the French pension system on a regular basis. Ironically, this was also recommended in the Charpin report.

CONCLUSION: COMMISSIONS AS POLICY-MAKERS?

This comparative analysis has shed light on the three research questions outlined in the introduction. First, governments have gained important insights from the creation of public commissions. Commissions have functioned as powerful instruments of learning. For example, the British Pensions Commission and the first report of the COR established a much needed detailed picture of their pension systems. Their research publications – but not necessarily their recommendations – are widely accepted by all major policy actors as representing an accurate and impartial picture of their respective pension systems. This has helped to focus the discussion on how to reform a pension system.

Second, commissions have used numerous tools to ensure that their work has significant and lasting political influence. For example, in the UK, the members of the Pensions Commission relied heavily on civil servants to conduct their research, ensuring that key measures were supported by major policy actors. With regard to the former, the same civil servants were involved in drafting the White Paper and were inspired by their work with the Pensions Commission. In the Swedish case, the creation of a broad endorsement of a proposal made by the Working Group on Pensions ensured that public pensions did not become an issue of intense political disagreement, as in the 1950s. Third, there is strong evidence to suggest that commissions have had a lasting influence on policy. The proposals of both the British Pensions Commission and the Swedish Working Group on Pensions were adopted almost in total. Moreover, in the French case, key elements of the Charpin report were eventually adopted by the government in 2003 and 2007, and the COR has made important contributions to clarify the debate on pension reform.

Moving beyond France, Sweden, and the UK

Beyond the case studies, which have demonstrated the usefulness of the theoretical elements developed in this paper, two other findings have strong potential for future research on the policy impact of commissions. First, as stressed in a comparative study of pension commissions in the US and Japan, sequencing matters a great deal (Kato 1991). The Swedish Working Group on Pensions benefited greatly from the previous Pension Commission. The Working Group was allowed to justify the non-inclusion of interested parties and it jump-started discussions on reform and an analysis of its consequences. In the British case, the Pensions Commission would never have seen the light of day if the recent policies developed by Labour had been efficient. It was a sense of urgency about adopting pension policies in the light of recent failures, the search for a Blair legacy, and the need for a proposal with strong support from most interested parties that prompted the government to be so supportive of the commission.

Second, overusing commissions can backfire and send a signal that a government is incapable of governing (Long 1994). France represents a clear case where pension commissions have been far too numerous, often created to avoid making a decision. Within this context, it is difficult for any commission to have a genuine influence on policy; interested parties opposed to the general direction of a commission can undermine it, knowing that another venue may bring more positive results.

An interesting finding from these case studies is the lack of substantive learning from abroad in the elaboration of pension reform proposals in all three countries. While policy-makers have acknowledged a basic insight into what is being done in other EU countries, it remains extremely difficult to translate this into reform proposals because key institutions and policies surrounding pensions are strongly entrenched within distinctive national settings. Nonetheless, this has not prevented various pension commissions from learning important policy lessons, as indicated by this study. These were internal processes operating within national settings.

However, there are a few exceptional cases where learning from abroad has been acknowledged as playing a critical role in pension reform within the EU. Ironically, it has not been the EU, but rather the World Bank (WB), which has had the most influence across Europe in facilitating learning and the diffusion of pension policies. Swedish pension reform has been highly praised by the WB (Holzmann and Palmer 2006) and it has already been adopted by Poland and Latvia. Norway is currently reforming its pension system and a few elements of Swedish pension reform, such as the life income principle, were inspired by its Nordic neighbor. However, one should exercise caution before reaching a premature conclusion that these cases demonstrate the increasing popularity of learning from abroad. For example, the introduction of the Swedish reform in Latvia has been triggered by the inability of its public administration to gather the necessary expertise and capabilities to implement successful economic policies following its independence (Tavits 2003), conditions unlikely to be replicated elsewhere. In the Norwegian case, the introduction of measures similar to Sweden's was facilitated by the fact that their pension system shared many characteristics of the old Swedish system (pre-1994).

ACKNOWLEDGEMENTS

The author would like to thank Michelle Egan, Anthony Zito, and the anonymous referees for generous comments and Anna-Maria Luponio and Mike Torunian for research assistance.

NOTE

1 In the same vein, there are no significant hurdles for this type of political executive to adopt the recommendation of a commission (regardless of who established it).

REFERENCES

Ashford, D.E. (1986) *The Emergence of the Welfare States*, Oxford: Basil Blackwell.
Béland, D. (2001) 'Does labor matter? Institutions, labor unions and pension reform in france and the United States', *Journal of Public Policy* 21: 153–72.
Béland, D. (2005) *Social Security: History and Politics from the New Deal to the Privatization Debate*, Lawrence, KS: University Press of Kansas.
Bradford, N. (1998) *Commissioning Ideas: Canadian National Policy Innovation in Comparative Perspective*, Toronto: Oxford University Press.
Bulmer, M. (1983) 'An Anglo–American comparison: does social science contribute effectively to the work of governmental commissions?', *American Behavioral Scientist* 26: 643–68.
Bulmer, M. (1993) 'The royal commission and departmental committee in the British policy-making process', in B.G. Peters and A. Barker (eds) *Advising West European*

governments: Inquiries, Expertise and Public Policy, Edinburgh: Edinburgh University Press, pp. 37–49.

Chapman, R.A. (1973) 'Commissions in policy-making', in R.A. Chapman (ed.), *The Role of Commissions in Policy-making*, London: George Allen & Unwin, pp. 174–88.

Charpin, J.-M. (1999) *L'avenir de nos retraites*, Paris: La documentation française.

Conseil d'orientation des retraites (COR) (2001) *Retraites: renouveler le contrat social entre les générations*, Paris: La documentation française.

Cox, R.H. (2001) 'The social construction of an imperative: why welfare reform happened in Denmark and the Netherlands but not in Germany', *World Politics* 53: 463–98.

de la Porte, C. and Nanz, P. (2004) 'The OMC – a deliberative-democratic mode of governance? The cases of employment and pensions', *Journal of European Public Policy* 11: 267–88.

Department for work and pensions (2006) *Security in Retirement: Towards a New Pensions System*, London: The Stationery Office.

Featherstone, K. (2005) '"Soft" co-ordination meets "hard" politics: the European Union and pension reform in Greece', *Journal of European Public Policy* 12: 733–50.

Guillemard, A.-M. (1986) *Le déclin du social: Formation et crise des politiques de la vieillesse*, Paris: Presses Universitaires de France.

Heclo, H. (1974) *Modern Social Politics in Britain and Sweden*, New Haven, CT: Yale University Press.

Hogwood, B.W. and Peters, B.G. (1982) 'The dynamics of policy change', *Policy Sciences* 14: 225–45.

Holzmann, R. and Palmer, E. (eds) (2006) *Pension Reform: Issues and Prospects for Non-financial Defined Contribution (NDC) Schemes*, Washington, DC: World Bank.

Inwood, G.J. (2005) *Continentalizing Canada: The Politics and Legacy of the Macdonald Royal Commission* Toronto: University of Toronto Press.

Kato, J. (1991) 'Public pension reform in the united states and Japan', *Comparative Political Studies* 24: 100–26.

Levitt, B. and March, J.G. (1988) 'Organizational learning', *Annual Review of Sociology* 14: 319–40.

Lindblom, C.E. (1959) 'The science of "muddling through"', *Public Administration Review* 19: 79–88.

Long, M. (1994) 'The correct use of commissions', *International Review of Administrative Sciences* 60: 505–11.

March, J.G. (1991) 'Exploration and exploitation in organizational learning', *Organization Science* 2: 71–87.

Marier, P. (2008) *Pension Politics: Consensus and Social Conflict in Ageing Societies*, London: Routledge.

Molin, B. (1965) *Tjänstepensionsfrågan*, Göteborg: Akademiförlaget.

OECD (2005) *Pensions at a Glance: Public Policies Across OECD Countries*, Paris: OECD.

Park, Y.H. (1972) 'The government advisory commission system in Japan', *Journal of Comparative Administration* 3: 435–67.

Pensions Commission (2004) *The First Report of the Pensions Commission*, London: Pensions Commission.

Pensions Commission (2005) *The Second Report of the Pensions Commission: A New Pension Settlement for the Twenty-first Century*, London: Pensions Commission.

Peters, B.G. (2001) *The Politics of Bureaucracy*, New York: Routledge.

Pierson, P. (1996) 'The new politics of the Welfare State', *World Politics* 48: 143–79.

Pierson, P. (2000) 'Increasing returns, path dependence, and the study of politics', *American Political Science Review* 94: 251–66.

Premfors, R. (1983) 'Governmental commissions in Sweden', *American Behavioral Scientist* 26: 623–42.
Rose, R. (1991) 'What is lesson-drawing?', *Journal of Public Policy* 11: 3–30.
Salter, L. (2003) 'The complex relationship between inquiries and public controversy', in A. Manson and D. Mullan (eds), *Commission of Inquiry: Praise or Reappraise?*, Toronto: Irwin Law, pp. 185–209.
Sheriff, P.E. (1983) 'An Anglo-American comparison: does social science contribute effectively to the work of governmental commissions?' *American Behavioral Scientist* 26: 669–80.
SOU (1994) *Reformerat pensionssystem*, Stockholm.
Tavits, M. (2003) 'Policy learning and uncertainty: the case of pension reform in Estonia and Latvia', *The Policy Studies Journal* 31: 643–60.
Teulade, R. (2000) *L'avenir des systèmes de retraite*, Paris: Les Éditions des Journaux Officiels.
Tsebelis, G. (2002) *Veto Players: How Political Institutions Work*, Princeton, NJ: Princeton University Press.
Wheare, K.C. (1955) *Government by Committee*, Oxford: Oxford University Press.
Wilson, F.L. (1987) *Interest-group Politics in France*, Cambridge: Cambridge University Press.
Zito, A.R. (2001) 'Epistemic communities, collective entrepreneurship and European integration', *Journal of European Public Policy* 8: 585–603.

European agencies as agents of governance and EU learning

Anthony R. Zito

INTRODUCTION

Environmental policy, given its interconnection with scientific uncertainty and diverse societal concerns, presents fundamental challenges for political organizations. This reality is doubly problematic given the complex nature of the European Union (EU) policy-making process. Learning approaches to EU integration suggest: (a) how EU actors define both their environmental policy and organizational management problems, and (b) how they formulate philosophies and actions to cope with this complexity.

This article disaggregates the EU system, assuming that the EU's institutional complexity provides numerous potential fora for learning. It takes a meso approach, focusing on two institutions and their evolution: the European Environment Agency (EEA) and the Environment Agency of England and Wales (EA). The core research questions are: under what conditions do agencies pursue organizational and policy innovation, and what are the implications of such innovation for the relationships between environmental agencies and their organizational context? Learning approaches may provide insights into how EU and national organizations, acting as agents, can transform the nature of their relations with the principals, but institutional context sets strong limits on this potential.

The choice of agencies reflects 'the most different case approach' within the EU context. The EA is on a completely different scale from the EEA: the largest European environmental agency versus the smallest in terms of staff, the former wielding immense regulatory scope versus the latter's information-centred governance; budgetary resource differences; and the possibilities for intervention by the relatively cohesive British state executive compared to the EU multi-headed hydra (Williams 2005: 85). These hugely different agencies facilitate a comparison of the degree to which they confront similar contextual dynamics and internal impulses.

The next section presents the analytical propositions. The third section investigates the origins of the EEA and the EA respectively, in both cases asking how the founding negotiations frame the relationship between agency (agent) and principal(s), and explores their historical evolution, focusing on their organizational adaptation to context (organizational learning) and policy learning.

THEORETICAL OVERVIEW

Principal–agent propositions

Notions of principal–agency have elucidated numerous important EU relationships between bureaucratic organizations (the agents) and principals, the political authorities (Egan 1998). Assuming that bureaucrats manipulate the system to maximize their budget because of their information advantages, principal–agent theorists postulated that politicians/principals anticipate such manipulation and assert their long-term control over their agents by setting various controls (McCubbins *et al.* 1987). Further assumptions include: (1) bureaucrats have personal preferences that conflict with the principals' concerns; (2) the delegation of authority to agents gives the bureaucrats information advantages (McCubbins *et al.* 1987: 246–7).

Because of the prohibitive costs of monitoring and sanctioning such bureaucratic behaviour, the principals establish control mechanisms (e.g. clearly defined administrative procedures and oversight processes), but do not require to specify or even know the detailed policy outcomes (McCubbins *et al.* 1987: 256–61). Agency discretion occurs if the agency manages to engage in opportunistic behaviour, known as 'shirking', that is more costly for the principal (Kassim and Menon 2003: 122).

Structural disagreement

Moe's framework (1984: 773) questioned key principal–agent assumptions (i.e. that the agency possesses no internal conflict and that the principals agree) and the amount of control that principals can actually impose. Multiple interests and principals operate in all democratic systems. Moe's structural perspective expects a dominant advocacy coalition consisting of the government and its associated constituencies to build administrative structures insulating their achievements from politics. The opposing coalitions protect their voice in the structural design of the bureaucracies by imposing structures that subvert effective performance and politicize agency decisions (Moe 1989: 273–7).

The agency's characteristics are the product of strategic design exercised by politicians and affected interests. Since no singularity of interest exists, the design of the personnel decisions and administrative goals reflect a much more chaotic discussion than the principal–agent approach predicts. No one succeeds in achieving their goals for agency design: opposing coalitions seek to impose structures that inhibit agency performance and enhance external control while the coalition in power defends the agency and even counter-attacks with its own structures (Moe 1989: 281–5). The Moe framework expects agencies to face a path-dependent situation where the structural choices of the agency's creation endure and dominate over future changes, leading to a largely static and incoherent equilibrium for the agencies.

Historical institutionalist propositions

Sharing characteristics of Moe's more rationalist approach, historical institutional perspectives provide an alternative explanation for agency change and stasis. The complex EU institutional process places significant constraints on agency choices, forcing agency adherence to past norms and decisions. Environment agencies are also slow to change and do so incrementally to reflect enshrined norms and rules. Although institutions resist change in favour of current norms, change is possible without hypothesizing learning (Streeck and Thelen 2005: 18–31). For example, agencies may keep the basic set of rules and resources but face redirection by newly elected governments, or some grouping of principals, towards a new set of goals and objectives that transform the agency's role.

Learning propositions

Waterman *et al.* (2004: 24–46) conceptualize the implications of relaxing two principal–agent assumptions (conflicts over goals are inevitable, and agents have more information than principals). They argue that the principal–agent model is only one (albeit frequent) scenario (Waterman *et al.* 2004: 24–31). They argue for the possibility of competing principals as well as agencies, and that the principals may sometimes possess considerable knowledge. Neither the principals nor the agents are likely to have unitary outlooks. Agencies have incentives to ally with principals who share their goals/outlooks, and vice versa. Both agencies and other interest groups are strongly motivated to share information with supporting coalitions; consequently, the situation of information asymmetry decreases.

Information and learning are core dynamics that can transform the principal–agent relationship as both sets of actors learn gradually about policy and their own organizations (Waterman *et al.* 2004: 37–42). Carpenter (2001: 14–35, 353–67) has explored how bureaucracy can build autonomy and establish direct links to the citizens and the new associations. Bureaucracies need stable legitimacy for themselves and their policies, so they push policy innovation (Carpenter 2001: 14–18). Autonomy exists when agencies can make the first decisive moves towards a new policy, establishing an agenda or the most popular alternative, which becomes too costly for politicians and organized interests to ignore. Principal–agent adherents would define such behaviour as shirking. However, there is a significant possibility that cannot be subsumed in this approach: namely, that agencies can *transform* the preferences or the configuration of the principals (the public, organized interests, and politicians). Agencies operating with discretion may exert bureaucratic entrepreneurship (Carpenter 2001: 30–1). Here the agency leadership experiments with new programmes and introduces innovations to existing programmes while gradually convincing the diverse political coalitions to value the new innovation and the agencies themselves.

Agency actors sustain this preference shift by using recognized legitimacy in the policy area, by building superior ties to the public and/or media, or by establishing reputations for impartiality and dedication to the public good. Agencies operating in the classic principal–agency scenario seek to develop advocacy coalition scenarios or even more secure policy subsystem and technocracy relationships where stability, recognition and legitimacy define the agency role. This article articulates the conditions under which agencies deviate from the principal's goals (i.e. shirking) but also the conditions where those goals are transformed (learning processes).

Learning approaches and constraints

This special issue's introductory article presents the main learning approaches used here: 'lesson drawing', 'social learning' and 'organizational learning' (see also Bennett and Howlett 1992). 'Lesson drawing' articulates how programmes change by learning about new instruments. This distinction focuses on what is being learnt. This involves a more instrumental form of policy learning where actors and organizations seek to improve their performance over time – without changing fundamental values and perceptions. 'Social learning' encompasses the policy learning process where new worldviews are learnt, triggering radical shifts in policy paradigms. Differentiating these two concepts is difficult given their definitional ambiguity and interrelatedness. Both involve searching for and using information from outside the organization and both processes should impact on each other given the environment agencies' policy tasks.

Organizational learning is 'the development of structures and procedures that improve the problem-solving capacity of an organization and make it better prepared for the future' (Olsen and Peters; cited in Common 2004: 37). It is useful to differentiate between this focus on how organizations learn and adapt in their organizational setting and the concepts of social learning and lesson drawing which focus on the organization's policy output. The distinction indicates an important yet overlooked learning dimension: how do actors adjust their political strategy? Table 1 outlines some of the possibilities for agency learning and coalition-building. The table examines agency behaviour in terms of how it seeks to manipulate innovation and the political arena to influence its principal–agent relationship.

Situation A suggests that the agency is entrenched in a stable political relationship that its officials either desire or are forced to maintain. This could take the form of: an agent with certain information advantages yet still controlled by principals; or a policy community/triangle where there is a policy goal consensus, and perhaps even relatively equivalent levels of principal–agent knowledge. Learning and change are still possible in this scenario (e.g. incremental adaptation or lesson drawing that does not modify the organizational strategy and worldview), but they are less important and unlikely to transform the agency, the principals or the mutual relationship. The agency may shirk at the margins by learning new organizational strategies or developing new policy instruments that escape the principals' control mechanisms. Both the principal–agent and the Moe approaches expect this scenario to dominate future agency performance.

Situation B relates a similar pattern, although incremental adjustments to political strategy are more likely. This scenario occurs in changing political circumstances when power is shifting (e.g. changes in government) or the actor coalitions are more fluid. Organizational learning is possible, but again is unlikely to be transformational in the way the agency, or its principal–agent relationship, operates. Changes in tactics and alliances that do not reflect substantive policy learning processes are most likely, and shirking is possible.

Situation C involves substantial coalition innovation through endogenous processes although external pressures may also figure. All three forms of learning outlined above may factor in improving agency performance and coping strategies; this may cause shirking from aims set by the principal.

The key difference between this and Situation D is that Situation D encapsulates the process where the learning dynamics (potentially all three types) are harnessed by entrepreneurship. The agency seeks a wider actor coalition to embrace this knowledge and embed it into its own rules and behavioural

Table 1 Learning strategies

Dimensions of agency activity	Maintain/Safeguard arena	Expand political arena
Innovation is stable	(A) Policy subsystem (iron triangle–policy community); or classic principal–agent	(B) Political engagement and advocacy coalition building on entrenched ideas
Innovation is pushed	(C) Internal coalitional and organizational learning	(D) Expansive advocacy coalition – entrepreneurship

norms. It is this political and entrepreneurial act of taking the learning outcome, and using it to inform and perhaps transform the wider principal–agent relationship that goes beyond principal–agent conceptions. The act of learning successful entrepreneurial skills in a particular context is likely to constitute organizational learning.

COMPARING ENVIRONMENTAL AGENCIES

The EEA origins

On 17 January 1989, the Commission President Jacques Delors mentioned the regional agency idea while addressing the European Parliament (EP). Several Members of the European Parliament (MEPs) had filed motions for creating an agency in 1987 and 1988 (EP 1987). Delors' speech, calling for the establishment of a precursor to a pan-European environment agency, gave the idea crucial momentum (Brown 1995). This partially reflected a growing awareness that the European Community (EC) environmental policy's continual expansion demanded an equivalent implementation focus.

The EC arena had already recognized the need for high quality environmental data to support policy formulation and monitoring. In 1985, CORINE (Co-ordinating Information on the Environment) began investigating data-gathering and co-ordinating member state environmental data (Bailey 1997: 148–9). Nevertheless, the lack of quality EC-level data troubled Commission officials who faced producer criticism that Commission environmental proposals lacked a sound scientific basis (Brown 1995). The 1988 Rhodes European Council Summit specifically requested better information on the state of the environment, empowering the Commission response (Schout 1999: 86).

Although all member states announced basic support for the concept, specific positions quickly diverged. The British government, preferring a data co-ordinator, warned against a new agency receiving regulatory and inspection powers that duplicated other agencies' work (Brown 1995). In contrast, the Green and Socialist MEPs wanted an agency with regulatory teeth. The Environment Commissioner, Ripa di Meana, and other agency supporters campaigned for autonomous status (Majone 1997). Although the EP lacked the co-decision power in the 1980s to block Council agreement, the EP Environment Committee pushed hard to give the EEA power to inspect and monitor member state compliance (Ladeur 1996).

While the top Commission leadership vocalized strong interest in the agency idea, others in Directorate-General (DG) Environment feared EEA duplication of its own work (House of Lords 1995: 9). Delors' proposal surprised many in DG Environment; this fear of a potential competing agent subsequently coloured relations (EEA interview, 2007; Schout 1999: 87).

On 21 June 1989, the Commission formally proposed the creation of the EEA and an information/surveillance network. The purpose was to co-ordinate the enactment of Community and national environmental policies, assess the impact of environmental actions, provide modelling and forecasting methodologies, and harmonize and store data (Commission of the EC 1989). The Environment Ministers agreed to establish the agency in principle on 19 September, but the proposal was weakened by member state representatives (particularly the British and Spanish). Ripa di Meana and others accepted this reality, arguing that any further EEA enhancement should be a future development (Brown 1995). This member state position, together with increasing recognition given to subsidiarity, gave a strong impetus to the network governance idea (Schout 1999). The EP only accepted this weakening of its initial vision with the provision of a review procedure. This procedure means that the Council must consult the EP before the review of EEA tasks (Bailey 1997).

The Council negotiations on the agency proposal on 28 November reached many key decisions. The Council was split over the agency's membership: the UK, Denmark, Germany, Italy and the Netherlands favoured allowing non-EC states to join; Belgium, Luxembourg, Portugal and Spain opposed this (Brown 1995). The Council debated extensively the decision-making process (unanimity versus qualified majority voting) for locating elements of the EEA network and for deciding the EEA multi-annual programme. Finally, the agency location proved problematic: each member country, except Luxembourg, wished to be host (Majone 1997). The Council deferred this last debate to achieve an agreement.

A Council Regulation established the EEA and 'a European environment information and observation network' (EIONET) on 7 May 1990, without locating the agency operations (Council of the EC 1990: 2). The Regulation set the EEA the objective of providing the EC with 'objective, reliable and comparable information at European level enabling them to take requisite measures to protect the environment, to assess the results of such measures and to ensure that the public is properly informed about the state of the environment'. The Regulation granted the agency legal autonomy but also required it to maintain close links with Community institutions and member states (Council of the EC 1990: 3).

Regulation Article 3 emphasized that the agency's activities should 'avoid duplicating the existing activities of other institutions and bodies'. This was problematic because EC institutions, most notably the Statistical Office of the European Communities (EUROSTAT), already gathered environmental information (House of Lords 1995). Article 20 stipulated that the Council review the situation after two years, in consultation with the EP, and decide whether to extend the EEA's tasks.

The Council created an agency charged with providing information and co-ordinating this information through the means of networks (Vos 2003: 119–20). This differentiated it from the older EC agencies that lacked the scope for network creation; e.g. the European Centre for the Development of Vocational Training. The EEA represented the embodiment of 'network governance', where more decentralized networks replace the 'top-down' mechanisms of governing society associated with the state.

In the EEA's creation, one set of principals, the member states, dominated several key decisions. At one level the EEA is located in a classic principal–agent role with a very constrained role in co-ordinating information (gathered by others) and a network (Ladeur 1996). Nevertheless, the differing principals' negotiating positions are reflected in some of the original Regulation's ambiguities. The Regulation is unclear about whether the agency can directly influence policy formulation (Majone 1997). Ambiguity surrounds the EEA's relationship with the Commission. The EEA management board's composition (including EP, Commission and member state representatives) also embedded the presence of the various principals who disagreed over the agency's scope.

Moe's approach better explains some of the Regulation's tensions than a strict principal–agent approach. The EEA had a long list of tasks, but the Commission and some member states particularly underscored the information-gathering. The EP wanted the EEA to monitor implementation while certain member states hoped the EEA could steer EC policy through informational devices (Schout 1999: 90). Moe's notion of a clash of interests also resonates with the three-year struggle over the EEA's location (Carvel 1993). The decision became linked to the location of the other newly formed EC institutions and the EP's continued presence in Strasbourg (European Parliament 1990: 7–8). When the Strasbourg site was confirmed and the number of new institutions reached a sufficiently high level for a horse trade, the Danes, keen on the environment agency's symbolic value, secured the EEA.

The EA origins

In his first speech on the environment as Prime Minister on 8 July 1991, John Major announced his government's desire for a combined environmental agency (Carter and Lowe 1995: 38–9). This proposal was not self-evident. The Conservative government's White Paper had only recently rejected this alternative, enabling the institutions under consideration – Her Majesty's Inspectorate of Pollution (HMIP), the National Rivers Authority (NRA) and the Waste Regulation Authorities (WRAs) – to establish themselves more firmly (United Kingdom 1990). Moreover, the proposal clashed with the UK environmental tradition of fragmented, decentralized and informal regulatory administration and behaviour (Carter and Lowe 1995). The agencies involved in environmental regulation and management were quite disparate (the EA was created out of 86 predecessor organizations – see Bell and Gray 2002: 90). The relatively newly formed and small HMIP was composed of various inspectorates and had a new statutory role of taking a cross-media, integrated environmental approach. The 1989 Water Act united the ten regional water authorities of England and Wales into the enormous NRA. The WRAs were part of the local authorities, tasked with the role of waste treatment, storage and disposal (Department of the Environment 1991).

Although Major's announcement involved various electoral considerations, it chimed with social learning shifts occurring in the policy arena. There was an increasing learning process recognizing that the absence of a unified administration was leading to the regulation of emissions in one medium simply displacing pollution into another medium. The Royal Commission on Environmental Pollution and other actors pushed the integrated pollution control concept, which emphasized the need for rationalizing administrative structures (Carter and Lowe 1995: 41–3). The creation of HMIP and the NRA already reflected this, but many sought further steps.

European environmental regulation was also shifting UK environmental structures (interview with national expert, 2006). The more informal, piecemeal UK environmental approach had to confront the detailed EC regulatory stipulations (Haigh 1986). Although the various UK agencies, such as the NRA, had developed European divisions and officers, these sections were enmeshed in increasing detail and lacked a strategic perspective on European developments (Ward *et al.* 1995: 48–9). This reactive mode meant that the agencies seldom had direct involvement in the various EU specialist committees framing and generating new EC policy. Commission officials often perceived these UK agencies as having a marginal role while Whitehall departments controlled Brussels access.

Furthermore, European actors had difficulty in discerning the specific agency roles in the unfamiliar, complex UK system. Agencies such as the NRA lacked an explicitly defined relationship to the EU policy structure; their uniqueness in the European context rendered it difficult to form relationships with European networks (Ward *et al.* 1995: 49–51).

Although most actors expressed superficial support for Major's proposal, within Whitehall, the Department of the Environment (DoE) and the Ministry of Agriculture, Fisheries and Food (MAFF) contested policy control. At stake was ministerial control over parts of the river authority functions when the NRA lost some of these functions in its agency transfer (Carter and Lowe 1995: 38–47). Consequently, the government set up a consultation process until January 1992.

Circulated in 1991, the consultation paper offered four options: (1) an agency that absorbed HMIP responsibilities and local authority control over waste regulation but left the separate NRA's water authority; (2) an umbrella body that co-ordinated the separate NRA and HMIP activities; (3) an agency combining HMIP, NRA and WRAs; and (4) an agency combining the three bodies but leaving a partial NRA managing river, water and fisheries (Department of the Environment 1991).

The Confederation of Business Industry wanted a unified agency centred on the HMIP, with which it had excellent professional relations. Water amenity/industry and rural interests backed a strong NRA. Environmental non-governmental organizations supported a unified agency but worried that amalgamation would damage the strong statutory authority located within the NRA. The departmental row within Whitehall continued and even extended to disputes concerning overall responsibilities for coastal protection (Carter and Lowe 1995: 48–9).

The Conservative government chose the third solution. The 1995 Environment Act established the EA, an agency covering England and Wales, but not Scotland (United Kingdom 1995). The agency's principal aim was protecting and enhancing the environment, taken as a whole, thus contributing to the global goal of sustainable development (EA, undated). Although sponsored by one department (the DoE), the EA had links to the Welsh Office and to MAFF. Government grants provided 30 per cent of the agency funding, while environmental charges would finance the remainder. The agency's work fell into two categories: (1) environmental protection including the regulating of controlled waste management, protecting and improving the quality of various bodies of water and groundwater, regulating major industrial processes; and (2) water management concerning water resource, flood defence, fisheries, recreation, conservation and navigation (United Kingdom 1995: section 6; EA, undated). Underlying these aims was a considerable debate over how to incorporate officials from the diverse government bodies (McMahon 2006: 146). There was a fundamental tension in the specific principles that the bodies wanted incorporated into the new agency. The organizational amalgamation reflected the desire to retain the strengths of the three core bodies while also pleasing their separate constituencies. However, this effort devised a rather incoherent administrative structure reflecting these concerns and creating tensions within the new organization. Moe's framework is persuasive in this history.

The officials in each of the bodies hoped that the EA would reflect the key organizational principles of their own institution. The NRA, the largest of the three bodies in terms of staffing and budget, wanted the EA organization to follow 'natural environmental boundaries and particularly river basins' (McMahon 2006: 147–74). HMIP officials feared that such an approach would create a larger NRA, with HMIP losing their professional philosophy and their close professional links to business. The WRAs wanted an organization based on local authority boundaries. The eventual outcome reflected the organization of the biggest EA segment – the NRA.

Another critical issue focused on whether the organization should reflect functional media divisions or a set of cross-cutting and functionally integrated themes. This suggested the idea of multi-skilled teams that HMIP, with its integrated pollution control outlook, found the best fit.

The ensuing agency had a small head office, regional managers who set regional strategies and area officials who resolved local issues (EA interviews, 2007). The agency, in incorporating a more integrated approach to regulatory tasks, also added a matrix structure organized around nine overarching themes; it required regional and area actors to work across the themes. The underlying idea was to inculcate at the more local level different officials with different functional expertise and skills working together as a multi-skilled team. What resulted was an organizational system that, especially below the national level, posed its staff with unfamiliar rules and norms. Consequently, the staff felt that the agency had made inadequate allowance for their adjustment to the new complex organization (McMahon 2006: 147–74).

The EEA evolution

Following the adoption of Regulation 1210/90, a DG Environment task force started the EEA groundwork. The first stage of the EEA development occurred from 1990 to 1995, focusing on baseline information and assessments on individual environmental themes (IEEP and EIPA 2003: 26; House of Lords 1995). This preliminary effort involved further development of the CORINE data inventories and building relationships with other institutions. The latter usually took the form of protocols/MoUs (Memorandums of Understanding – see House of Lords 1995). With the Commission task force disbanding in 1994, a small agency staff of six began a recruiting process that expanded the agency to 55 staff with a budget of 18.6 million European currency units (ECUs) by 1999 (Caspersen 1999: 72; House of Lords 1995). In order to achieve its three basic aims of networking, monitoring and reporting, the EEA followed a five-year Multi-annual Work Programme. The essential EEA organization involved a director's office, an administrative department, three operational departments, a management board and a scientific committee. Given the agency's small size and the Regulation's stipulations, the EEA necessarily embraced becoming a 'new kind of "networking bureaucracy"'(Caspersen 1999: 72).

Given the explicit mandate to build a network system using an extant structure, the EEA had to engage with national institutions. Within the EIONET network there were nine European Topic Centres (ETCs), which are groupings of specialist research organizations (EEA, undated). Perhaps even more important were the National Focal Points (institutions charged with assisting the EEA in preparing and implementing the work programme and EIONET's development). Regulation Article 14 specifically instructs the EEA to co-operate actively (without duplicating effort) with other international organizations, specifically mentioning bodies such as the United Nations and its specialized agencies (Council of the EC 1990). The Regulation required the EEA to have a global networking scope.

The original Regulation foreordained the first EEA change: namely, a Commission report to review the agency's performance after two years, with proposals concerning additional tasks, for the Council's consideration (Council of the EC 1999: 1). Postponed for two years, the Regulation revision process started in 1997. It had the potential to develop organizational learning and push the EEA in two contrasting directions: (a) a mechanism for expanding EEA powers, as some actors intended the original compromise; or (b) a monitoring tool for the principals concerning performance and the constraint of those tasks. Without adequate support of clients/principals, the review could become negative, leading to constraints or even reduced powers.

The resulting Regulation 933/1999 did not dramatically change the EEA's path but added important nuances. The revised Article 2 changed the aims 'to provide the Community and the Member States with the objective information necessary for framing and implementing sound and effective environmental policies' (Council of the EC 1999: 2). This gave scope to the understanding that the EEA was not merely a collector of databases but had an explicit policy function. The Regulation specified that the agency utilize the data generated by EUROSTAT and the national statistical offices, underlining the EEA's position as merely one collector of environmental data. This revised Regulation prompted the agency to become more focused on reforming (i.e. streamlining and systematizing) information systems and on sectoral integration and prospective analysis (IEEP and EIPA 2003: 26). It also required internal reviews of the agency's performance and efficiency; it further mandated the submission of a 2003 report to the principals (the Commission, Council and EP), assessing the agency's progress regarding the 'Community's overall policy on the environment' (Article 20, Council of the EC 1999: 2).

The consultants, Arthur Andersen, conducted the 1994–2000 evaluation of performance and efficiency, importantly affirming the need for the agency and EIONET. The evaluation praised the network for linking the agency to capacity-building at the national level (IEEP and EIPA 2003: 26–7). It argued that the agency's work needed to fit more closely with the principal clients' needs, but that it could not serve all users and policy areas given extremely limited resources. Acting as a monitor for the principal–agent linkage, the review argued that the EEA's role needed to shift from supplying stand-alone products (such as reports) to providing services to the policy-making actors. Such a recommendation could encompass a strong element of task expansion to include influencing the policy process. The 2003 review (IEEP and EIPA 2003) also led to an explicit Council statement enshrining the EEA role as serving the entire EU as an independent body (EEA interview, 2007; Council of the EC 2003).

Another potential controlling device for the principals was the EEA management board, which directly incorporates the various principals (member state representatives, Commission officials and EP appointees). While the board must approve the EEA work programme and various organizational/staffing decisions, this is more a negative form of control rather than the ability to manage the EEA's direction. Furthermore, the board's increasing size (with enlargement) exacerbates these limits. The board acts as information conduit and network for the EEA and its principals.

The core principal–agent relationships are evolving. The relationship with DG Environment, the key interlocutor between the Commission and the EEA, has ambiguities given the Commission's role as guardian of the treaties and the location of the EEA budget within the DG Environment budget. The DG has special control over it and can make proposals. This has nurtured a perception among some DG officials that the EEA takes its money and should do its bidding (EEA interview, 2007; IEEP and EIPA 2003: 62–3). A 1990s effort of the EEA leadership to enlist the EP as a counterweight principal to the Commission created further difficulties; it did not transform the generally tepid MEP interest (EP official interview, 2007). Since 2000, however, both the Commission and the EEA have built a more collaborative relationship despite some continued differences of opinion about the EEA role in policy implementation and effectiveness (IEEP and EIPA 2003: 42–3). This partly reflects a politically more discrete and sensitive EEA approach and relationship to the DG, compared to relations between senior management in the 1990s (EEA and EP official interviews, 2007; IEEP and EIPA 2003: 60–2). Regular interaction at both the top and lower management levels has aided mutual communication and understanding (EEA interviews 2007).

This suggests substantial agency organizational learning over time about discerning the boundaries of its roles (EEA interview, 2007). A key example was the EEA commitment to the Environment Data Centre; the high-level Commission leadership generated this idea to share database management between the EEA, DG Environment, EUROSTAT and the Joint Research Centre. The EEA conducted an internal reorganization to solidify its co-operation (EEA 2006: 50). One core internal EEA change has involved restructuring its teams and mid-level management and an increased focus on technical and management training (EEA interview, 2007). The 2001–04 restructuring increased mid-level management authority to supervise project managers and to provide more focused groups for studying issues, as well as data integration across policy sectors and environmental themes (EEA 2004: 26–8). This move partly signalled to the principals the EEA commitment to fundamental aims-centred data collection and interaction with the Commission, EUROSTAT and other institutions. The Commission's thinking also evolved. Its 2003 review acknowledges the importance of the EEA's role and accepts a potential extension of EEA support activities 'along the entire range of stages of the policy cycle' (Commission of the EC 2003: 10; EEA interview, 2007).

The EEA has also gradually developed stronger links to the Council and like-minded member states (IEEP and EIPA 2003: 42). The EEA has undertaken various collaborative efforts, including the development of conferences and the provision of background notes. The EP Environment Committee perceives itself as a client/principal and has asked the agency for numerous *ad hoc* reports. The Committee emphasized the need for background material on Commission legislative proposals and related member state activity. This request was partly a conscious EP effort to boost EEA scope to conduct discrete, limited policy analysis. MoUs between the EEA and EP concretized this effort (EP official interview, 2007).

The policy role has been integral in the EEA evolution from report writing and maintaining information integrity. In the 1990s, the Directors General of DG Environment viewed themselves as the chief client and actor responsible for policy; the EEA's main focus should be data collection. The 1998 and 2000 budget discussions triggered a heavy DG push for the EEA to downgrade lower priority tasks (IEEP and EIPA 2003: 38–40, 61–2). Nevertheless, the EEA actors understand that data-gathering and the provision of environmental information are ambiguous and not a neutral activity. Even mere data-organizing raises issues of policy problem perception and how policy works (EEA interviews, 2007).

Changing EU policy demands have supported this organizational and instrumental learning (IEEP and EIPA 2003: 28–9). Thus, the Cardiff Process and the Sixth Action Programme generated particular policy requests (by the clients/principals) that the agency could respond to with specific information. Since 1998, the EEA has worked with the Commission and the Council Presidency in actual policy development in such areas as the greenhouse gas monitoring mechanism. EEA staff have made presentations to the informal Environment Councils (IEEP and EIPA 2003: 32).

The EEA has exploited its network agency role to build closer ties with actors both inside and outside the EU process. The EEA management have stressed the importance of staff networking, which sometimes challenges EEA officials from highly technical backgrounds. The EEA officials carefully follow the Regulation, which has enough ambiguity to allow limited task expansion (EEA interviews, 2007). For the EIONET to function properly, the EEA must interact with member state officials, scientific experts, civil society stakeholders and the EU institutions.

EEA officials observe the regulatory requirement to engage with international organizations without duplicating effort. They engage with third countries and international institutions in order to showcase policy knowledge and networking and data-collection ideas, based on EU experience (EEA interviews, 2007).

Although the EEA has embedded itself in an extensive policy network and has moved towards policy assessment, this ongoing process can still meet resistance from various quarters. Accordingly, EEA officials focus on discrete and restricted aims. Nevertheless, public criticism can be swift. The EEA made two initial efforts to assess the policy effectiveness of directives (reports on packaging waste implementation and on urban waste water treatment). The waste report encountered substantial industry criticism (consultant interview, 2007). The EEA's careful response to this criticism fits with its broader organizational approach: to remain careful about the data, its analysis and the resulting claims (*ENDS* 2005a; 2005b).

The EA evolution

Since its 1996 creation/amalgamation, much of EA learning has been internal (Situation C). The EA involved a complex new structure and new features (e.g. matrix structures). Many members of staff from HMIP and the WRAs perceived the new organization as essentially a NRA 'takeover', forcing a considerable management adjustment on their part (McMahon 2006: 156–7). The 1996–98 transition also saw a lack of management consensus about agency tasks and processes. The communication and co-ordination problems and newness generated a substantial period of low morale (EA interview 2007; House of Commons Select Committee on Environment 2000). Many EA staff complained that the move had destroyed their sense of mission (EA interviews, 2007).

One particular EA challenge was to overcome this view and build organizational cohesion. Another complexity involved the principals that the EA answers to. The EA principals include the government, particularly the Department for Environment, Food and Rural Affairs (DEFRA) in London, and the relevant House of Commons and Welsh Assembly bodies.

From 2002 to 2009, the EA has undergone considerable changes. People have moved around and out of the EA; over time the tensions have eased if not completely disappeared (EA interviews, 2007). The head office sets agency policy and defines how localities interpret legislation, but the regions conduct the direct regulation. EA management restructured the headquarters into three areas: the policy-setting unit, the unit translating policy into detailed regional instructions, and the science department. The reorganization's focus was to ensure that a consistent policy and set of instructions trigger a uniform decision-making process at the regional level (EA interview, 2007; House of Commons Environment Committee 2006: 16–17). Simultaneously facing significant budget constraints and concerns about agency priorities, the EA management changed the focus of its priorities for the scientific team several times, abolishing national centres and altering the balance between priorities. This pressure on budgetary resources reflects a larger policy pressure on the agency. In 2007, the agency had to implement a 5 per cent government efficiency savings target and a short-term severe DEFRA spending cut to meet an agriculture overspend (EA, consultant interviews, 2007).

National pressures are not solely budgetary: the UK government has set a premium on quantifiable targets to demonstrate agency efficiency. The last two years have witnessed the agency considering how to make long-term cuts in various areas. However, some areas, for example, increased flood defences (arguably reflecting a new kind of policy problem), are ring-fenced but also an enormous drain on agency resources and effort (EA official, consultant interviews, 2007). External constraints such as the 2007 flooding and the DEFRA budgetary crisis have disrupted EA planning.

The EA displays evidence of an instrumental learning with social learning elements: one example is the major rethink of how the agency regulates industry. This is most concretely demonstrated by the modernizing regulation initiative, which existed within the agency even before becoming a Blair government priority. This is partly recognition that the management of regulation must be done to maximize efficiency, given the kind of constant resource constraints mentioned above (DEFRA 2003: 12–16; House of Commons Environment Committee 2006: 13–15).

There is some evidence of organizational learning, with the EA leadership and representatives working hard to shape both international and regional networking and thinking. EA Chairman John Harman gave considerable attention to the networks of the Heads of Environmental Protection Agencies; the EA was one of the network's primary leaders. The network discusses various issues and experiences, including how agency leaders conduct both political and policy strategy within their respective contexts (EEA actor interview 2007).

The EA has steered some of the network's stances, including the 2006 Prague meeting's emphasis on the positive impact of regulation. With DEFRA, the EA is also active in the Implementation and Enforcement of Environmental Law (IMPEL) network and EEA networking activities. The EA pushed the better regulation agenda heavily in these fora (EA interviews, 2007).

The EA's EU and international relations office undertakes a number of international networking projects. Multilateral and bilateral networking is a priority to extend the EA impact. One should avoid overstatement as the relatively small staff and budget must highlight national priorities (e.g. flooding; EA interview, 2007).

The recognition that the EA is a competent authority for implementing EU regulations necessitated agency involvement in discussions concerning new EU measures. However, the policy community recognized that EA involvement varied significantly, depending on the policy area, and generally was relatively reactive and less strategic before 2000 (consultant interview, 2007). Gradually, the Commission has learned to listen to the agency and recognize that it has a significant voice which is distinct from the government (consultant, EA interviews, 2007).

This separateness from the principal, the UK government, has been recognized internationally. The Commission finds the agency's evidence-based approach useful to its argumentation; the EA also pushed the better regulation agenda in EU discussions (EA interviews, 2007). The EA influenced the EU process which formulated, for example, the general structure and specific (e.g. groundwater) provisions of the Water Framework Directive (EA official interview, 2007). Similarly, the EA has promoted the UK emphasis on risk-based calculations in formulating environmental management, such as the Contaminated Land Directive (EA interview, 2007). Although the EA has an EU strategy and a Concordat of Understanding to undertake various roles at the EU level, DEFRA, which is both a principal and a competing agent in these circumstances, prescribes EA policy engagement with the Commission (EA interview, 2007; House of Commons Environment Committee 2006: 29). DEFRA is protective of its policy-making and EU representative role; it takes agency people to support its Council negotiations, but the agency would not solely represent the UK. Similarly, DEFRA prevents the EA from being the main interlocutor in the EEA network. Finally, the EA must follow the ministerial/principal line (EA interviews, 2007).

CONCLUSIONS

A comparison of these two agencies must always acknowledge their fundamental differences. The EEA is an information and network agency, while the EA has strong regulatory powers. Ignoring CORINE, the EEA started from scratch; the EA amalgamated with the NRA and other bodies within the UK system.

Nevertheless, there are interesting similarities. Both agencies started as political ideas for limited organizations that were rendered more complicated during negotiations by the widely disparate decisional actors' interests; both histories conform strongly to Moe's depiction of the structural choices and negotiations that occur at the start of an agency's history. This theoretical explanation dominates the findings as well as the individual histories, posing challenges for the agencies to overcome. The dynamics that these initial decisions create, accord substantially with the path-dependent expectations of the historical institutionalist approach. For example, the EEA has scrupulously followed the dictates of its founding regulation.

The evolving histories make a substantial if secondary case for learning concepts. This may also reflect the nature of environmental governance where there is some convergence in an isomorphic sense towards information and informal/formal networking; such processes occur in other significant agencies, including the United States Environment Protection Agency (Hoornbeek 2000). Political and budgetary constraints may also be forcing agencies down particular paths.

There is strongest evidence for organizational learning and lesson drawing as expected in Situation C. Both agencies underwent substantial management and organizational changes that reflect agency adjustment to internal developments and external pressures. Simultaneously, both agencies have invested heavily in networking and building relationships with the principals that require the heaviest engagement. The EEA has advanced further in this task expansion – partly because it had the greater distance to travel: its growing presence in policy analysis compares starkly with the EA's large, inherited regulatory responsibility. The latter has sought to build a reputation at the EU level. Inherent in this organizational learning was an increased appreciation of the role of networks and information, indicating an increased understanding of how to use instruments to advance organizational aims (both organizational learning and lesson drawing). Both agencies seem involved in social learning, but a definitive statement needs systematic research across all policy areas. The example of the EA pushing hard for new understanding of regulations, necessitating some rethinking of policy values and principles, is suggestive. It is arguable that the strongest social learning was embedded in the creation of both agencies, recognizing the different implementation problems in the EC and UK systems.

The question of whether or not the agency–principal relationships reflect the principal–agent model requires further systematic study across policy areas. In the historical overviews, key principals have monitored and controlled agency behaviour. The EEA's history highlights periodic EEA reviews, the management board, and the founding regulation. DEFRA controlled the policy decisions, the EA budget and EU access. Both agencies have shown a concerted effort to improve their internal organization but also to reach out to their specific principals and other actors through networking (organizational learning). This suggests that some expansive coalition-building is altering relations. These changes are closer to notions of shirking than actual transformation of the principal–agent relations in both cases.

One dynamic that gives scope to both shirking and the potential for transformation is the reality of multiple principals *and* multiple agents. Both agencies have to negotiate their relations with other competing agencies and principals carefully. In particular, where institutions are both the competing agent and the principal (i.e. DEFRA and the Commission), this creates a particularly difficult context for the agency to transform.

ACKNOWLEDGEMENTS

The author thanks the Leverhulme Trust and the British Academy for their support of this research project, and also Chad Damro, Michelle Egan, two anonymous policy officials and two anonymous referees for their comments.

REFERENCES

Bailey, P. (1997) 'The changing role of environmental agencies', *European Environmental Law Review*, May: 148–55.
Bell, D. and Gray, T. (2002) 'The ambiguous role of the Environment Agency in England and Wales', *Environment Politics* 11(3): 76–98.
Bennett, C. and Howlett, M. (1992) 'The lessons of learning: reconciling theories of policy learning and policy change', *Policy Sciences* 25(3): 275–94.
Brown, L. (1995) 'Advocacy coalitions and the founding of the European Environmental Agency', manuscript, University of Florida.
Carpenter, D. (2001) *The Forging of Bureaucratic Autonomy: Reputations, Networks, and Policy Innovation in Executive Agencies, 1862–1928*, Princeton, NJ: Princeton University.
Carter, N. and Lowe, P. (1995) 'The establishment of a cross-sector environment agency', in T. Gray (ed.), *UK Environmental Policy in the 1990s*, Basingstoke: Macmillan, pp. 38–56.
Carvel, J. (1993) 'EC financial centre goes to Frankfurt', *The Guardian*, 30 October.
Caspersen, O. (1999) 'The European Environment Agency', *Global Environmental Change* 9(1): 71–5.
Commission of the EC (1989) *Proposal for a Council Regulation (EECP) on the Establishment of the European Environment Agency and the European Environment Monitoring Information Network*, COM (89 303 Final).
Commission of the EC (2003) *Report from the Commission to the Council: Review of the European Environment Agency*, COM (2003 800 Final, 22/12).
Common, R. (2004) 'Organisational learning in a political environment: improving policy-making in UK Government', *Policy Studies* 25(1): 35–49.
Council of the EC (1990) 'Council Regulation (EEC) No. 1210/90 of 7 May 1990 on the Establishment of the European Environment Agency and the European Environment Information and Observation Network', *Official Journal of the European Communities L 120* 11(05): 1–6.
Council of the EC (1999) 'Council Regulation (EEC) No. 933/1999 of 29 April 1999 Amending Regulation (EEC) No. 1210/90', *Official Journal of the European Communities L 117* 05(05): 1–4.

Council of the EC (2003) 'Council Regulation (EC) No. 1641/2003 of 22 July 2003 Amending Regulation (EEC) No. 1210/90', *Official Journal of the European Communities L 245* 29(09): 1–3.
Department for Environment, Food and Rural Affairs (DEFRA) (2003) *Review of Legislation Affecting Integration Within the Environment Agency: Final Report*, London: DEFRA.
Department of the Environment (1991) *The Government's Proposals for a New, Independent Environment Agency*, London: Ministry of Agriculture, Fisheries and Food.
EA (Environment Agency) (undated). Memo.
EEA (European Environment Agency) (undated) *Eionet Connects*, Copenhagen: EEA.
EEA (2004) *Annual Report 2003*, Luxembourg: Office for Official Publications of the EC.
EEA (2006) *Annual Report 2005*, Luxembourg: Office for Official Publications of the EC.
Egan, M. (1998) 'Regulatory strategies, delegation and European market integration', *Journal of European Public Policy* 5(3): 485–506.
ENDS Environment Daily (2005a) 'EEA evaluates effectiveness of EU green laws', 7 October.
ENDS Environment Daily (2005b) 'Packaging chain challenges EEA over prevention', 19 December.
European Parliament (1987) *Motion for a Resolution Pursuant to Rule 63 by Richard Cottrell MEP on the Creation of a European Environmental Protection Agency*, B2-1549/87.
European Parliament (1990) *Report Drawn Up on Behalf of the Political Affairs Committee on the Seat of the European Environment Agency*, A3-117/90.
Haigh, N. (1986) 'Devolved responsibility and centralization: effects of EEC environmental policy', *Public Administration* 64(2): 197–207.
Hoornbeek, J. (2000) 'Information and environmental policy: a tale of two agencies', *Journal of Comparative Policy Analysis: Research and Practice* 2(2): 145–87.
House of Commons Environment, Food and Rural Affairs Committee (2006) *The Environment Agency*, Seventh Report of the Session 2005–2006, HC 780-1, London: Stationery Office.
House of Commons Select Committee on Environment, Transport and Regional Affairs (2000) *The Environment Agency*, Sixth Report of the Session 1999–2000, HC 34-1, London: HMSO.
House of Lords Select Committee on the European Communities (1995) *European Environment Agency*, Session 1994–1995, HL Paper 29, London: HMSO.
IEEP (Institute for European Environmental Policy) and EIPA (European Institute for Public Administration) (2003) *Evaluation of the European Environment Agency: An IEEP/EIPA Study*, Brussels and Maastricht: IEEP and EIPA.
Kassim, H. and Menon, A. (2003) 'The principal–agent approach and the study of the European Union: promise unfulfilled?', *Journal of European Public Policy* 10(1): 121–39.
Ladeur, K. (1996) *The New European Agencies: The European Environment Agency and Prospects for a European Network of Environmental Administrations*, Working Paper RSC 96/50, Florence: EUI.
Majone, G. (1997). 'The European Environmental Agency and the politics of structural choice'. Lecture, Summer Symposium on the Innovation of Environmental Policy, University of Bologna, 21–25 July.
McCubbins, M., Noll, R. and Weingast, B. (1987) 'Administrative procedures as instruments of political control', *Journal of Law, Economics, and Organization* 3(2): 243–77.
McMahon, R. (2006) *The Environmental Protection Agency: Structuring Motivation in a Green Bureaucracy*, Brighton: Sussex Academic Press.

Moe, T. (1984) 'The new economics of organization', *American Journal of Political Science* 28(4): 739–77.
Moe, T. (1989) 'The politics of bureaucratic structure', in J. Chubb and P. Peterson (eds), *Can the Government Govern?*, Washington, DC: Brookings Institution, pp. 267–329.
Schout, A. (1999) 'The European Environment Agency (EEA): heading towards maturity', in M. Everson, G. Majone, L. Metcalfe and A. Schout (eds), *The Role of Specialised Agencies in Decentralising EU Governance*, Brussels: CEC, pp. 81–174.
Streeck, W. and Thelen, K. (2005) 'Introduction: Institutional change in advanced political economies', in W. Streeck and K. Thelen (eds), *Beyond Continuity: Institutional Change in Advanced Political Economies*, Oxford: Oxford University Press, pp. 1–39.
United Kingdom (1990) *This Common Inheritance: Britain's Environmental Strategy*, London: HMSO.
United Kingdom (1995) *The Environment Act 1995*, HMSO: http://www.hmso.gov.uk/acts/acts1995/Ukpga_19950025_en_1.htm
Vos, E. (2003) 'Agencies and the European Union', in T. Zwart and L. Verhey (eds), *Agencies in European and Comparative Law*, Oxford: Intersentia, pp. 113–47.
Ward, S., Talbot, H. and Lowe, P. (1995) 'Environmental agencies and Europe: a case of missed opportunities?', *ECOS* 16(2): 47–53.
Waterman, R., Rouse, A. and Wright, R. (2004) *Bureaucrats, Politics, and the Environment*, Pittsburgh: University of Pittsburgh.
Williams, G. (2005) 'Monomaniacs or schizophrenics? Responsible governance and the EU's independent agencies', *Political Studies* 53(1): 82–99.

Governance and learning in the post-Maastricht era?

Michelle Egan

Over the past several decades, there has been an increased focus on new approaches to improving European governance. While we have seen a surge of academic research on conceptualizing such transformations based on concepts of markets, networks and hierarchy, or reflexive, participatory or deliberative modes of governance, the integrating of ideas within different contexts, and understanding the importance of policy learning, can add value to current debates surrounding the political and administrative changes in Europe. Specifically, why do some countries adopt ideas and policies from other domestic contexts? Under what conditions does the need for solutions to political and societal problems lead to the transfer of policy ideas designed for another political system? How does the diffusion of ideas to different countries or regions take place? The concept of policy learning, an idea that has emerged within comparative public policy, has generated significant debate about its empirical and normative assumptions in explaining policy innovation and change, policy diffusion and convergence, and policy failure (May 1992; Bennett and Howlett 1992; Hall 1993; Radaelli 2000; Weyland 2006; Evans 2006).

The concept of policy learning is important in the context of globalization as the diffusion of norms, rules and institutions has undermined national autonomy, and provided for cross-national networks of collaboration, learning and cooperation at the international level. Within Europe, different member states have often emulated, borrowed, copied or imitated their neighbors.

Privatization has spread rapidly across Europe, with many nationalized banks, utilities and transportation networks shifting away from state ownership. Yet the mechanisms of privatization vary, with different levels of divestiture and ownership, models of corporate governance, and mechanisms of regulatory oversight (Schamis 2001). Such diffusion of liberal economic ideas has not, however, led to convergence of outcomes as different varieties of capitalism demonstrate the resilience of national economic models (Hall and Soskice 2001; Hancke *et al.* 2007). Similarly, Sbragia shows that different models of federalism are the result of reviewing prior models and explicitly drawing lessons from foreign experience in order to map out different institutional configurations of territorial authority (Sbragia 1992). The same argument is made by Pastor who noted that the European model was viewed as having limited relevance to the North American experience of integration. Yet the lack of deep integration has generated significant externalities that could be addressed by adopting common policies such as regional development, customs union and coordinated macroeconomic policies (Pastor 2001). The design of institutions, the adoption of policies, and the diffusion of goals and ideas lead to the question: what are the causal mechanisms to explain why policy learning takes place in some contexts but not others? Despite the difficulties in comparing the significance of policy learning in relation to other factors in terms of causality, this special issue is designed to map out how new tools and instruments of governance can evolve in response to changes in different policy environments.

Each paper in this issue is looking at reasons for reform and change which lie in different endogenous and exogenous incentives created by existing institutions and policies. Various theoretical frameworks of learning provide different explanations in the European context, drawing on models of uncertainty, advocacy coalitions, institutional isomorphism, organizational and network governance to explain the nature and causes of learning in affecting policy outcomes. Yet explaining policy change has generated a diversity of terminology from notions of political learning developed by Heclo (1974), policy-oriented learning developed by Sabatier (1998), lesson-drawing analysed by Rose (1991), and social learning discussed by Hall (1993) that leads some critics to question the value of policy learning as an explanatory tool. Although the papers do not just describe instances of policy transfer – or learning – but the underlying coercive, mimetic and normative rationales, they often share an explanatory role with other plausible mechanisms for the diffusion of policies including the impact of policy styles (Richardson 1982; Vogel 1986), policy diffusion (Walker 1969) or policy succession on European policy-making (Peters and Hogwood 1982). This concluding summary seeks to assess the extent to which the papers in this volume can provide analytic leverage and historical narratives about policy change as there are several complementary, yet distinct, notions of policy learning found in the emerging literature in this area (see Bennett and Howlett 1992: Introduction). Not only does the literature emphasize different factors as fostering policy learning, they also differ substantially on the subject of learning, its object and its effects.

MODES OF LEARNING

The papers in this issue pick up four different types of learning – organizational, social, policy and instrumental – outlined in the introduction. They point to the formal organizational capacities that exist for learning within different policy areas, though some address the informal learning environment. All the papers point to a myriad of tools and instruments that have been tried, adopted or emulated for learning. These include market models that are based on exchange modes of governance, hierarchical models based on statutory rules and guidance, network models that are based on expert communities or issue networks, and normative models that are based on values, norms or prescriptive modes of governance. Zito's (2009) focus on environmental agencies emphasizes the importance of goal displacement and its effect on organizational learning. Farrell (2009) points to inherent power dynamics that strategically limit the promotion of European governance norms and ideas. Schout (2009) points to how the structural environment shapes bureaucratic incentives, and that organizational learning is affected by statutory objectives, market incentives, and hierarchical systems of governance. Radaelli (2009) evaluates whether regulatory impact assessment and better regulation have improved regulatory quality. Despite widespread emulation, and the potential for concentrated benefits, Radaelli illustrates the obstacles to learning within different national contexts. Marier (2009) highlights the importance of learning as an essential element of evaluation outcomes. He notes that the impact of different regulatory traditions and institutional design can affect organizational learning in contentious areas such as pension reform. Montpetit (2009) challenges the policy styles used to differentiate European and American policy environments, by arguing that the issue networks surrounding biotechnology do not produce different 'learning styles'. The often-cited classification of European governance as consensus, communicative and deliberative may also be applicable in the US. This suggests that Lowi's categorization that policy shapes politics may have some heuristic value in that regulatory, distributive, redistributive and constituent policies may produce different learning dynamics.

So what do these papers tell us about the dynamics of European policy? To make sense of learning perspectives in the context of Europeanization, it is possible to distinguish between top-down perspectives where changes result from various systemic pressures and bottom-up pressures that are the result of domestic innovation and ideas that have fostered spillover effects. The results are often contradictory and unintended, and such processes may be the result of formal exchanges, horizontal coordination, peer socialization or informal networks. Policy learning is both constitutive of the changes in production and technology, and the result of societal and environmental changes. It is the tool that alters traditional modes of governance by reducing transaction costs, mitigating negative externalities, enhancing efficiency, and fostering new norms and values. To different degrees all the papers indicate that the process of learning is affected by organizational resources, institutional structures and the dispersion of authority, the logic of membership and the logic of access, and whether the policy mandate is statutory, advisory or deliberative. They also highlight that the cognitive reasoning that takes place among actors is one key element that can shape agenda-setting, problem-solving, evaluation and implementation albeit not the only factor that explains policy processes and outcomes. More broadly, they demonstrate the mutual engagement across scholarly boundaries as international relations scholars with their emphasis on norm diffusion engage with public policy scholars with their emphasis on organizational learning and administrative reform.

In response to criticism about when and under what conditions policy learning occurs, there has been some effort in the special issue to differentiate the identification from the reasons why they occur (see James and Lodge 2003). Several papers also emphasize the interplay between learning and emulation, and learning and diffusion to highlight the positive spillover effects. Others note that learning does not necessarily improve policy performance, thus the 'contagion' effect may also lead to learning that produces negative effects or magnifies the problem. But the literature remains diffuse in terms of explaining policy dynamics, with considerable variety of terminology, as scholars have identified learning characteristics that may be attributed *to a variety of factors*. Many analyses often combine institutional and ideational accounts, and focus on the socio-economic, ideological and geographic proximity of jurisdictions that learn from each other. Yet we puzzle over how to discern when learning does not take place, and whether this is intentional or unintentional. In short, we need to be much more precise about what single cases can illustrate, why specific cases are compared, what else can explain patterns of change, equilibrium or failure. How can such dynamics of learning, diffusion, emulation and so forth create their own effects that may displace, compound or blur the original problem? How then can we differentiate dysfunctional learning from policy failure?

CONCLUSION

Studying policy learning in practice will give us more theoretical and analytic leverage in understanding how structures, processes and performances are affected by organizational, institutional and individual learning. Though endowments matter in explaining outcomes so do policies. But there has been little agreement in the literature about the role that policy learning may play in accounting for policy change or for continuation of the status quo. Policy learning may also result in what Bachrach and Baratz termed 'the politics of non-decision-making' (Bachrach and Baratz 1962). Just because policy change is not evident it does not mean that deliberation, learning and assessment did not take place. We can, however, tease out some important implications and suggestions for further research from this special issue.

Methodologically, we can draw on a variety of tools including aggregate statistical studies, participant observation, structured interviewing and official documentation. Our studies can yield important insights by choosing different sectoral policy areas, which may result in convergence, complementarity or divergence in actual outcomes. However, we might move beyond the typical areas of health, welfare and environmental policy, as several papers in this volume have done, and think about whether the provision of public, private or collective goods affects learning outcomes. As policy-making is increasingly being carried out by non-state actors, through self-regulation, public–private partnerships, private enforcement or contracting out, the role of market incentives in shaping learning outcomes deserves further consideration. Much of the research on policy learning focuses on political considerations and deliberations but this may obscure economic variables that affect the learning process. For this reason, exogenous shocks, economic recession, court decisions and litigation could lead to shifts in policy-making. Thus, the changing environment could foster unintended consequences that require different policy responses. Because of the growth of transnational networks, policy learning can take place in multiple venues (Slaughter 2004). Such dense cooperation and interaction can foster exchanges of ideas, technical expertise and information, as well as the promotion of norms and values. It can also lead to forum shopping with different institutional arenas offering different menu choices and options.

However, we also recognize the asymmetric nature of this process where conditionality, sanctions and other pressures that foster compliance and convergence towards specific international norms or standards mean that the diffusion of policy is less benign than appears. This is especially the case in the European Union (EU) where bilateral trade agreements, accession negotiations and development assistance promote the 'normative power' of Europe (Youngs 2008). Although market liberalization principles have been 'exported' by the EU in competition policy (Damro 2006), trade (Büthe and Mattli 2005), data privacy (Heisenberg 2005) and capital markets (Quaglia 2005), the success of such globalization of European norms depends on the institutional capacity and governance practices in the emulating states (Farrell 2009).

The EU, the domestic political context for member states, and the internal effects of the EU in shaping 'learning beyond borders' provide a wealth of comparative analysis in understanding the dynamics of policy learning. Specific policy ideas or values may occur via a 'transmission belt' but, as we see in the case of the diffusion of liberal economic policies, they may be in conflict with different domestic values and norms. Despite being the target of Europeanization, many Central and East European countries have, despite broadly liberal patterns, opted for differential economic strategies in terms of welfare and social protection, macroeconomic stability, industrial policy and protection (Bohle and Greskovits 2007). Thus policy-making is comprised of multiple actors who, for a variety of reasons, deliberately pursue policy options that may have intended or unintended consequences, and may in fact block policy learning, adaptation or change. Is learning the result of bounded rationality? Or is learning the product of systematic rational evaluation? The question is whether this policy is the result of specific circumstances that reflect the best interests of firms or states or whether it is the result of suboptimal policy choices that are shaped by limited room for maneuver, lack of information, collective action dilemmas or past policy commitments (see Weyland 2006). Such debates with their focus on efficiency have to some degree become increasingly salient due to the public management movement that has generated an emphasis on managerialism, market incentives and performance-based outcomes (for a diversity of perspectives and critiques, see Majone 1997; Pollitt 1990). Better regulation, risk assessment and tradable permits reflect such initiatives and debates within Europe (Schout 2009; Radaelli 2009).

We can also differentiate where learning takes place in the policy process. Several papers have alluded to different types of learning in terms of the policy cycle. Some policy learning may occur early on in terms of the content of specific policies or in terms of the underlying values and philosophies, whereas other policy learning may occur later in terms of policy implementation and evaluation of specific issues. Thus, the learning may be the result of 'learning by doing' or incremental learning, or it may be the result of framing problems and directing attention to particular solutions (Schön and Rein 1994). Often, as Majone notes, marshalling arguments about policy problems, learning from mistakes, and recognizing the power to persuade others are critical features of policy-making (Majone 1989). Such discursive learning differs from the learning that may come about in administering policy, which may require shifts in regulatory or administrative rule-making to accommodate specific domestic political contexts (Zito 2009). And finally, learning may be organizational learning whereby bureaucratic agencies may learn from observing other organizations, borrowing from other agencies, or in the case of enlargement 'twinning patterns' that fostered socialization and learning between Eastern and Western Europe. For this reason, it is important to conceptualize policy learning as part of the interactive process of policy-making.

This raises another challenge for studies of policy learning. Mapping policy learning requires observing and explaining processes of change over time (see also Radaelli 2009). Thus, policy learning may not only be the diffusion of practices and ideas across boundaries, it may also be from one time period to another. Early advocates of European integration often referred to the economic success of the United States as evidence of the advantages of a large integrated economy (Egan 2008). This then raises a number of explanatory factors that shape the nature, extent and impact of policy learning. The path-dependent nature of policy choices may constrain policy change, since the 'lock-in' effects generated by decision rules or institutional barriers in the European context may come into play in governance transformations (Scharpf 1984; Pierson 1996). The specific timing of proposals may be related to the electoral cycle, as opportunistic policy-makers choose macroeconomic policies likely to generate lower unemployment rates and boost income (Lohmann 1992). Or it could be related to the issue attention cycle where the salience of an issue may command different levels of attention at different times (Downs 1972).

And finally, when policy is implemented – when the costs and benefits of policies are felt – is important. Many policies have lag times that ensure that the costs of implementation allow firms to make strategic adjustment in investment decisions or allow lag times in terms of compliance with statutory obligations (i.e. a learning curve). This may have an impact on the kind of reflexive learning that takes place within organizations.

Scholars of policy learning can draw upon a wealth of literature from international relations, business management, public policy and comparative politics, as attention has been given to the role of ideas and deliberation, persuasion and argumentation, norms and discursive structures in shaping the European polity. While the various papers analyze the shift towards modernizing regulation, rationalizing diverse policy instruments, and promoting of public goods, the full implications of this transformation of governance have not led to the more normative question of what kind of legitimacy is required in such a post-Maastricht governance era. Empirically, European integration attempts to address coordination problems or reduce transaction costs. The language of competitiveness, impact assessment, growth and market-based alternatives have come together as the political manifestation of an approach to European governance that differs from classic public administration (Radaelli 2009). Yet scholars have focused on the theoretical implications of the transformation of governance, in terms of democratic theory, social legitimacy and public accountability. Predominant among this discussion of the legitimacy of the regulatory state has been the procedural legitimacy of Majone, and its subsequent criticism (Joerges 2002). Notwithstanding these debates, what can we learn in practice? What has been learnt through using such reflexive or deliberative versus procedural approaches?

Certainly there is a theoretical expansion of the policy analysis literature along both comparative and historical dimensions, and a greater connectivity to other bodies of scholarship including those of neofunctionalism, constructivism and governance is welcome. Yet as many of the papers suggest, there needs to be more normative concern about government performance and accountability; more acknowledgment of inherited responsibilities and their effects on policy choices, and more work on the impact of bureaucratic organization on performance.

We have in recent years shifted from government to governance in delivering policies with an explosion of theoretical interest in this area, yet we have few studies of how collaborative governance, public–private partnerships or hybrid regimes work in practice. The changing policy dynamics of these new forms of governance can be viewed in terms of relational/trust factors as well as principal–agent models. How these new organizational forms engage in learning, how effective they are in the delivery of services, whether the rules and norms come from a business or public sector environment remain understudied. This excellent group of papers engages in a broad conceptual use of learning, drawing on a rich tradition in public administration and organizational analysis principal–agent literature that has seeped into European studies. As scholars focus increasingly on organizational learning and collaboration in multi-level, multi-jurisdictional contexts, they will benefit from engaging the broader public administration and policy management scholarship in the American domestic context.

Understanding policy dynamics, of which policy learning is one component, made me think about the relevance of Bardach's *Getting Agencies to Work Together* for the European context. Cooperation, mutual trust and inter-agency collaboration are key factors for Bardach. Yet if he provides the organizational tools and framework for improved policy learning, the transformation of governance in Europe raises many of the same issues expressed in Behn's *Rethinking Democratic Accountability*. As government performance has focused increasingly on oversight and surveillance, efficiency and results, it ignores the significant distinction between management in the public and private sector. Clearly we should consider the importance of performance and accountability not just in procedural terms implied by laws, regulations and statutory obligations, but in terms of fairness and equity which involves fulfilling public expectations (see also Scharpf 1999). The 'market place for ideas' (Farrell, citing Hall 1993) is also affected by public discourse, and the current antipathy or skepticism about European integration suggests that we might also look at the constraints that public opinion imposes on framing ideas. Such a view perhaps indicates why it is important to look at the political impact of learning, and see learning not just simply as a *process* that involves cognitive perception by networks, agencies or organizations. As Stone notes, 'analysis is itself a creature of politics; it is strategically crafted argument, designed to create ambiguities and paradoxes and to resolve them in a particular direction' (Stone 1997: 8).

ACKNOWLEDGEMENTS

My thanks to Anthony Zito and Claudio Radaelli for excellent comments and suggestions.

REFERENCES

Bachrach, P. and Baratz, M. (1962) 'Two faces of power', *The American Political Science Review* 56(4): 947–52.

Bardach, E. (1998) *Getting Agencies to Work Together*, Washington, DC: Brookings Institution.

Behn, E. (2001) *Rethinking Democratic Accountability*, Washington, DC: Brookings Institution.

Bennett, C. and Howlett, M. (1992) 'The lessons of learning: reconciling theories of policy learning and policy change', *Policy Sciences* 25(3): 275–94.

Bohle, D. and Greskovits, B. (2007) 'Neoliberalism, embedded neoliberalism, and neocorporatism: towards transnational capitalism in Central-Eastern Europe', *West European Politics* 30(3): 443–66.

Büthe, T. and Mattli, W. (2005) 'Accountability in accounting? The politics of private rule-making in the public interest', *Governance* 18(3): 399–429.

Damro, C. (2006) 'Transatlantic competition policy: domestic and international sources of EU–US cooperation', *European Journal of International Relations* 12(2): 171–96.

Downs, A. (1972) 'Up and down with ecology: the issue attention cycle', *The Public Interest* 28: 38–50.

Egan, M. (2008) 'The emergence of the US internal market', in J. Pelkmans, D. Hanf and M. Chang (eds), *The EU Internal Market in Comparative Perspective*, Brussels: Peter Lang Publishers, pp. 249–80.

Evans, M. (2006) 'At the interface between theory and practice – policy transfer and lesson drawing', *Public Administration* 84(2): 479–89.

Farrell, M. (2009) 'EU policy towards other regions: policy learning in the external promotion of regional integration', *Journal of European Public Policy* 16(8): 1165–84.

Hall, P. (1993) 'Policy paradigms, social learning and the state', *Comparative Politics* 25: 275–96.

Hall, P. and Soskice, D. (eds) (2001) *Varieties of Capitalism: The Institutional Foundations of Comparative Advantage*, Oxford: Oxford University Press.

Hancké, B., Rhodes, M. and Thatcher, M. (2007) *Beyond Varieties of Capitalism: Conflict, Contradictions, and Complementarities in the European Economy*, Oxford: Oxford University Press.

Heclo, H. (1974) *Modern Social Politics in Britain and Sweden*, New Haven, CT: Yale University Press.

Heisenberg, D. (2005) *Negotiating Privacy: The European Union, The United States, and Personal Data Protection (Politics/Global Challenges in the Information Age)*, Boulder, CO: Lynne Reinner.

James, O. and Lodge, M. (2003) 'The limitations of "policy transfer" and "lesson drawing" for public policy research', *Political Studies Review* 1(2): 179–93.

Joerges, C. (2002). 'The law in the process of constitutionalizing Europe', Arena Conference on Democracy and European Governance, Oslo.

Lohmann, S. (1992) 'Optimal commitment in monetary policy: credibility versus flexibility', *American Economic Review* 82(1): 273–86.

Majone, G. (1989) *Evidence, Argument and Persuasion in the Policy Process*, Yale, CT: Yale University Press.

Majone, G. (1997) 'The new European agencies: regulation by information', *Journal of European Public Policy* 4(2): 262–75.

Marier, P. (2009) 'The power of institutionalized learning: the uses and practices of commissions to generate policy change', *Journal of European Public Policy* 16(8): 1204–23.

Montpetit, E. (2009) 'Governance and policy learning in the European Union: a comparison with North America', *Journal of European Public Policy* 16(8): 1185–1203.

May, P. (1992) 'Policy learning and failure', *Journal of Public Policy* 12(4): 331–54.

Pastor, R. (2001) *Toward a North American Community: Lessons from the Old World for the New*, Washington, DC: Institute for International Economics.

Peters, G. and Hogwood, B. (1982) 'The dynamics of policy change: policy succession', *Policy Sciences* 14: 225–45.
Pierson, P. (1996) 'The path to European integration: a historical institutionalist analysis', *Comparative Political Studies* 29(2): 123–63.
Pollitt, C. (1990) *Managerialism in the Public Services: The Anglo-American Perspective*, Oxford: Blackwell.
Quaglia, L. (2005). 'The politics of financial services regulation and supervision in the EU'. Paper presented at the EUSA Biennial Conference, Nashville.
Radaelli, C. (2000) 'Policy transfer in the European Union: institutional isomorphism as a source of legitimacy', *Governance* 13(1): 25–43.
Radaelli, C. (2009) 'Measuring policy learning: regulatory impact assessment in Europe', *Journal of European Public Policy* 16(8): 1145–64.
Richardson, J. (ed.) (1982) *Policy Styles in Western Europe*, London: Allen & Unwin.
Rose, R. (1991) 'What is lesson-drawing?', *Journal of Public Policy* 11(1): 3–30.
Sabatier, P. (1998) 'The advocacy coalition framework: revisions and relevance for Europe', *Journal of European Public Policy* 5(1): 98–130.
Sbragia, A. (1992) *Europolitics*, Washington, DC: Brookings Institution.
Schamis, H. (2001) *Reforming the State*, Ann Arbor, MI: University of Michigan Press.
Scharpf, F. (1984) 'Economic and institutional constraints of full-employment strategies. Sweden, Austria, and Western Germany, 1973–1982', in J. Goldthorpe (ed.), *Order and Conflict in Contemporary Capitalism*, Oxford: Clarendon Press, pp. 257–90.
Scharpf, F. (1991) *Governing Europe*, Oxford: Oxford University Press.
Schön, D. and Rein, M. (1994) *Frame Reflection: Toward the Resolution of Intractable Policy Controversies*, New York: Basic Books.
Schout, A. (2009) 'Organizational learning in the EU's multi-level governance system', *Journal of European Public Policy* 16(8): 1124–44.
Slaughter, A. (2004) *A New World Order*, Princeton, NJ: Princeton University Press.
Stone, D. (1997) *Policy Paradox: The Art of Political Decision Making*, New York: Norton.
Vogel, D. (1986) *National Styles of Regulation: Environmental Policy in Great Britain and United States*, Ithaca, NY: Cornell University Press.
Walker, J. (1969) 'The diffusion of innovations among the American states', *American Political Science Review* 63(3): 880–99.
Weyland, K. (2006) *Bounded Rationality and Policy Diffusion: Social Sector Reform in Latin America*, Princeton, NJ: Princeton University Press.
Youngs, R. (2008) 'Is European democracy promotion on the wane?', Working Document #292, Brussels: Centre for European Policy Studies.
Zito, A.R. (2009) 'European agencies as agents of governance and EU learning', *Journal of European Public Policy* 16(8): 1224–43.
Zito, A.R. and Schout, A. (2009) 'Learning theory reconsidered: EU integration theories and learning', *Journal of European Public Policy* 16(8): 1103–23.

Index

Page numbers in *Italics* represent tables.
Page numbers in **Bold** represent figures.

access: logic of 145
accession negotiations 146
accountability 148, 149
acid rain policy 10
acquis 11
acquis communautaire 68, 78
ACTAL 24, 34, 36, 38, 53-4; control agenda 55-6; sanctions 56
adaptation 7, 75, 76; Africa-EU relations 71-3
administration costs 36
administrative burden programme 36
adversarial political systems 96-7
advocacy coalition framework (ACF) 5, 10; Sabatier 84-5
Africa: co-operation learning 73; diffusion in 12; discontent of EPAs 78; policy learning or adaptation 71-3; regional grouping 63; regional integration 69
Africa, Caribbean and Pacific group: Cotonou Agreement 68
Africa-EU: co-operation learning 73; policy learning or adaptation 71-3

Africa-EU Strategy (Lisbon 2007) 72, 75
African Union 73
agency drift 50
agency theory 16
agri-food biotechnology 88; policy transfer 95
agriculture 67
aid: effectiveness of 72; programmes 68
air transport 11
alarm raiser: commissions 107, 109, 110, 116-17
Americas: regional grouping 63
Andean Community 69
arbitration 87, 97
Argyris, C. 4
Arthur Anderson Consulting 133
ASEAN 71
Ashby, Ross 4
Asia: and EU 69; regional grouping 63; regional integration 71
Asia-Europe meeting (ASEM) 68, 71
assessment system: problems of 30
Association of British Insurers 115
Association of Southeast Asian Nations (ASEAN) 69

Index

authority 145
autonomy 125
aviation safety 12

Bachrach, P. 145
bad learning 9
Balladur, E. 110
Banerjee, A.V. 46
Baratz, M. 145
Barcelona process 70
Bardach, E.: *Getting Agencies to Work Together* 149
Barroso: President José Manuel 32
Barroso Commission 57
behavioural change 3
behaviouralism 4
Behn, E.: *Rethinking Democratic Accountability* 149
belief systems 84; learning 76
beliefs 12; core 5; and learning 66-7
Bell, D. 129
benchmarking 11, 54
benefit-cost principles 49
Bennett, C. 6
best practice 11, 87
better regulation (BR) 24, 28-30; Netherlands 33-9; organizational learning 30-3; organizational learning in Netherlands 35
Better Regulation Executive (BRE) 51; control agenda 55-6
bias 46
biotechnology actor survey: conclusion 97-8; consensus formation 94; discussion 94-7; distribution of respondents 89; hypothesises 91; introduction 88-90; learning intensity 91-3; learning tests 90-1; policy transfer 93; results 91-4, *92*; sources of policy inspiration **93**; variables 91

Blair, Tony 112, 118, 136
bloc-to-bloc diplomacy 63
blocked learning 9
Bomberg, E. 9, 10
Boswell, C. 57
box-ticking 38
brain: designing 4
Brazil 69
British Pensions Commission 105, 112, 114, 115, 117, 118
Brown, Gordon 58
Brunei 71
budgetary pressures 136
Bulmer, S. 9, 11, 88, 95
burdens reduction plans 58-9
bureaucratic capacities 27
bureaucratization 32

Canada: BAS 88; consensus formation 94; democratizing regulatory procedures 87; genetics policy 96; Macdonald Commission 108; pension policy 107; policy transfer 93-4
capacities 23, 34
capital markets 146
capitalism 143
Cardiff Process 13, 135
Central America: fta 69
certification 72
challenging opinions 84
change: levels of 65-6; as rational process 6; resistance to 5; third order 76
Charpin, J.-M. 105, 115-16, 117
Checkel, Jeffrey 66
China 69, 71
civil servants 91
climate policies 70
Co-ordinating Information on the Environment (CORINE) 127, 132, 137

co-ordination costs 23
coalition building 138
coalition innovation 126
CoCo 37
coercion 12, 26, 45, 46; IA 49
cognition 4
cognitive psychology 6
cognitive reasoning 145
collaboration 143, 149
collaborative governance 148
college 32
colonialism 72
commissions: alarm raiser 107, 109, 110, 116-17; analysis 106; appeasement 106; avoiding blame 106; compromise 106; defining 104; delay tactics 106; educating the public 106; elections 107; environment 109; idea shaker 108, 109, 110, 115-16; incrementalism 108, 109, 110; independence 109; killing proposals 106; and learning 103; learning capacity 102; mandate 109; membership 108; organizational learning 105; partisan motives 106; pension reform 110-19; policy engineer 108, 109, 110; policy impact of 118-19; as policy makers 117-19; role and importance in policy process 104-6; status quo 107, 109-10, 115-17; theoretical propositions 107-9; viability 109; welfare state reform 107-9; why governments rely on them 104-6
Committee on Economic Security: Roosevelt 108
Committee of Permanent Representatives (COREPER) 37
Common Foreign and Security Policy (CFSP) 63, 77

Common, R. 23
communication 5, 26; inter-subjective 4
communication-based instruments 13
Community method 26
competency trap 9, 105
competing advocacy coalitions 85
competition 26, 67, 72
competition policy 12, 146
competitiveness 26, 148
compromise 87; commissions 106
conditionality 67, 69, 146; and enlargement 68
Confederation of British Industry (CBI) 114, 115, 130
Conseil d'orientation des retraites (COR) 105, 117, 118
consensual knowledge 7, 12-13
consensual policy style 86
consensus 86; Wessels 87
consensus formation 89; by country 94
consensus-building 12
consensus-orientated networks: policy learning 86, 87
conservation 131
consistency 56
constitution 108
constructivism 4
constructivist approach 66
consumer policy 12, 72
Contaminated Land Directive 137
contracting out 146
convergence 6
cooperation 149
coordination problems 148
Copenhagen criteria 78
coping strategy 126
core beliefs 5, 66
core policy beliefs 85
corporatism 85

cost-benefit analysis: instrumental learning 49; UK 50
costs 36; reducing 148
costs and benefits: policy 148
Cotonou Agreement 72, 73; Africa, Caribbean and Pacific group 68; trade liberalization 72
court decisions 146
Cox, R.H. 108
crisis 2
Crossan, M. 4
currency: West Africa 69
customs union 143
cybernetics 6
Cyert, R. 4

Danish Commerce and Companies Agency 52
data privacy 146
decision making 6; expert knowledge 95; theory 4
delay tactics: commissions 106
deliberation 84; Europe and USA 85
Delors Committee 10
Delors, President Jacques 127
democracy: promotion of 76, 78
democratic accountability USA 86
democratic deficit 86
democratic experimentalism 13
democratic governance 73
democratizing regulatory procedures: USA and Canada 87
Denmark: EEA 129; IA 44; impact assessments (IAs) 51-2
Department of Business Enterprise and Regulatory Reform (BERR) 50-1
Department of the Environment (DoE) 130
Department for Environment, Food and Rural Affairs (DEFRA) 136, 137, 138, 139
deregulation 34; risk tolerant 50

Deutsch, K. 4, 5
development 68; European Consensus (2005) 74
development aid 76
development policy 67
di Meana, Ripa 127
dialogue of the deaf 85
diffusion 5-6, 49; leaders and importers 58; and learning 145; liberal economics 143; Netherlands 58; networks and emulation 54-5; studies 10-13
Diffusion of Innovations: (Rogers) 6
diffusion model: Netherlands 54
Directorate Generals (DGs) 24, 28, 29; IAs 32
Directors of Better Regulation of the EU 54
discursive learning 147
dispute resolution 97
dissatisfaction 2
divisionalization 28, 33
Doha Development Round 69
Dolowitz, D. 6
dominant advocacy coalition 123
double-loop learning 4, 7
downloading 12
Drake, Jeannie 114
Dudley, G. 10

Easterby-Smith, M. 23
Eberlein, B. 13
Eckardt, M. 9, 11
Economic and Financial Affairs Council (ECOFIN) 54
economic growth 78
economic incentives 25
economic liberalization 72
economic migration 70
Economic Partnership Agreements (EPAs) 70, 72, 74, 77; opposition to 79

economic variables: learning 146
economy: global 68
Egan, M. 17
Eising, R. 9, 12
electoral feasibility 50; policy setting 55
emissions 130
employment 73
employment strategy 65
emulation 46, 49-50, 54-5; and learning 145; Sweden 55
energy liberalization: policy learning 13
enlargement 14, 67, 75, 77; reasons for 69
entrepreneurship 6, 11, 127
environment 68, 70, 72; task force 38
Environment Act (1995) 131
Environment Agency of England and Wales (EA): budgetary pressures 136; comparison with EEA 137-9; evolution 135-7; instrumental learning 136; management difficulties 135; organizational learning 136; origins 129-31; social learning 136
Environment Councils 135
Environment Data Centre 134
Environmental Audit Committee: Russel, Dr Duncan 56
environmental governance: networking 138
environmental policy 65; introduction 122-3
epistemic community 10
equity 149
The EU and Africa: Towards a Strategic Partnership 70
EU Strategy for Africa (2005) 72
Europe: normative power of 146
European Centre for the Development of Vocational Training 128
European Commission 49; organizational learning 30-3; reform of 3; teachers 10
European Consensus (2005): development 74
European Court of Justice 85
European courts: jurisprudence 57
European Environment Agency (EEA): ambiguity 129; comparison with EA 137-9; evolution 132-5; origins 127-9
European Environment Information and Observation Network (EIONET) 128, 132, 133
European Monetary Union (EMU) 10
European Parliament 86
European Topic Centres (ETCs) 132
European Union (EU): and Asia 69, 76-7; BAS 88; committees 90; consensus formation 94; governance literature 22-3; membership and security 68; policy process 95; policy transfer 93-4; Presidencies 49, 54; representation and regional integration 70-1; rivalries 85
EUROSTAT 128, 133, 134
evaluation: Marier 144
exchange modes of government: market models 144
expert: independent 91
expert communities: network models 144
expert knowledge: decision making 95
expert networks 6
expertise 86-7

fairness 149

Farrell, M. 12, 16; power dynamics 144
Featherstone, K. 102
federalism 143
feedback 4
FIAS-World Bank 52
fiche 38, 44
Fillon, F. 110
financial crisis 10
financial market: internal market 10
firms 4
flawed learning 9
flexibility 26
flood defences 131, 136
formal exchanges 144
forum shopping 146
France: Charpin Report 105, 115-16, 117; genetics policy 96; Laraque commission 108; pension reform 103, 110, *111*, 115-16, 117; policy transfer 94
free trade 69, 108
fundamental beliefs 66

gender 91
genetic modification (GM) 89
genetics: human 88; policy transfer 95
Germany: policy transfer 94
Getting Agencies to Work Together: (Bardach) 149
Gilardi, F. 45
globalization 146; policy learning 142-3
goal displacement: Zito 144
gold plating 36
good governance: Africa 70
governance: exporting 76-8; and learning 13; pride in EU 83
governance learning 23, 24-5; better regulation 28-30; organizational learning *25*

governance turn 22, 39
Gray, T. 129
greenhouse gas monitoring 135
growth 55, 148
Grugel, J. 12

Haas, Ernst 6, 7, 10, 65, 74; adaptation 75-6
Haas, Peter 7
Hall, Peter 5, 65-6, 75, 78, 143; third order change 76
Harman, John 136
Heclo, H. 5, 143
Hedberg, B. 9
Her Majesty's Inspectorate of Pollution (HMIP) 129, 131, 135
herbicides 89
hierarchical belief system 67
hierarchical co-ordination 27
hierarchical governance 22
hierarchical legislation 26
hierarchical models: statutory rules and guidance 144
hierarchical norm setting 22
hierarchical steering 13
hierarchies 25-6, 97
Hills, Professor John 114
historical institutionalist propositions 124
horizontal co-ordination 28, 144
horizontal networks 86
human rights 69, 73, 76, 77
hybrid transfer 12

idea shaker: commissions 108, 109, 110, 115-16
ideas: market place for 65; policy 65
identity: EU 69, 76; and integration 70
Impact Assessment Board (IAB) 32
Impact Assessment Working Group 33

impact assessments (IAs) 16, 24, 26, 28, 29, 148; countries with long experience of 44; Denmark 51-2; description of 43-4; DGs 32; Netherlands 36, 37, 53-4; obligation 30; problems of 30; support mechanisms for 33; Sweden 52-3; templates 49-50; UK 51
Implementation and Enforcement of Environmental Law (IMPEL) 137
incentive-based mechanisms 26
incentives 67
incremental adaptation 126
incremental learning 147
incrementalism: commissions 108, 109, 110
independent regulators 87
India 69, 71, 77
Indonesia 71
industrial policy 146
information 45
information gathering 23
infrastructure 68
innovation 50, 95; domestic 144
institutional path dependency 3
institutionalist approach 138
institutionalized actors 10
instrument learning 23, 39, 46; better regulation 28-30
instrumental learning 50-4, 58; cost-benefit analysis 49; Environment Agency of England and Wales (EA) 136
instruments 6, 25-6; communication-based 13; design of 26-7; institutionalized 43; stability of 39
integration: and identity 70; levels of 70; policy making 86; understanding 1

integration theories: and learning 9-14
integrators 28
intellectual property rights 72
inter-regional co-operation 68
interest group politics 85, 91
internal market: financial market 10
International Monetary Fund 72
international relations networks 6-7
interviews: problems with 45
isomorphism 87
issue networks 144

Japan 71; pension commissions 118
Jervis, R. 6
jobs 55
Joint Africa-EU Strategy (Lisbon 2007) 72, 75
joint learning 95
Joint Research Centre 134
Jordan, A. 13, 37
Jospin, Lionel 115-16, 117
Juppé, Alain 115
jurisprudence: European courts 57

Kelemen, D.R. 85
Kerber, W. 9, 11
Kerwer, D. 13
Kinnock reforms 30, 33
Knill, C. 26
knowledge: strategic, symbolic and substantiating 55; and time 45; usages of 46; utilization 43, 45
Kohler-Koch, B. 95
Kok, Wim 34
Könberg, Bo 110

labels: policy transfer 12
laboratory federalism 11
labour standards 72
language 66; change in 4
Laraque commission: France 108

Lascoumes, P. 27
Latvia: pensions 119
law: rule of 76
lay knowledge 45
Le Galès, P. 27
leadership 3, 10
learning: alternative sources of 91; approaches 125-7; and beliefs 66-7, 76; and commissions 102, 103; concepts 2; conditions for 14, 66, 74; constraints 11, 125-7; definition 65; and diffusion 145; dynamics 126; economic variables 146; empirical analysis of 45-50; and emulation 145; in EU and USA 3; first and second order 67, 75-6; and governance 13; individual 65; intensity 89; levels in EU governance debate 24-9; modes *8*, 144-5; mutual 65; and neofunctionalism 10; obstacles to 144; organization 75; policy improvement 59; policy process 147; political-strategic 50; poor conditions for 9; propositions 124-5; socialization 77; strategies *126*; and time 9; types and expectations *48-9*; types of *47*
learning curve 148
learning styles: Montpetit 144
learning theory 1-2, 3-9; USA 14
Legal Service 30
legislation 13, 39; scrutiny 44
legitimacy 87, 96, 125, 148; networks 87
legitimacy deficit 86, 87, 90, 93; policy development 98
Lenschow, A. 26
lesson drawing 6, 125, 126, 143; EEA and EA 138
liberal economics: diffusion 143

liberalization 34
Lisbon EU-Africa summit 74
Lisbon process 13, 29, 55
Lisbon Treaty 3
litigation 146
logic of appropriateness 66
logic of consequentiality 66
Lomé Agreements 72, 73, 75
Lowi, T.J. 144
Lyles, M. 23

Macdonald Commission: Canada 108
Majone, G. 147, 148
Major, Prime Minister John 129
Malaysia 71
management: difficulties 135
managerialism 147
Mandelson, Peter 51
March, J. 4
Marier, P. 11, 16; evaluation 144
market access 71
market incentives 146, 147
market liberalization 146
market models: exchange modes of government 144
markets 25-6
Marsh, D. 6
matrix structures 135
May, Peter 45, 46
Members of the European Parliament (MEPs) 24
membership 145
Mercosur 12, 68
micro changes 1
Middle East policy 70
migration 73; economic 70
Millennium Development Goals 70, 73
Ministry of Agriculture, Fisheries and Food (MAFF) 130
Minztberg's synthesis 27

misperception 6
mobility 73
Moe, T: framework 123, 124, 126, 129, 131, 138
Montpetit, E. 16, 83; learning styles 144
Morgan, K. 11
multilateralism 76
Mutz, D.C. 85

National Association of Pension Funds 115
National Audit Office: IA 51
National Focal Points 132
National Pension Savings Scheme (NPSS) 114
National Rivers Authority (NRA) 129, 130, 131, 135, 137
negotiation 87
neofunctionalism 6-7, 10; and learning 10
Netherlands 24; better regulation in 33-9; BR agenda and EU policy making 37-9; BR related organizational learning *35*; diffusion 58; diffusion model 54; IAs 37, 44, 53-4; policy making 39; reducing costs 54; standard cost model 55; welfare state 34
network models: expert communities 144
networked governance 13, 22, 26
networking: EEA 135; environmental governance 138; multilateral and bilateral 137
networking bureaucracy 132
networks 5, 13, 14, 25-6; cross-national 143; dispersal of power 86; elites 10; emulation and diffusion 54-5; governance 2, 128; informal 144; learning 5, 13; legitimacy 87; transnational 146

New Zealand 106
Nijland, Jeroen 54
non-decision making: politics of 145
non-governmental organizational (NGO) networks 10
non-learning model 85
non-state actors: policy-making 146
normative models 144
normative power of: Europe 146
normative suasion 68
norms 144; exporting 76-8
Norway: pensions 119
null hypothesis 45, 46, 57-8

objectives: standardization of 27-8
open markets 78
open method of co-ordination (OMC) 2, 11, 13, 14, 26, 65; and organizational learning 5
Organization for Economic Co-operation and Development (OECD) 49, 52, 56; pension reform 103
organizational cohesion 136
organizational exploration 4
organizational inquiry 4
organizational learning 4-5, 7, 23, 125; better regulation 30-3; BR-related *31*; Commission 30-3; commissions 105; definition of 23; EA 136; EEA 134, 135; EEA and EA 138; governance learning *25*; literature 23; and open method of co-ordination (OMC) 5; unpacking 27-8
Ostrom, E. 13
oversight 149
Owens, Susan 43, 44

packaging waste 135
Padgett, S. 9, 12, 88, 95
paradigms 6

Paré, I. 88
partisan effects 46
Pastor, R. 143
peace 73
peer socialization 144
pension commissions: Japan 118; USA 118
pension policy: Canada 107; learning 103; Sweden 107
pension reform 11; automatic enrolment 106; commissions 110-19; France 103, 110, 115-16; France, Sweden and UK *111*; Greece 102; lack of learning 102; policy engineers 112-15; Sweden 103, 110-11; UK 103
Pensions Act (2007) 112
Pensions Commission 112
Pensions Policy Institute 115
perception 6
performance 148, 149
persuasion 84
Philippines 71
pluralism 85, 96
Poland: pensions 119
policy: change 142; community 5; convergence 142; core beliefs 66; costs and benefits 148; diffusion 45, 142; effectiveness 135; efficiency 87; electoral feasibility 55; experience from different countries 90; failure 142; ideas 65; innovation 142; learning 143; legitimacy deficit 98; middlemen 5; transfers 87
policy engineers: commissions 108, 109, 110; pension reform 112-15
policy learning 5, 45, 46, 142, 144; Africa-EU relations 71-3; analytical framework 65-7; consensus-orientated networks 86; definition from Sabatier and Zafonte 84; dynamics of 146-7; energy liberalization 13; EU 84-8; framework 65, 79; globalization 142-3; promotion of regional integration 64; thought alteration 89; time 147
policy making: commissions 117-19; comparison between USA and Europe 85-6; competition for access 85; non-state actors 146
policy transfer 12, 65, 90, 93-4, 142; human genetics 95; labels 12
political learning 5, 7, 46, 55-7, 143
political reform 68
political strategy: adjusting 126
politics: avoiding 85
politics of non-decision making 145
Pollack, M.A. 86
pollution 130
positive sum games 2
power 23
power dynamics: Farrell 144
power politics 45
prescriptive governance 144
presidency: rotating 10
principal agent model 123, 124, 126, 129, 138, 148-9
private enforcement 146
privatization 143
problem-solving 23
process 23
Prodi Commission 57
professional knowledge 45
professionalization: training 28
public criticism 135
public interest 90
public opinion 149
public-private partnerships 146, 148

quality 34
quality assurance 50
quantity 34

Radaelli, C.M. 11, 16, 29, 87; legitimacy 96; regulatory quality 144
Raffarin, J-P. 110
rational policy analysis 58
rational policy theory 2
recession 146
red tape 54
referenda failure 3
reflexive learning 46, 148
reform 11
regional blocs 12
regional development 143
regional integration 73; Africa 69; Asia 71; EU representation 70-1; European Commission's definition 64; goals of 69, 77; promoting 67-70; research on 64; support for 63
regionalism 64, 70
regulation: better 29-30, 137
regulation theory 59
Regulatory impact assessment (RIA) *see* impact assessments (IAs)
regulatory quality 26; Radaelli 144
Regulatory Reform Group 54; control agenda 55-6
regulatory regimes 11
Rethinking Democratic Accountability: Behn 149
Rhodes European Council Summit (1988) 127
Richardson, J. 10
risk-tolerant deregulation UK 50
Risse-Kappen, T. 95
roadmap 32
Rogers, Everett: *Diffusion of Innovations* 6
Roosevelt: Committee on Economic Security 108
Rose, R. 9, 143
rotating presidency 10

routine 5
Royal Commission on Environmental Pollution 130
Russel, Dr Duncan: Environmental Audit Committee 56

Sabatier, P. 5, 84, 85, 88, 143; heuristic 46
sanctions 56, 146
Santer Commission: fall of 2
Sbragia, A. 143
Scharpf, F.W. 97
Schön, D. 4
Schout, A. 13, 15, 37; structural environment 144
scrutiny: legislation 44
Secretariat General (SG) 24, 29; work planning and IAs 32
security 69, 73; Africa 70; Eastern Europe 68; and EU membership 68
Security Strategy (2003) 74
self-regulation 146
September 11th 74
shadow of the hierarchy 11, 15
shirking 123, 125, 126
Simon, Herbert 4
Singapore 71
Single European Act 85
single-loop learning 4, 7
Situation C 138
Skogstad, G. 87
social conflict 7
social learning 6, 46, 65, 95, 125, 143; EA 136
social networks 49
socialization: learning 77
soft co-ordination 12
soft power 83, 84, 95
South Africa 69
South Asian Association for Regional Co-operation (SAARC) 71

South Korea 71
Soviet Union: effect of collapse 68
Spain: EEA 128
spillover 7, 10, 144
spinning 7
standard cost model 55, 57; Netherlands 55; UK 55
standardization 34, 72; of objectives 27-8
status quo: commissions 107, 109, 110, 115-17
statutory rules and guidance: hierarchical models 144
steel policy 10
Steinbrunner, J. 6
Stoiber Group 33
Stone, D. 149
strategic planning and programming (SPP) 30
Streeck, W. 85
structural disagreement 123-4
structural environment: Schout 144
surveillance 149
sustainability 26
sustainable development 70; tests 36
Sustainable Economic Growth, Regional Integration and Trade 70
Sweden: commissions 106; emulation 55; IA 44; impact assessments (IAs) 52-3; pension policy 107; pension reform 103, 110-11, *111*, 116; pro-business regulation model 58
Swedish Pension Commission 116
Swedish Working Group on Pensions 112, 114, 115, 117, 118
symbolic learning 7, 46, 58
symbolic politics 30

tax measures 26
technical assistance 68, 76
testing ideas 106
Thailand 71
Thatcher, M. 107, 112
third order change 76
thought alteration: policy learning 89
time 12; and knowledge 45; and learning 9
time-dimension: bias 46
Towards a New Asia Strategy 71
trade 67, 72, 73, 76, 146; agreements 68, 77, 146; Asia 69; Cotonou Agreement 72; liberalization 69; standards 72
trade not aid 67, 72, 73-4
Trade Union Congress (TUC) 114, 115
training: professionalization 28
transmission belt 146
transmission process 5
transnational networks 146
Transport Task Force 38
trust 85, 149
Turner, Adair 114
twinning patterns 147

UK Pensions Commission report 114
United Kingdom (UK): BAS 88; BR 34; cost-benefit analysis 50; and EEA 127, 128; genetics policy 95-6; IA 44, 51; pension reform 103, *111*, 112; reducing costs 54; regulatory panel 56; risk-tolerant deregulation 50; standard cost model 55
United Nations (UN) 132
United States of America (USA) 57; adversarial politics 85; BAS 88; cost-benefits analysis 50; deliberation 85; democratic accountability 86; democratizing regulatory procedures 87; genetics policy 95-6;

learning theories 14; pension commissions 118; policy transfer 93-4
United States Environment Protection Agency 138
unlearning 9
updating 45
uploading 5, 12
utilities 11

value change 4
value for money 72
values 144
variables 45-6
Verdun, A. 10
Verheugen, Vice President G. 54
vertical authority 97
veto players 108
veto points 11, 12
Vietnam 71

wage war 55
war on terror 69
Washington Consensus 75
waste management 131

Waste Regulation Authorities (WRA) 129, 135
waste water treatment 135
Water Act (1989) 129
Water Framework Directive 137
water management 131
Waterman, R. 124
Weiss, Carol 43, 44
welfare 146
welfare state 103; Netherlands 34; reform 107-9
Wessels, W.: consensus 87
West Africa: currency 69
Wiener, J.B. 55
World Bank 34, 56, 72, 118
World Trade Organization (WTO) 69

Zafonte, M.A. 84, 88
Zalm, Gerrit 58
zero learning 45-6
zero sum games 2, 22
Zito, A.R. 10, 16, 105; goal displacement 144